FRONTEX AND NON-R

Since the Frontex Border Agency's establishment in 2004, its activities have foregrounded the complexity and difficulty of protecting the human rights of those seeking access to the European Union (EU). In this connection, protection from *refoulement* should be paramount in the Agency's work. By navigating through the intricacies of Frontex's structure and working methods, this book answers abiding questions: which circumstances would trigger EU responsibility if violations were to occur in Frontex's joint operations? What is the legal standing of the principle of *non-refoulement* in relation to Frontex's activities? Can Frontex be entrusted with an exclusive search and rescue mandate? This book offers a theoretical and practical insight into the legislative intricacies of Frontex's work, examining the responsibility of the EU and scrutinising the interaction of international law and EU law with a focus on the principle of *non-refoulement*.

ROBERTA MUNGIANU is Assistant Professor at the University of Copenhagen Faculty of Law. She conducts research and teaches in the field of migration and human rights.

FRONTEX AND NON-REFOULEMENT

The International Responsibility of the EU

ROBERTA MUNGIANU

Faculty of Law, University of Copenhagen

CAMBRIDGE
UNIVERSITY PRESS

CAMBRIDGE
UNIVERSITY PRESS

University Printing House, Cambridge CB2 8BS, United Kingdom

One Liberty Plaza, 20th Floor, New York, NY 10006, USA

477 Williamstown Road, Port Melbourne, VIC 3207, Australia

314-321, 3rd Floor, Plot 3, Splendor Forum, Jasola District Centre, New Delhi - 110025, India

79 Anson Road, #06-04/06, Singapore 079906

Cambridge University Press is part of the University of Cambridge.

It furthers the University's mission by disseminating knowledge in the pursuit of education, learning and research at the highest international levels of excellence.

www.cambridge.org
Information on this title: www.cambridge.org/9781107590069
DOI:10.1017/9781316459904

First published 2016
First paperback edition 2018

A catalogue record for this publication is available from the British Library

Library of Congress Cataloging in Publication data
Names: Mungianu, Roberta, 1980– author.
Title: Frontex and non-refoulement : the international responsibility
of the EU / Roberta Mungianu.
Description: New York : Cambridge University Press, 2016. | Series: Cambridge
studies in european law and policy
Identifiers: LCCN 2016021029 | ISBN 9781107133570 (hardback)
Subjects: LCSH: Refoulement. | Refoulement – European Union countries. |
Refugees – Legal status, laws, etc. – European Union countries. | Asylum,
Right of – European Union countries. | Human rights – European Union
countries. | European Agency for the Management of Operational Cooperation
at the External Borders of the Member States of the European Union. |
European Union. | BISAC: LAW / International.
Classification: LCC KZ6530 .M86 2016 | DDC 342.2408/3–dc23
LC record available at https://lccn.loc.gov/2016021029

ISBN 978-1-107-13357-0 Hardback
ISBN 978-1-107-59006-9 Paperback

CONTENTS

ACKNOWLEDGEMENTS

I would like to thank all those who, in each their way, have made this book possible.

This book is an adaptation of my doctoral thesis that I have defended at the University of Copenhagen in 2014. It would not have been possible to carry out my doctoral research without the thoughtful supervision of Morten Broberg. My immense gratitude goes to him for his support, invaluable advice and encouragement which were essential throughout the entire doctoral research process. My sincere thanks go to Bart van Vooren, who co-supervised my work and has always been a supportive and caring colleague and friend. I also wish to thank the Faculty of Law at the University of Copenhagen and its staff who hosted me and provided a truly intellectually stimulating research atmosphere. I warmly thank Helle Krunke and all my colleagues at the Centre for Comparative and European Constitutional Studies at the Faculty of Law for allowing me to be part of the best possible work environment.

I am profoundly indebted to Marise Cremona, Jens Vedsted-Hansen and Ebrahim Afsah, who served as members of my doctoral thesis committee, for their generous and extremely valuable advice, which has helped me to improve the manuscript. The book has also greatly bene-fitted from the critical insights and comments of Steve Peers, Mikael Rask Madsen, Yoshifumi Tanaka, Lars Holmberg, Gregor Noll, Ramses A. Wessel and Francesco Messineo. I am deeply grateful to them all.

My research for this book has been partly conducted at the European University Institute, Florence, Italy. I am grateful to the Institute and its staff for allowing me to benefit from their excellent research environment and for so warmly welcoming me.

My thanks go also to the personnel of Frontex Border Agency for their availability in answering my questions and for helping me to clarify some aspects of the work conducted by the Agency.

I wish to thank the series editors, Jo Shaw and Laurence Gormley, and the three anonymous reviewers for their comments and suggestions.

I owe my thanks to Elizabeth Spicer for her excellent assistance from the drafting of the original proposal to the submission of the manuscript and the editorial staff at Cambridge University Press for guiding me through to final publication. I acknowledge Jens Christian Dalsgaard for his very valuable contribution in the editing of the book. I remain solely responsible for any errors that the book may still contain.

Finally, I express my warmest thanks to my family for their never-ending care and love; to my friends in Denmark and around the world for their encouragement and support; and to Henrik just for being there. This book is dedicated to Aisha, who has generously allowed me to meet the so-called 'other'.

***

The law stated in the text, to the best of the author's knowledge, is current as of 1 May 2015.

When this book goes to press, political agreement is sought on a proposal by the European Commission for a regulation of the European Parliament and of the Council on a 'European Border and Coast Guard', repealing the Frontex Regulation (COM 2015, 671 final). If such instrument is adopted, it may be necessary for the reader to reconsider some findings and arguments of this book in the light of the new rules.

I wish to acknowledge that Chapters 2 and 3 of this book have been published in an earlier version in the *European Journal of Migration and Law* 15 (2013) 359–385, R. Mungianu, 'Frontex: Towards a Common Policy on External Border Control'.

TABLE OF CASES

Permanent Court of International Justice and International Court of Justice

United Nations International Criminal Tribunal for the Former Yugoslavia

Court of Justice of the European Union and Opinions of the Advocate General

European Commission of Human Rights and European Court of Human Rights

United Nations Human Rights Committee

United Nations Committee against Torture

Inter-American Commission on Human Rights

International Tribunal for the Law of the Sea

Domestic case law

United States

United Kingdom

The Netherlands

TABLE OF LEGISLATION

Treaties and other international instruments

EU Law Instruments

EU Primary Law

EU Secondary Law

Introduction

1.1 Frontex Border Agency in an EU Legal and Political Setting

Immigration is increasingly perceived as an economic and cultural risk to European Union (EU) society. Populist parties across the EU are flourishing, and they reflect political pressures which are volatile and significant. Efforts designed to control irregular migration have been prioritised on both national and EU political agendas. In 2004, the EU established Frontex Border Agency (hereinafter Frontex or the Agency) with the aim of ensuring Member State operational cooperation at the EU's external borders and curbing flows of irregular migrants in the framework of an EU common policy. Frontex's border control practices – through which the EU and its Member States aim to prevent irregular migrants from entering EU territory – are now very salient in political, societal and legal dimensions. Yet measures taken to alleviate security concerns date from a time well before 2004, and this fuller context constitutes the political milieu out of which Frontex has grown. The entry into force of the Treaty of Amsterdam, integrating the Schengen *acquis* into the framework of the EU, has given the EU powers to develop policies on asylum, immigration and border control. Additionally, policy developments since the 1999 European Council meeting in Tampere have focused on the importance of ensuring the surveillance of external borders and the management of migratory flows.[1] The European Council in Tampere identified the development of common rules on asylum and immigration as a policy priority for the building of an Area of Freedom Security and Justice in the

---

[1] European Council, Tampere 15 and 16 October 1999, 16/10/1999, No. 200/1/99. See also European Council, Laeken, 14 and 15 December 2001, 14/12/2001, No. 300/1/01; European Council, Seville, 21 and 22 June 2002, 24/10/2012, No. 13463/02; European Council, Thessaloniki, 19 and 20 June 2003, 1/10/2003, No. 11638/03; European Council, 'The Hague Programme: Strengthening Freedom, Security and Justice in the European Union', OJ 2005 No. C53, p. 1; and European Council, 'The Stockholm Programme – An Open and Secure Europe Serving and Protecting the Citizens', 2 December 2009, OJ 2010 No. C115, p. 1.

EU.[2] Recently, in its Communication 'The Global Approach to Migration and Mobility', the European Commission reiterated the importance of preventing and reducing irregular migration and trafficking in human beings in the context of developing the external dimension of the EU's Area of Freedom Security and Justice.[3]

Clearly, though, a preoccupation with security must not be the only EU priority in the management of irregular migration. The EU and its Member States are bound by protection obligations towards third-country nationals, and the permutations of these commitments must be scrutinised and kept clearly in view. International law and EU law uphold a framework of protection for those individuals trying to escape persecution and ill treatment. The prohibition against returning individuals to non-EU countries where they may be at risk – the so-called principle of non-refoulement – is at the core of the protection regime and must inform the policy choices of the EU as a whole. According to the EU Treaties,[4] the EU is founded on the values of respect for human dignity, freedom, democracy, equality, the rule of law and respect for human rights.[5] Specifically, the Treaty on the Functioning of the EU requires the EU to develop a common policy on asylum in order to deal with any third-country national requiring international protection and to ensure compliance with the principle of non-refoulement.[6]

Given this legal and political setting, Frontex's mandate is that of a specialist EU body responsible for managing operational cooperation at the EU's external borders. It supports Member States' border control activities. According to the Frontex Regulation, Frontex must carry out risk analysis so that the EU and its Member States can improve the management of the external borders; provide training at the EU level for national instructors of border guards; develop relevant scientific research; manage lists of technical equipment provided by the Member States; provide assistance in organising joint return operations; and

---

[2] The European Council brought this matter up at its meeting in Tampere because net migration to Europe rose to over 700,000 in 1999, having declined over the previous decade. See H. Brücker and Others, 'Managing Migration in the European Welfare State', www.frdb.org/upload/file/paper1_23jun01.pdf (accessed 13 November 2015), 5.

[3] Communication from the Commission to the European Parliament, the Council, the Economic and Social Committee and the Committee of the Regions: 'The Global Approach to Migration and Mobility', COM (2011) 743 final.

[4] Consolidated versions of the Treaty on European Union and the Treaty on the Functioning of the European Union, OJ 2010 No. C83, p. 1.

[5] Article 2 of the Treaty on European Union (TEU).

[6] Article 78 of the Treaty on the Functioning of the European Union (TFEU).

facilitate operational cooperation between Member States and third countries. In 2011, the Frontex Regulation was amended by Council Regulation (EU) 1168/2011 so as to enhance the role of Frontex and bring it into line with a policy objective of introducing an integrated management of the external borders of the Member States.[7] Importantly, Frontex's control of the EU's external borders presently extends to coordinating joint operations at land, sea and air borders. Joint operations consist of the deployment of additional border guards and technical equipment to those EU border areas that are under significant pressure. The aim is to prevent third-country nationals circumventing border controls at the EU's external borders by making border checks and carrying out border surveillance. Such activities may involve a refusal of entry to EU territory, or the interception of third-country nationals before they reach the EU's borders, or a refusal of onward passage. It is in the realm of these activities that the potential for violating the principle of non-refoulement arises (notably, if individuals are returned to territories where they may be at risk). Frontex's activities have intensified within the mandate outlined, and this, in turn, intensifies the need to address persistent areas of contradiction or potential risk which pertain to the Agency's legal setting. One such problem arises from the Agency's increasing dependence on Member States' contributions in terms of equipment and deployed personnel. Another is an inadequate self-monitoring mechanism relating to compliance with fundamental rights obligations which has generated concerns with the European Ombudsman and which may adversely affect Frontex's operations. A further unresolved issue involves the risk that the Agency's support of border control activities conducted by third countries with poor human rights records may call into question the legality of its action in the external sphere. There is also a need to deal prudently with pressure

---

[7] Council Regulation (EC) 2007/2004 of 26 October 2004 establishing a European agency for the management of operational cooperation at the external borders of the Member States of the European Union OJ 2004 No. L349, p. 1 as amended by Regulation (EC) 863/2007 of the European Parliament and the Council of 11 July 2007 establishing a mechanism for the creation of Rapid Border Intervention Teams and amending Council Regulation (EC) 2007/2004 as regards that mechanism and regulating the tasks and powers of guest officers OJ 2007 No. L199, p. 30 and by Regulation (EU) 1168/2011 of the European Parliament and the Council of 25 October 2011 amending Council Regulation (EC) 2007/2004 establishing a European agency for the management of operational cooperation at the external borders of the Member States of the European Union OJ 2011 No. L304, p. 1 (hereinafter the Frontex Regulation). Article 1 of the Frontex Regulation. I will analyse the concept of integrated border management in Chapter 2, Section 2.2.2.1.

and questions as to whether Frontex should be more urgently involved in search and rescue at sea operations in a climate intensified by the rising number of migrants dying in failed bids to cross the Mediterranean.

At first sight, control of the external borders of the EU seems to have a strictly territorial dimension. According to the Schengen Borders Code, which contains the rules governing the movement of persons across EU borders, the control of the external borders consists of border checks carried out at border crossing points and 'surveillance of borders between border crossing points and the surveillance of border crossing points outside the fixed opening hours'.[8] The intensification of Frontex's joint operations has contributed to moving the borders of the EU.[9] In some instances, the borders have moved from the territorial borders of the Member States to the high seas where Frontex's joint operations take place. In other instances, the EU's borders are now sometimes within the territories of third countries – a process facilitated by working arrangements between Frontex and third countries, by international agreements between Member States and third countries, and by Frontex's contribution in setting up the EU's Network of Immigration Liaison Officers (ILOs), operating in the territories of third countries. ILOs consist of Frontex's officers deployed in third countries with the aim of collecting information for operational use and identifying third-country nationals.[10]

Defining the EU's borders for the purposes of Frontex's joint operations is essential to effectively examine the application of the principle of non-refoulement, since it is the attempt to enter the EU that gives meaning to the prohibition of refoulement. Patrolling the territorial waters, the contiguous zone and the high seas entails preventing irregular migrants from reaching the territories of the EU. Also, by virtue of agreements with various third countries, Member States are allowed to patrol their territorial waters whose shores border the Mediterranean in order to prevent the transit of irregular migrants towards the EU. This has been part of joint operations.[11] It is also

---

[8] Regulation (EC) 562/2006 establishing a Community Code on the rules governing the movement of persons across borders (Schengen Borders Code), OJ 2006 No. L105, p. 1, Article 2 (10) and (11).

[9] For a detailed analysis of other factors contributing to the moving of the borders of the EU, see Jorrit J. Rijpma and M. Cremona, 'The Extra-Territorialisation of EU Migration Policies and the Rule of Law' (2007) *EUI Working Papers Law*, 2007/01.

[10] European Parliament and Council Regulation (EU) 493/2011 of 5 April 2011 amending Council Regulation (EC) 377/2004 of 19 February 2004 on the creation of an immigration liaison officers network OJ 2011 No. L141, p. 1.

[11] See Joint Operation Hera I and Joint Operation Hera II 2006, www.frontex.europa.eu (accessed 13 November 2015).

possible that in the future there will be agreements on joint operations between the EU and the third countries whereby the Member States' border guards will be deployed in third countries' territories with the aim of apprehending irregular migrants. Such arrangements may be made in the context of operational cooperation through Frontex. In this respect, the Frontex Regulation states that Frontex 'shall facilitate the operational cooperation between Member States and third countries' and that 'when concluding bilateral agreements with third countries ... Member States may include provisions concerning the role and competencies of the Agency'.[12] The aim of these arrangements is to prevent irregular migrants crossing EU borders. Any action which results in returning individuals to territories where they may be at risk may trigger the application of the principle of non-refoulement.

1.2 Aim and Scope

Within this context of broader, unresolved difficulties, my book examines the legal setting for joint operations between Frontex Border Agency and the EU Member States – operations which may result in push-back of third-country nationals trying to reach EU borders to countries where they may experience persecution, torture and other ill treatment in violation of the principle of non-refoulement. The book's abiding question is this: 'Which precise legal circumstances may expose the EU and its Member States to incurring responsibility for breaches of the principle of non-refoulement in Frontex's joint operations?'

What characterises joint operations under Frontex's auspices is that they enact a complex interdependence between the EU and its Member States. The media frequently reports push-back operations which occur off the coasts of Malta and Italy and at the Greek–Turkish border.[13] In many cases, it is alleged that push-back operations take place in the context of joint operations coordinated by Frontex. For instance, in December 2012 it was reported by the media that Syrian refugees, leaving Syria during the uprising against the rule of President al-Assad, tried to cross the Evros River into northern Greece. Without being registered, they were pushed back into Turkey by Greek border guards, thus facing the risk of being sent back to Syria. This push-back seems to

---

[12] Article 14(1) and (7) of the Frontex Regulation.
[13] *Human Rights Watch*, 30 January 2014, www.hrw.org (accessed 13 November 2015); *MaltaToday*, 9 July 2013 www.maltatoday.com (accessed 13 November 2015).

have taken place in the context of a joint operation coordinated by Frontex.[14] At issue here are various forms of legal exposure: and while the vulnerability and legal standing of irregular migrants garner media attention and loom largest in popular consciousness, this book focuses on the insufficiently scrutinised network of legal responsibility of the EU and its Member States related to the plight of these people.[15] I also wish to emphasise that the purposes of my book are not punitive. My analysis is not a prosecutorial search for specific infractions committed by Frontex, the EU or the Member States. The premise is that violations of the principle of non-refoulement *may* occur during Frontex's joint operations and that they *may* trigger the responsibility of the EU and of the Member States – and that these risks remain high unless the legal setting is sufficiently studied, applied and, if need be, reformed. A vital

---

[14] *The Guardian*, Friday 7 December 2012, www.theguardian.com (accessed 13 November 2015).

[15] Until now, this topic has only been explored to a rather limited extent in the literature dealing with the principle of non-refoulement; see e.g., V. Moreno Lax, '(Extraterritorial) Entry Controls and (Extraterritorial) Non-refoulement in EU Law' in M.C. Foblets and P. De Bruycker (eds.), *The External Dimension(s) of EU Asylum and Immigration Policy* (Bruylant, 2011); Efthymios Papastavridis, 'The EU and the Obligation of Non-refoulement at Sea' in F. Ippolito and Seline Trevisanut (eds.), *Migration in the Mediterranean: Mechanisms of International Cooperation* (Cambridge University Press, 2016) and in works dealing with Frontex border control activities see J. Rijpma, 'Building Borders: The Regulatory Framework for the Management of the External Borders of the European Union' (DPhil thesis, European University Institute, 2009); and J. Rijpma, 'Frontex: Successful Blame Shifting of the Member States?' (2010), www .realinstitutoelcano.org (accessed 13 November 2013); and E. Papastavridis, ' "Fortress Europe" and Frontex: Within or Without International Law?' (2010) 79 *Nordic Journal of International Law* 75; J. Rijpma, 'Hybrid Agencification in the Area of Freedom, Security and Justice and Its Inherent Tensions: The Case of Frontex' in M. Busuioc, M. Groenleer and J. Trondal (eds.), *The Agency Phenomenon in the European Union – Emergence, Institutionalization and Everyday Decision-making* (Manchester University Press, 2012). Some very valuable contributions map extraterritorial migration-control mechanisms (including Frontex's border control activities) in connection with possible breaches of human rights and refugee rights, in particular the principle of non-refoulement, but they do not focus on a specific border control mechanism; see the contributions in B. Ryan and V. Mitsilegas (eds.), *Extraterritorial Immigration Control: Legal Challenges* (Martinus Nijhoff, 2010); T. Gammeltoft-Hansen, *Access to Asylum: International Refugee Law and the Globalisation of Migration Control* (Cambridge University Press, 2011); and M. den Heijer, *Europe and Extraterritorial Asylum* (Hart Publishing, 2012). Specifically on the European readmission policy, see N. Coleman, *European Readmission Policy: Third Country Interests and Refugee Rights* (Martinus Nijhoff, 2009). In a 2011 article Guy S. Goodwin-Gill has specifically addressed the issue of the responsibility of Frontex and Member States and the principle of non-refoulement in the context of interception at sea; see G. S. Goodwin-Gill, 'The Right to Seek Asylum: Interception at Sea and the Principle of Non-refoulement' (2011) 23 *International Journal of Refugee Law* 443.

complementary thread running through my analysis of international responsibility is my examination of the specificities of Frontex's mandate which endeavours to further our understanding of the legal position of the EU vis-à-vis the management of its external borders.

A comprehensive approach is adopted in addressing the book's abiding question, cited above. Structurally, this involves the use of sub-questions. First, the book looks at the underlying reasons for the establishment of operational cooperation at the external borders of the EU. The focus is on how Frontex Border Agency was shaped and defined by the setting up of a common policy on external border control in the fast-developing EU Area of Freedom Security and Justice. This part of the book also addresses the way Frontex's joint operations are structured in order to understand the circumstances in which the EU and its Member States may incur responsibility for violations of the principle of non-refoulement.

Second, inter-dependent questions are studied. Since Frontex's joint operations bring together the EU and its Member States, should responsibility for joint operations fall upon the EU (via its agency, Frontex), the involved Member States or both? Frontex is an EU body and its mandate is to enable Member States in their exercise of border controls at the EU's external borders. Since such external border control activities may directly result in individuals not reaching Member State territories to submit asylum applications, the question of the EU's responsibility – via Frontex – matters significantly. On this point, the Frontex Regulation provides that 'the responsibility for the control and surveillance of external borders lies with the Member States'.[16] However, Frontex's operational capabilities have been strengthened, especially since the adoption of the amendments to the Frontex Regulation. Frontex's mandate now seems to entail more than the simple coordination of joint operations. This concern was recently expressed by the Parliamentary Assembly of the Council of Europe with these words:

> A dangerous mindset still exists which views Frontex's activities as being no more than those of Member States, with responsibilities lying with individual Member States and not with the Agency. While progress has been made in accepting that this is not always the case, the recourse to this argument is still too frequently made when looking at issues involving human rights responsibilities.[17]

[16] Article 1(2) of the Frontex Regulation.
[17] Parliamentary Assembly of the Council of Europe, 'Frontex: Human Rights Responsibility', Resolution 1932 (2013); see also 'Frontex: Human Rights Responsibility', Recommendation 2016 (2013).

Thus, a vision much clearer than this 'mindset' and a fuller understanding of who may be responsible for breaches of human rights and refugee rights in the context of joint operations are necessary.

Third, consideration is given to push-back operations which, if they occur, may have the potential to trigger EU and Member State responsibility if they result in the return of an individual to a territory where he or she is likely to face persecution, torture or other ill treatment in violation of the principle of non-refoulement. This principle is included in both international human rights instruments and EU primary and secondary legislation. This plethora of legal sources embodying the principle of non-refoulement prompts an investigation of what the principle consists of in EU law and whether protection against refoulement is ensured in the specific relevant legislation on Frontex's joint operations. The principle of non-refoulement acquires particular relevance in the case of Frontex's joint operations, since Frontex's action is carried out in different legal regimes (i.e. from the territories of the Member States to, potentially, the territories of third countries). An analysis of the extent to which protection is provided pursuant to the principle in the different legal regimes sheds light on the obligations of the EU, through Frontex, and the Member States when carrying out such operations. Moreover, EU legislation on Frontex's joint operations and external border control, especially after the 2011 amendments, indicates the importance of the principle of non-refoulement when joint operations are carried out by Frontex and the Member States: 'the mandate of the Agency should therefore be revised while ensuring that all measures ... fully respect fundamental rights and the rights of refugees and asylum seekers, including in particular the prohibition of refoulement'.[18]

1.3   Structure of the Book

By examining the tension and interplay between intergovernmentalism and supranationalisation in the EU, Chapter 2 explores the impetus for setting up a common policy on external border control through an analysis of EU policy papers. Additionally, this chapter examines the competence of the EU to establish the common policy, juxtaposing this with what I have chosen to term 'safeguard clauses' of Member State sovereignty. Chapter 2 offers an analysis of the EU common policy that includes the relevant features of operational cooperation at the external

---

[18]   Recital 9 of the Frontex Regulation.

borders through Frontex. The first of the aforementioned sources of legal risk and compromise – Frontex's escalating reliance on Member States' contributions – is a dynamic which is illustrated throughout the chapter.

Chapter 3 builds upon Chapter 2's definitions of the legal and political framework and examines the legal and political interests which have specifically shaped Frontex's present role. It achieves this by: (i) drawing upon the division of competence between the EU and its Member States illustrated in Chapter 2; (ii) examining the structure of Frontex, including an analysis of its legal personality and the structure of the joint operations it carries out; (iii) analysing the current relevant features and future directions of the European Border Guard Teams. The European Border Guard Teams are pools of border guards seconded by Member States and deployed in Frontex's joint operations. The teams contribute to the implementation of operational aspects of external border management at land, air and sea borders. Chapter 3 offers an account of the Member States' interests which illustrates their involvement and responsibility for the establishment of Frontex and the development of its mandate as of when the relevant legislation was drafted. The problematic presence within Frontex's structure of a 'self-monitoring', inadequate mechanism of compliance with fundamental rights obligations is presented and analysed in this chapter.

Chapter 4 considers the potential responsibility of the EU and its Member States for internationally wrongful acts and draws upon two different bodies of law: public international law and EU external relations law. After examining the issue of the EU's legal personality, I proceed in this chapter to identify the most suitable approach in establishing the EU's responsibility. The choice is between the organic model of attribution and the competence model of attribution. After arguing in favour of the traditional organic model as reflected in the International Law Commission's Article on Responsibility for International Organisations, I apply this model by examining the responsibility of the EU and its Member States by attribution via Frontex, studying cases of derivative responsibility pertaining to the EU for the internationally wrongful acts of its Member States. The analysis explores a theoretical problem: How *may* the EU and its Member States be held accountable should any violation occur in Frontex's joint operations? Conversely, the chapter does not seek to assess EU/Member States' responsibility by attempting citations of any previous violations tied to specific operational circumstance. The third legally problematic dynamic impacting Frontex's activity – potential support by the Agency for border control activities conducted by authorities of third countries with poor human rights records – is analysed in this chapter.

Chapter 5 analyses the interconnection of international law sources and EU law sources in order to examine what constitutes the principle of non-refoulement in the EU setting, whereas Chapter 6 examines the juridical space in which a State is responsible for ensuring that an individual is protected against return to persecution, torture or other ill treatment by analysing the relevant provisions of international law sources and case law. The international law sources include the 1951 Convention relating to the Status of Refugees, the Convention against Torture, the International Covenant on Civil and Political Rights and the European Convention on Human Rights.[19] This chapter also examines whether the principle of non-refoulement is customary international law. Additionally, the chapter studies the nature of protection from refoulement afforded by EU legislation concerning Frontex's joint operations. The EU's legal sources include the EU Treaties, the general principles of EU law, the EU Charter of Fundamental Rights, the Schengen Borders Code, the Frontex Regulation and the EU Sea External Border Regulation.[20] Both Chapters 5 and 6 consider the conflicting EU priorities of security and border control, on the one hand, and protection of third-country nationals escaping persecution, on the other hand.

Building upon the analysis conducted in Chapters 5 and 6, Chapter 7 analyses the interaction between the legal regime for search and rescue at sea and the principle of non-refoulement. A section of the chapter is devoted to illustrating the problems related to any possible increased involvement of Frontex in search and rescue at sea operations. These issues constitute the fourth problematic legal dynamic affecting Frontex's activity underpinning the book's argument.

---

[19] 1951 Convention relating to the Status of Refugees (189 UNTS 137); 1984 Convention against Torture and Other Cruel, Inhuman or Degrading Treatment or Punishment (1465 UNTS 85); 1966 International Covenant on Civil and Political Rights (999 UNTS 171); 1950 European Convention for the Protection of Human Rights and Fundamental Freedoms (213 UNTS 222).

[20] Charter of Fundamental Rights of the European Union OJ 2010 No. C83, p. 1; Regulation (EU) 656/2014 of the European Parliament and of the Council of 15 May 2014 establishing rules for the surveillance of the external sea borders in the context of operational cooperation coordinated by the European agency for the management of operational cooperation at the external borders of the Member States of the European Union OJ 2014 No. L189, p. 93.

It is also part of this study to create scenarios in which violations of the principle of non-refoulement may take place in the context of Frontex's joint operations. These constitute very useful indications of: (i) the extent to which the EU and its Member States *may* be responsible and (ii) how violations of the principle *may* be avoided by Frontex. Chapter 8, based on the analytical foundation of the previous chapters, identifies and explores such scenarios according to a sequential method. First, I look at the case law on the principle of non-refoulement of the Court of Justice of the European Union, the European Court of Human Rights, the Human Rights Committee and the Committee against Torture, as well as of national courts. The case law provided by these decision-making bodies identifies contentious situations and assesses whether such situations led to breaches of the principle of non-refoulement. Second, I examine problematic situations arising from the interviews which I conducted at Frontex's headquarters in Warsaw, Poland, in November 2012. In these interviews, the interviewees describe border control practices of Frontex and the Member States which seem to contain problematic aspects in relation to violations of the principle of non-refoulement. Third, I also review the legislation on Frontex's joint operations. The Sea External Borders Regulation sets forth the rules for sea border operations coordinated by Frontex and lists the measures which may be taken in the course of Frontex's surveillance operations at the sea external borders. Potential triggers of the EU and Member States' responsibility are explored in joint operations at sea and on land. The chapter identifies scenarios in which not only human resources but also technical means such as radar and thermos-visors are employed to protect the EU external borders.

This book has been developed out of core material contained in my doctrinal analysis of primary legal sources and literature research. It is supported by: (i) the result of the semi-structured qualitative interviews with Frontex's personnel conducted at Frontex's headquarters; and (ii) operational plans of Frontex's joint operations and other documents provided by Frontex upon request. An examination of the political context in which the legislation concerning Frontex was drafted is paramount in order to give a comprehensive understanding of the topic. As part of this process, I analyse EU documents selected for their bearing on inter-institutional procedures between those EU institutions relevant to the legal measures under consideration.

Together with the coordination of joint operations, Frontex has the tasks of arranging for rapid interventions and coordinating joint return operations. In rapid interventions, Frontex deploys personnel in the territory of a requesting Member State 'faced with a situation of urgent and exceptional pressure, especially the arrival at points of the external borders of large numbers of third-country nationals trying to enter the territory of that Member State illegally'.[21] Frontex's joint return operations consist of assisting the Member States in returning third-country nationals irregularly present in their territories.[22] This book will deal with Frontex's joint operations with operational structures that are used both for rapid interventions and for joint return operations.

I use the term 'European Community' to refer to the legal and political entity after the entry into force of the Treaty of Maastricht in 1993 and the integration of the Schengen *acquis* into the framework of the European Community with the Treaty of Amsterdam in 1999. I use the term 'European Union' to refer to the legal and political entity after the entry into force of the Treaty of Lisbon in 2009. In this respect, the EU superseded and replaced the European Community. The term 'third-country nationals' is used interchangeably with the term 'individual', when referring to those affected by potential violations of the principle of non-refoulement. The term 'refugee' indicates a third-country national who has been granted refugee status; an 'asylum seeker' indicates an individual who has applied for asylum and is waiting for a decision on this application. The term 'individual in need of international protection' indicates both potential refugees and people who may be awarded a subsidiary protection status pursuant to the EU Qualification Directive.[23]

Finally, it is necessary to make an observation about the EU borders. Frontex was set up to improve the integrated management of the external borders of the Member States of the EU. The Schengen Borders Code states that 'external borders means the Member States' land borders, including river and lake borders, sea borders and their airports, river ports, sea ports and lake ports, provided that they are not internal borders'.[24] The Frontex

---

[21] Article 8a of the Frontex Regulation.   [22] Article 9 of the Frontex Regulation.
[23] Council Directive 2004/83/EC of 29 April 2004 on minimum standards for the qualification and status of third-country nationals or stateless persons as refugees or as persons who otherwise need international protection and the content of the protection granted OJ 2004 No. L304, p. 12; and recast Directive 2011/95/EU of the European Parliament and of the Council of 13 December 2011 on standards for the qualification of third-country nationals or stateless persons as beneficiaries of international protection, for a uniform status for refugees or for persons eligible for subsidiary protection, and for the content of the protection granted OJ 2011 No. L337, p. 11.
[24] Article 2(2) of the Schengen Borders Code.

Regulation defines the 'external borders of the Member States' as 'the land and sea borders of the Member States and their airports and seaports, to which the provisions of Community law on the crossing of external borders by persons apply'.[25] In my book, I refer interchangeably to the EU's external borders and the external borders of the Member States, meaning the borders of the Member States to which the provisions of EU law on the crossing of external borders by persons apply. EU law on the crossing of external borders by persons refers to that part of the Schengen *acquis* which consists of the 1985 Agreement, the 1990 Schengen Convention[26] and measures implementing the Convention which were integrated in the Treaty establishing the European Community and the EU Treaties by the Treaty of Amsterdam in 1999. Since the entry into force of the Treaty of Lisbon in 2009, the Schengen *acquis* applies to all Member States except the United Kingdom and Ireland.[27] Furthermore, Iceland, Lichtenstein, Norway and Switzerland are non–Member States associated with the implementation, application and development of the Schengen *acquis*,[28] and they participate in Frontex's activities and in the

---

[25] Article 1a(1) of the Frontex Regulation.

[26] The Schengen Acquis – Convention implementing the Schengen Agreement of 14 June 1985 between the Government of the States of Benelux Economic Union, the Federal Republic of Germany and the French Republic on the gradual abolition of checks at their common borders, OJ 2000 No. L 239, p. 19; Treaty of Amsterdam OJ 1997 No. C340, p. 1.

[27] Council Decision 2000/365/EC of 29 May 2000 concerning the request of the United Kingdom of Great Britain and Northern Ireland to take part in some of the provisions of the Schengen *acquis*; Council Decision 2002/192/EC of 28 February 2002 concerning Ireland's request to take part in some of the provisions of the Schengen *acquis*. See also Recitals (25) and (26) of the Frontex Regulation and Recitals (27) and (28) of the Schengen Borders Code. Denmark has opted in to all measures building upon the Schengen *acquis* according to Protocol No. 22 on the position of Denmark to the TEU and TFEU.

[28] Agreement of the Council of the European Union and the Republic of Iceland and the Kingdom of Norway concerning the latter's association with the implementation, application and development of the Schengen *acquis*, OJ 1999 No. L176, p. 36; Agreement between the European Union, the European Community and the Swiss Confederation on the Swiss Confederation's association with the implementation, application and development of the Schengen *acquis*, OJ 2008 No. L53, p. 52; Council Decision 2011/350/EU of 7 March 2011 on the conclusion, on behalf of the European Union, of the Protocol between the European Union, the European Community, the Swiss Confederation and the Principality of Lichtenstein on the accession of the Principality of Lichtenstein to the Agreement between the European Union, the European Community and the Swiss Confederation on the Swiss Confederation's association with the implementation, application and development of the Schengen *acquis*, relating to the abolition of checks at internal borders and the movement of persons, OJ 2011 No. L160, p. 19.

implementation of the Schengen Borders Code.[29] In this connection, Marise Cremona and Jorrit J. Rijpma have observed that 'it is the Schengen external borders that have become the focus of legislative activity for the purpose of migration control'.[30] This book focuses primarily on the EU's land and sea borders.

---

[29] Recital (23) of the Frontex Regulation and Recitals (23) and (24) of the Schengen Borders Code.

[30] See Rijpma and Cremona, 'The Extra-Territorialisation of EU Migration Policies and the Rule of Law', 12.

2

At the External Borders of the EU

2.1 Intergovernmentalism and Supranationalisation

EU integration is a dynamic process in which intergovernmental cooperation and supranationalisation must co-exist in complex ways. These methods of taking action alternate or prevail depending on the subject policy area.
Early in this chapter, we will approach fuller working definitions of these
categories and examine their legal evolution. Yet prior to this, I wish to begin
with a composed, condensed scene: a setting in which we might consider the
EU's increasingly complex working methods at its borders, noting the ways
such interwoven methods begin to raise the responsibility questions which
underpin this book. As we know, many of those who approach the EU's
external borders have faced very brutal forms of uncertainty. On their part,
the physical urgency of simply leaving their disempowered transit overrides
other considerations. Yet as a vessel, piloted by people smugglers, bobs
silently within towing distance of an Italian island, its engines cut, awaiting
the dawn and a response from authorities, a network of responsibilities has
been activated which is so vast and inter-connected that legal precision and
clarity are vital but hard to access and ensure. Our study will be situated in
this emergent space. The EU's network of responsibilities is under pressure
to collaborate in a densely inter-dependent framework while still managing
forms of compliance. It is faced, in our envisaged scene, by a vessel cruelly
overloaded with people. The contradictions facing this illustrative vessel are
instructive: it may be met by a national authority, but if it is met by a joint
operation, additional complexities silently swarm upon the scene. If the EU
is represented here by Frontex, the scene presents us with coordinating,
supervising figures who are nevertheless simultaneously agents directly
representing national sovereignty. Frontex is present in this scene because
of an ambitious, growing process of supranationalisation, and yet it is held in
check by all manner of legal conditions relating to national sovereignty.
Explication of this intricate legal setting becomes essential, providing my
project with its drive and purpose.

Throughout my discussion, the term 'European Union' will refer specifically to the institutions which carry out the governmental functions of external border control: the European Council, the Council, the Commission and the Parliament. Intergovernmental cooperation is a mode of governance whereby national executives of the EU Member States negotiate with each other to achieve common objectives. Accordingly, the EU level is a framework that facilitates and enhances negotiations among Member States and ensures coordination among them. Conversely, supranationalisation is a mode of governance characterised by the competence of the EU to legislate in a specific policy area. Supranationalisation means that centralised EU governmental structures, here, the EU institutions, exercise power on policy areas within the territory of the Member States as a consequence of the conferral of power from the Member States to the EU within those policy areas.[1]

This chapter is concerned with the legal setting for operational cooperation at the EU's external borders: a mechanism set up for the efficient implementation of these common rules on standards and procedures for the control and surveillance of the external borders of the EU. Since 2004, operational cooperation has been supported by the Border Agency Frontex. As such, operational cooperation has evolved to be central to the intricate, inter-dependent process of EU integration. Policy developments since the Tampere European Council[2] have demonstrated recognition of the importance of closer cooperation and mutual technical assistance between the border control services of the Member States to ensure the surveillance of the EU's external borders and the management of migration flows. As part of its development, operational cooperation has always entailed a degree of strategy and negotiation: it has become a way of inhabiting the space of intergovernmental governance, relying upon it, while nonetheless seeking to alter it. It has been understood as a way to overcome the weaknesses of national management of the external borders, primarily with the involvement of the executives of the Member States, and with the EU only ensuring a framework for

---

[1] For an analysis of EU integration as a dynamic process, see A. Stone Sweet and W. Sandholtz, 'European Integration and Supranational Governance' (1997) 4 *Journal of European Public Policy* 297; A. Moravcsik, 'Preferences and Power in the European Community: A liberal Intergovernmentalist Approach' (1993) 31 *Journal of Common Market Studies* 473; T. A. Börzel, 'Mind the Gap! European Integration between Level and Scope' (2005) 12 *Journal of European Public Policy* 217.

[2] European Council, Tampere 15 and 16 October 1999, Presidency Conclusions.

negotiations among them.[3] In the process, operational cooperation has become part of a movement towards supranationalisation. The 2002 Commission Communication 'Towards Integrated Management of the External Borders of the Member States of the European Union'[4] and the 2006 Justice and Home Affairs Council Conclusions, which introduced the concept of 'integrated management system' for the external borders,[5] have confirmed operational cooperation as a component of a common policy on external border control. Together they contribute to a context of significant negotiation, and it is here that we must situate the setting up by the EU institutions of a common policy based on the integrated management of the external borders involving the activities of Frontex, under whose auspices operational cooperation is realised.

Thus, while supranationalisation accrues influence, features of inter-governmental cooperation must certainly still pertain to Frontex's structure, motivated by the sovereignty power exercised by Member States on issues concerning the controls of the external borders. Accordingly, the additional step towards greater supranationalisation constituted in the setting up of a European Corps of Border Guards, as provided for by the Commission since 2002, has not yet been endorsed by Member States concerned with the loss of sovereignty and autonomy in internal security issues. Significantly, when Frontex was established, and most recently in the 2011 amendment of the Frontex Regulation, the Member States were involved via the Council as part of the decision-making process. Thus, the EU institutions and the Member States are jointly responsible for the establishment of Frontex and the development of its mandate.

Supranationalisation on external border control by EU institutions cannot take place without taking into consideration the fact that Member States retain primary responsibility for the surveillance and control of their own external borders. This primary responsibility is expressed at the level of EU primary legislation by several provisions concerned with the maintenance of law and order and the safeguarding of internal security, cooperation and coordination between Member

---

[3] See the establishment in 2002, within the framework of the Strategic Committee for Immigration, Frontiers and Asylum (SCIFA) – part of the Council's working structure – of a Common Unit entrusted with the coordination of border practitioners in the Member States.

[4] European Commission, Communication from the Commission to the Council and the European Parliament 'Towards Integrated Management of the External Borders of the Member States of the European Union' COM(2002) 233 final.

[5] European Council, 2768th session of JHA Council meeting, Brussels, 4 and 5 December 2006.

States for national security purposes and the geographical demarcation of Member States' borders. The competence of the Member States in this regard must be respected when setting up an EU common policy on external border control.

Importantly, the fact that Member States have primary responsibility for the surveillance and control of their own external borders affects Frontex's activities and generates problems in the execution of the Agency's mandate – namely, Frontex is dependent on Member States' contributions in terms of equipment and deployed personnel. Before the launch of a new joint operation, there must be a call on Member States to contribute in this respect. The launch of operation Triton in November 2014 provides a telling illustration. The operation is designed to help Italy cope with the high number of migrants crossing the Mediterranean and to avoid similar humanitarian tragedies to the one which occurred a mile from the Italian island of Lampedusa in March, 2013, where 366 migrants from Africa drowned. At the time of writing, the operation is expected to cost 2.9 million euros a month and to require the deployment of two surveillance aircraft, six vessels and two helicopters. The positive outcome of the joint operation depends on contributions from France, Finland, the Netherlands, Spain, Portugal and Iceland, which is a non-EU member.[6]

Confronted with this interwoven legal setting, we must analyse the division of competence between the EU and its Member States in joint operations coordinated by Frontex. My immediate focus will be on examining the broader division of competence between the EU and its Member States in establishing a common policy on external border control, of which operational cooperation under Frontex is a part. The outcome of this analysis will, in turn, be taken up in Chapter 4 and used to scrutinise the responsibility of the EU and its Member States.

The relaxation of the EU's internal border controls and thus the necessity of strengthening its external borders are at the core of the gradual transformation of the EU into an Area of Freedom, Security and Justice. Strengthening the EU's external borders has required creating an approximation of national rules on surveillance and control of persons crossing the external borders. This has entailed conferring on the

---

[6] On joint operation Triton, www.frontex.europa.eu (accessed on 13 November 2015). On the contribution to Frontex by Member States in terms of technical equipment for border control and surveillance, see S. Carrera, 'The EU Border Management Strategy – Frontex and the Challenges of Irregular Migration in the Canary Islands', *CEPS Working Document* No. 261/March 2007, 10.

EU the competence to legislate in the policy area of external border control, giving enhanced powers to the EU institutions, especially after the entry into force of the Treaty of Lisbon. Following the entry into force of the Treaty of Lisbon, Article 67(2) of the Treaty on the Functioning of the European Union (TFEU) sets out the competence of the EU to frame a common policy on external border control. The purpose of this approximation within the EU legislative framework is to ensure that the border authorities of each Member State apply the same set of rules for preventing threats to internal security, such as irregular migration and human trafficking. This approximation of national rules on external border control within the EU legislative framework started with the integration into EU law of the Schengen Convention[7] and other measures adopted by the Schengen Executive Committee, in particular the Common Manual for Border Guards[8] (the Schengen *acquis* on external border controls), with the entry into force of the Treaty of Amsterdam in 1999. This development was strengthened with a Decision on border signs[9] and a Regulation on the stamping of documents,[10] together with several amendments to the Common Manual, which led to the adoption in 2006 of a Regulation establishing the Schengen Borders Code (SBC) bringing together all EU and Schengen rules on internal and external borders.[11]

I propose to examine the extent to which the EU may establish a common policy on external border control pursuant to the Treaty on European Union (TEU) and TFEU and what competence remains to the Member States (Section 2.2). I do not propose to address the issue of (horizontal) delegation of power from EU institutions to independent

---

[7] Convention implementing the Schengen Agreement of 14 June 1985 between the Governments of the States of the Benelux Economic Union, the Federal Republic of Germany and the French Republic on the gradual abolition of checks at their common borders OJ 2000 No. L239, p. 19.

[8] Common Manual OJ 2002 No. C313, p. 97.

[9] Council Decision of 29 April 2004 determining the minimum indications to be used on signs at external border crossing points OJ 2004 No. L261, p. 119.

[10] Council Regulation (EC) 2133/2004 of 13 December 2004 on the requirement for the competent authorities of the Member States to systematically stamp the travel documents of third-country nationals when they cross the external borders of the Member States and amending the provisions of the Convention implementing the Schengen Agreement and the common manual to this end OJ 2004 No. L369, p. 5.

[11] European Parliament and Council of the European Union, Regulation (EC) 562/2006 of 15 March 2006 establishing a Community Code on the rules governing the movement of persons across borders (Schengen Borders Code) OJ 2006 No. L105, p. 1.

agencies, as addressed by the Court of Justice in the *Meroni* cases.[12] Finally, some conclusions will be offered (Section 2.3).

2.2 The EU Power to Develop a Common Policy on External Border Control

2.2.1   An Area of Shared Competence

According to Article 4(2)(j) TFEU, in the establishment of a common policy on border control the EU's exercise of power is shared with the Member States. This means that the Member States can adopt legislation autonomously as long as the EU has not adopted legislation on the same matter.[13] When the EU takes action, the shared competence allows the EU to regulate the matter exhaustively, and this excludes the power of Member States with regard to the adoption of legislation in that field.[14] However, it is also possible that the EU may exercise its power, but not exhaustively. In this case, the Member States are only prevented from adopting legislation on the same matter on which the EU has legislated.[15] Thus, the application of shared competence works in ways which mean that when the EU legislates on a particular matter it correspondingly limits the competence of the Member States to regulate the same matter autonomously. This also means that whenever the EU adopts further legislation the dividing line will – in effect – move.[16] However, the Treaties include 'restraints' to the exercise of the EU's power on the maintenance of law and order and the safeguarding of the internal security of the EU Member States, preventing the EU from fully regulating this policy area.[17]

---

[12] Case 9/56 *Meroni* [1957] ECR 11 and Case 10/56 *Meroni* [1958] ECR 53. As I will show in Section 2.2, Frontex is the result of a (vertical) transfer of power from the Member States to the EU rather than a delegation of power from an EU institution. On this point, see R. Dehousse, 'Misfits: EU Law and the Misfits of European Governance', *Jean Monnet Working Paper* 2/2002, 13.

[13] Article 2(2) TFEU.

[14] A. von Bogdandy and J. Bast, 'The Federal Order of Competences' in A. von Bogdandy and J. Bast (eds.), *Principles of European Constitutional Law* (Hart/CH Beck/Nomos, 2011), 290. See also P. P. Craig, 'Competence and Member State Autonomy: Causality, Consequence and Legitimacy' in H. W. Micklitz and B. de Witte (eds.), *The European Court of Justice and the Autonomy of the Member States* (Intersentia, 2012); L. Azoulai (ed.), *The Question of Competence in the European Union* (Oxford University Press, 2014).

[15] Article 2(2) TFEU.

[16] von Bogdandy and Bast, *The Federal Order of Competences*, 292.

[17] Article 4(2) TEU and Articles 72, 73 and 77(4) TFEU.

2.2.2   The Common Policy on External Border Control

2.2.2.1   Treaty Basis

The development of a common policy on external border control, part of which includes Frontex's operational cooperation, started with the integration of the Schengen *acquis* in the Treaty of Amsterdam and the consequent inclusion of the rules on crossing external Schengen borders embodied in the 1990 Schengen Convention and in the Common Manual on Border Controls. Article 62(2)(a) of the Treaty establishing the European Community (TEC) envisaged power for the European Community (now the EU) to adopt 'measures on the crossing of the external borders of the Member States which shall establish standards and procedures to be followed by Member States in carrying out checks on persons'.[18] These were 'flanking measures with respect to external border controls' aimed at counterbalancing the relaxation of the internal borders of the EU.[19]

Since the entry into force of the Treaty of Lisbon, the provisions on external borders have been revised. Article 67(2) TFEU provides that the EU must 'frame a common policy . . . on external border control, based on solidarity between Member States'. Article 77 TFEU states:

1. The Union shall develop a policy with a view to: . . . (b) carrying out checks on persons and efficient monitoring of the crossing of external borders (c) the gradual introduction of an integrated management system for external borders.
   . . .
2. For the purposes of paragraph 1, the European Parliament and the Council, acting in accordance with the ordinary legislative procedure, shall adopt measures concerning: (b) the checks to which persons crossing the external borders are subject (d) any measure necessary for the gradual establishment of an integrated management system for external borders.

In comparison with the pre-Lisbon situation, the main change brought about by the Treaty of Lisbon has been the EU's recognition of the power to frame a common policy on external border control by the gradual introduction of an 'integrated management system'.

There are different interpretations of what 'integrated management system' means and, accordingly, the extent of power that the EU has in

---

[18] Article 62(2)(a) TEC. See also Article 61 TEC on the measures which must be adopted to establish progressively an Area of Freedom, Security and Justice.
[19] Article 61(a) TEC.

developing its common policy.[20] A wide interpretation looks at the definition of the concept of 'integrated border management' (IBM) given in 2006 by the JHA Council conclusions.[21] The definition describes five dimensions relating to criminal law, policing, expulsion, customs cooperation and internal security. In 2005, when the concept of IBM was being developed, Peter Hobbing observed that 'IBM rules cannot easily be located within just one framework; they are spread across a number of legal and administrative instruments', including the crossing of external and internal borders and police cooperation.[22] According to a second narrower interpretation of the concept of 'integrated management system' put forward by Steve Peers, the former solution is difficult to realise from a legal perspective.[23] This is due to the fact that, for each of the above-mentioned five fields, the Treaties provide for different legal bases subject to different rules. There is in the Treaties no definition of 'integrated border management' and, in the absence of any definitions, the different provisions constituting legal bases in criminal law, policing, expulsion, customs cooperation and internal security should prevail as *lex specialis*. According to this narrower interpretation, 'integrated management system' may be considered as entailing border control together with activities connected with the management of the external borders. In the words of Peers, Article 77(c) TFEU 'should be understood to cover the regulation of the link between external border control and the activities regulated pursuant to other provisions of the Treaty', but with a separation when the activity carried out falls within a field different from the management of the borders.[24] In this author's opinion, the more encompassing interpretation of the concept of 'integrated management system', which brings together five dimensions belonging to different

---

[20] The development of 'a common policy on integrated management of external borders' was first proposed by the European Commission in 2002 in its Communication 'Towards Integrated Management of the External Borders of the Member States of the European Union', see note n. 4, para 20. For an analysis pre-Lisbon on how Frontex constitutes a step forward in setting up an EU common policy on external border control, see H. Jorrit, 'Construction of a European Institutional Model for Managing Operational Cooperation at the EU's External Borders: Is the Frontex Agency a Decisive Step Forward?', *CEPS Challenge Paper* No. 6, Brussels, 2007.

[21] European Council, 2768th session of JHA Council meeting, Brussels, 4 and 5 December 2006.

[22] See P. Hobbing, 'Integrated Border Management at the EU level' in S. Carrera and T. Balzacq (eds.), *Security versus Freedom? A Challenge for Europe's Future* (Ashgate Publishing, 2006), 165.

[23] S. Peers, *EU Justice and Home Affairs Law* (Oxford University Press, 2011), 157.

[24] *Ibid.*, 157.

fields, appears to be more in line with the EU's political goals as expressed in the Council's conclusions. This is supported by Article 21(3) TEU, which requires the EU to 'ensure consistency between the different areas of its external action and between these and its other policies', since the management of the external borders arguably has an external component. In fact, for our purposes, the Frontex Regulation requires Frontex to facilitate operational cooperation with third countries 'within the framework of the external-relations policy of the Union'.[25] Nevertheless, from a legal perspective the obstacles pointed out above make it difficult to support the encompassing interpretation of the phrase 'integrated border management'. Therefore, in my analysis I will follow the narrow interpretation, according to which the 'integrated management system' only includes border control together with all activities linked with the management of the external borders.

In sum, although the power of the EU to establish an 'integrated management system' according to the Treaties appears to be less encompassing vis-à-vis what emerged from the relevant policy papers, the Treaty of Lisbon has arguably introduced relevant changes which point towards the development of a common policy on border control.

2.2.2.2 Administrative Cooperation and the Standing Committee on Internal Security

We must now analyse Articles 71 and 74 TFEU, which are relevant for the establishment of a common policy on border control. Article 71 TFEU, which was introduced by the Treaty of Lisbon, confers on the Council the power to set up a common policy on external border control by providing for the establishment within the Council of a Standing Committee for the promotion and strengthening of internal security within the EU. Although the Committee lacks the power to conduct operations or adopt legislative measures, it may foster cooperation between the Member States' border authorities and may 'evaluate the general direction and efficiency of operational cooperation ... identify possible shortcomings or failures and adopt appropriate recommendations to address them'.[26] Frontex representatives may be involved in the work of the Committee, which

---

[25] Article 14 of the Frontex Regulation.
[26] Article 71 TFEU. But see J. Rijpma, 'Hybrid Agencification in the Area of Freedom, Security and Justice and Its Inherent Tensions: The Case of Frontex' in M. Busuioc, M. Groenleer and J. Trondal (eds.), *The Agency Phenomenon in the European Union – Emergence, Institutionalization and Everyday Decision-making* (Manchester University Press, 2012), 86.

was established in 2010.[27] Article 74 TFEU (formerly Article 66 TEC) states: 'the Council shall adopt measures to ensure administrative cooperation between the relevant departments of the Member States . . . as well as those departments and the Commission'.[28] As Peers has observed, if Article 74 TFEU is compared with other provisions of Title V, it will be seen that the wording of Article 74 TFEU is very limited and does not give the Council the competence to adopt substantive law. Therefore, Article 74 TFEU cannot constitute the legal basis for measures of a substantive nature concerning Title V of the TFEU. However, it can be the legal basis for measures concerning issues such as exchanges of personnel.[29] Hence, Article 74 TFEU constitutes the legal basis of the Frontex Regulation along with Article 77(2) TFEU, which constitutes the legal basis for substantive measures. By adopting the Frontex Regulation, the EU uses administrative cooperation for 'the efficient implementation of common rules on standards and procedures for the control of the external borders', as stated in the SBC.[30] In particular, the Frontex Regulation requires the Member States to make personnel available for the setting up of European Border Guard Teams to be deployed in the territories of different Member States.[31]

In order to understand the way this provision operates, it is worth drawing a comparison with Article 197(2) TFEU, which also provides for administrative cooperation and applies to all policy areas in the Treaties unless otherwise provided for. Article 197(2) TFEU provides:

> The Union *may* support the effort of Member States to improve their administrative capacity to implement Union law . . . *No Member State shall be obliged to avail itself of such support.* The European Parliament and the Council . . . shall establish the necessary measures to this end, *excluding any harmonisation of the law and regulations of the Member States.*[32]

Article 197(3) TFEU provides:

> The Article . . . shall also be *without prejudice to other provisions of the Treaties providing for administrative cooperation* among the Member States and between them and the Union.[33]

---

[27] Council Decision 2010/131/EU of 25 February 2010 on setting up the Standing Committee on operational cooperation on internal security OJ 2010 No. L52, p. 50.
[28] Article 76 TFEU provides for a proposal from the Commission or an initiative by a quarter of all EU Member States.
[29] Peers, *EU Justice and Home Affairs Law*, 57.   [30] Recitals (1) and (2) SBC.
[31] Article 3b of the Frontex Regulation.   [32] Emphasis added.   [33] *Ibid.*

It follows from Article 197(3) TFEU that administrative cooperation under Article 74 TFEU constitutes a *lex specialis* rule vis-à-vis administrative cooperation under Article 197(2) TFEU. Accordingly, this last-mentioned provision does not apply to operational cooperation at the external borders for the realisation of a common policy on border control. A comparative analysis of Article 74 TFEU and Article 197 TFEU therefore makes it possible to identify the features of administrative cooperation under Article 74 TFEU. Firstly, it explicitly follows from Article 197(2) TFEU that the EU may support Member States in pursuing administrative cooperation and, furthermore, that the Member States are not obliged to take part in such cooperation, even though it is established. Conversely, Article 74 TFEU specifies that the EU has the power to set up administrative cooperation between the relevant departments of the Member States, as well as between those departments and the Commission. It is therefore mandatory for the Member States to take part in this cooperation. Secondly, Article 197(2) TFEU provides that, in establishing administrative cooperation, the EU institutions involved must exclude 'any harmonisation of the laws and regulations of the Member States'. Administrative cooperation under Article 197 TFEU is an area in which the EU has competence to support, coordinate or supplement the Member States' actions.[34] It is an area of competence where 'the Union's role is typically to adopt broad guidelines or incentive measures, or to facilitate the exchange of information about best practice', but where legally binding acts of the Union 'are not capable of harmonising national laws or having pre-emptive effects vis-à-vis domestic competence'.[35] Whereas Article 197(2) TFEU thus lays down that the EU institutions must exclude 'any harmonisation of the laws and regulations of the Member States', Article 74 TFEU does not include this wording. Therefore, administrative cooperation under Article 74 TFEU is not simply a mechanism to help the Member States improve their administrative capacity, as under Article 197(2) TFEU, but also an instrument given to the EU to regulate the policy area: notably, under the Frontex Regulation the legislator is doing more than merely adopting guidelines concerning the operations conducted by Member States. The Frontex Regulation establishes the Member States' obligations when they manage their external borders. In particular, it

---

[34] Article 6(g) TFEU.
[35] A. Dashwood, M. Dougan, B. Rodger, E. Spaventa and D. Wyatt, *European Union Law* (Hart Publishing, 2011), 104. See also J. Schwarze, 'European Administrative Law in the Light of the Treaty of Lisbon' (2012) 18 *European Public Law* 294.

requires that 'the Agency shall draw up and further develop a Code of Conduct applicable to all operations coordinated by the Agency'.[36] Thirdly, while Article 197 TFEU only provides for administrative cooperation between the Member States, Article 74 TFEU provides for administrative cooperation between the departments of the Member States, *as well as* between those departments and the Commission. This shows how, under Article 74 TFEU, the activities carried out by the Member States must be linked with those carried out by EU institutions. It follows, then, from the analytical comparison above that Article 74 TFEU empowers the Council to adopt binding measures to foster cooperation between the Member States and the Commission in the field of external border control.

In sum, the main change brought about by the Treaty of Lisbon with regard to the establishment of a common policy on external border control is giving power to EU institutions to introduce an 'integrated management system' pursuant to Article 77 TFEU. The concept of an 'integrated management system' must be interpreted narrowly to include only those activities that are connected with the management of the external borders, despite the broader definition of 'integrated management system' given in 2006 by the JHA Council conclusions. Furthermore, Articles 71 and 74 TFEU give the Council instruments to foster cooperation between the EU Member States and the Commission in the field of external border control. Article 71 TFEU facilitates cooperation between Member States to strengthen internal security within the EU; Article 74 TFEU empowers the Council to adopt binding measures for fostering administrative cooperation between the Member States and the Commission.

2.2.3   Power Remaining with the Member States

2.2.3.1   The 'Safeguard Clauses' in the TFEU on Member State Sovereignty

Crucial to the analysis now are the 'restraints' in the TFEU which prevent the EU from fully exercising its power to develop a common policy on border control. These 'restraints' – or 'safeguard clauses' regarding Member States' sovereignty, if we take a Member State perspective – concern the responsibility of the Member States for the maintenance of

---

[36] Article 2a of the Frontex Regulation.

law and order, as well as internal security and administrative cooperation to safeguard national security.[37]

2.2.3.2   Article 72 TFEU

Article 72 TFEU provides that the development of an Area of Freedom, Security and Justice should not affect the exercise of the responsibilities incumbent upon EU Member States with regard to the maintenance of law and order and safeguarding of internal security. This provision, which includes border control, means that the use of coercive measures, in order to enforce measures adopted pursuant to the provisions of the Treaties on the Area of Freedom, Security and Justice, is left to Member States' authorities.[38] Coercive measures against individuals include arrest, detention and the use of force.[39] According to Peers, the restraint provided for in this provision concerns 'the execution of operational measures necessary to implement EU rules' and does not represent 'a restriction on the subject matter which the EU is competent to address'.[40] For our purposes, the EU has adopted the SBC and the Frontex Regulation, both of which contain provisions on the use of coercive measures. However, the use of these coercive measures is a prerogative of the authorities of the Member States.

2.2.3.3   Article 73 TFEU

According to Article 73 TFEU, which was introduced with the Treaty of Lisbon, it must be *'open to Member States* between themselves and under their responsibility'[41] to organise forms of administrative cooperation to safeguard their national security. This provision concerns the possibility of coordination and cooperation between the competent authorities of the Member States in matters of national security.

---

[37] There is a further restraint in Article 77(4) TFEU which excludes the exercise of EU competence on the geographical demarcation of Member States' borders, in accordance with international law.

[38] See Peers, *EU Justice and Home Affairs Law*, 54. See also D. Kostakopoulou, 'An Open and Secure Europe? Fixity and Fissures in the Area of Freedom Security and Justice after Lisbon and Stockholm' (2010) 19 *European Security* 151, 154–156.

[39] Kostakopoulou, 'An Open and Secure Europe?', 154–156.

[40] *Ibid.*, 55. See also K. Hailbronner, 'Introduction into the EU Immigration and Asylum Law' in K. Hailbronner (ed.), *EU Immigration and Asylum Law: Commentary on EU Regulations and Directives* (CH Beck Hart Nomos, 2010), paras 11–12. On the limits to the exercise of EU power under Article 4(2) TEU in respect of Article 72 TFEU, see Peers, *EU Justice and Home Affairs Law*, 56.

[41] Emphasis added.

However, the provision does not prevent the EU from setting up forms of cooperation and coordination on national security issues; the only limit is that such coordination by the EU must not entail law-enforcement power exercised by the EU itself. In other words, in so far as the EU limits itself to the role of coordinator without any law-enforcement power, and in so far as the Member States are free to engage in a form of cooperation among themselves, Article 73 TFEU has been respected.

Article 73 TFEU, like Article 72 TFEU, leaves to the Member States the competence to exercise only law-enforcement power. If the legislator had wished to give greater competence to the Member States than that provided in Article 73 TFEU, it would arguably have chosen a more explicit wording, such as in Article 79(5) TFEU. This provision states that the power of the EU to develop a common immigration policy '*shall not affect the rights of Member States* to determine volumes of admission of third-country nationals'.[42] For our purposes, with the adoption of the Frontex Regulation, Article 2(2) allows the Member States to 'continue cooperation at an operational level with other Member States and/or third countries at external borders'.[43] However, Member States' power to regulate the management of external borders among themselves without the intervention of Frontex can only be exercised under two conditions: (i) 'such cooperation complements the action of the Agency' and (ii) such cooperation must be 'without prejudice' to Frontex's competence.[44] According to the Frontex Regulation, the Member States must 'refrain from any activity which could jeopardise the functioning of the Agency or the attainment of its objectives'.[45] The problem to be investigated here is the extent to which this provision of the Frontex Regulation may infringe Article 73 TFEU.

At first glance, a violation could be envisaged since the conditions posed by the provision in the Frontex Regulation impose limitations on the establishment of the above-mentioned cooperation among Member States. On this point, Anneliese Baldaccini has observed that 'under the terms of the Regulation, the role of the Member States vis-à-vis Frontex is to supplement or complement activities carried out by Frontex, and to refrain from activities that can jeopardise the functions of the Agency. This rather suggests a reduction of Member State autonomy in this

---

[42] Peers, *EU Justice and Home Affairs Law*, 55, emphasis added.
[43] Article 2(2) of the Frontex Regulation. The same provision is embodied in Article 16(3) SBC.
[44] Article 2(2) of the Frontex Regulation.   [45] *Ibid.*

field'.[46] I share this view concerning the reduction of Member State autonomy, but in my opinion this view must be qualified. In fact, the reduction of Member State autonomy, consisting of the limitations posed on Member States to regulate the management of external borders under Article 2(2) of the Frontex Regulation, is nothing more than the exercise of power by the EU to arrange forms of coordination and cooperation on internal security issues, which are permitted by Article 73 TFEU. In this case, there is no violation of Article 73 TFEU. There would only be such a violation if the limitations posed by Article 2(2) of the Frontex Regulation reduced State autonomy to the extent that Frontex exercises law-enforcement functions. This is not the case, as I will show in Chapter 3 when I analyse the composition and secondment of European Border Guard Teams.[47] As we have seen, the deployment of personnel from Member States to the European Border Guard Teams, in compliance with the division of competence between the EU and its Member States under EU law, and in particular Articles 72 and 73 TFEU, is a feature of Frontex's structure which generates problems in the functioning of the Agency. The Agency depends on contributions from the Member States to carry on its operations and also greatly relies on Member States' interventions.

In sum, Article 72 TFEU leaves to the Member States the competence to exercise law-enforcement power when enforcing measures adopted pursuant to EU provisions on operational cooperation and border control. Importantly, Article 72 TFEU does not restrict the areas in which the EU can adopt legislation. Article 73 TFEU leaves it to the Member States to engage in forms of administrative cooperation on matters of national security. Equally, the EU can establish such forms of cooperation as long as the exercise of law-enforcement power stays with the Member States. According to Article 73 TFEU, the EU must limit itself to coordinating administrative cooperation between Member States, without itself exercising any law-enforcement power. In this respect, the limitations posed by the Frontex Regulation on Member States to continue cooperation at an operational level with other Member States constitute an exercise of EU power under Article 73 TFEU.

---

[46] A. Baldaccini, 'Extraterritorial Border Controls in the EU: The Role of Frontex in Operations at Sea' in B. Ryan and V. Mitsilegas (eds.), *Extraterritorial Immigration Control – Legal Challenges* (Martinus Nijhoff, 2010), 234.

[47] Chapter 3, Section 3.4.

2.3   Conclusions

In this chapter we have been concerned with the division of competence between the EU and its Member States in Frontex's joint operations. The setting up of a common policy on border control after the entry into force of the Treaty of Lisbon empowers the EU to gradually introduce an 'integrated border management', which, in narrow terms, includes only those activities that are connected with the management of the external borders. Further, Article 74 TFEU enables the EU to set up administrative cooperation at the EU level. Article 71 TFEU facilitates this cooperation between Member States to strengthen internal security within the EU.

In establishing a common policy on external border control, the EU must respect the competence pertaining to the Member States: firstly, the competence of the EU Member States on the exercise of law-enforcement power when the Member States enforce measures adopted pursuant to provisions on operational cooperation and border control, and secondly, the competence of the Member States to engage in forms of administrative cooperation in matters of national security. The primary responsibility of the Member States in the surveillance and control of the external borders makes Frontex notably dependent on the contributions of the Member States in terms of equipment and personnel. The Agency tends to greatly rely on Member States' intervention and the positive outcome of joint operations can be affected by a lack of Member States' contribution in this respect.

Frontex Border Agency

Contradiction and Complexity

3.1 Setting the Scene

In this chapter, I examine the role presently played by Frontex Border Agency in the management of the external borders of the EU. Specifically, I scrutinise the legal terms framing the Agency's participation, drawing attention to areas of contradiction and complexity. To set the scene for these detailed questions, we might return briefly to our hypothetical vessel, adrift within the range of Italy's coastline, about to encounter a hybrid of national and European authority. We might gather some of this chapter's questions around a visualisation of what such an encounter means legally; because if it *is* a joint operation that becomes tasked with such a vessel and its occupants, there are many issues buried deep in the network of shared responsibility that require excavation and focused legal consideration. Consider, for instance, the complex legal standing of the Frontex Agency as a vessel partly staffed by its representatives approaches the scene: the Agency carries the label of 'autonomous', but is simultaneously compromised and inter-dependent in this matter as we shall see; some of its founding language is that of independence, but its structure and planning retain ties to the Commission which, though embedded and indirect, are no less significant for this; it can 'initiate' an operation but must rely on national resources to do so; it contains a self-monitoring element in its code of compliance which constitutes an opening for potential problems; it has been entrusted with 'increased coordination' but must seek to achieve this without a standing staff of its own border guards, relying on secondment and an additionally intricate relationship with EU Member States to do this; and it is situated in an elaborate and ceaseless interplay with sovereign nations regarding tasks and powers that require it to coordinate without taking over national prerogatives. All of this creates a fabric of legal complexity which invites problems and violations if it is insufficiently studied and understood. It is precisely this complexity, then, which we must now scrutinise.

Amendments to the Frontex Regulation in 2011 established an 'enhancement' of the role of Frontex 'in line with the objective of the EU to develop a policy with a view to the gradual introduction of the concept of Integrated Border Management',[1] which is at the core of the common policy on border control. The amendments to the Frontex Regulation concern: (i) the obligation for Frontex to draw up a Code of Conduct applicable to all operations; (ii) detailed provisions on the organisational aspects of joint operations and pilot projects and, in particular, the drawing up and content of an operational plan for each operation; (iii) the setting up of European Border Guard Teams; (iv) the possibility for Frontex to acquire, lease, own or co-own technical equipment with a Member State; (v) improved risk analysis and training of border guards; (vi) the improvement of return cooperation; (vii) several new provisions on information exchange and data protection; (viii) extended provisions on Frontex's cooperation with EU agencies, international organisations and third countries; and (ix) the obligation for Frontex to develop a Fundamental Rights Strategy.[2]

I contend that the concept of an 'integrated management system' in Article 77(2)(d) must be given a narrow interpretation, referring to border control, together with those activities which are connected with the management of the external borders.[3] Thus, operational cooperation through Frontex is excluded from fulfilling any functions beyond the management of the external borders, such as customs cooperation or criminal law, as the broader interpretation of the concept of 'integrated management system' would require.

Article 20(c) of the Frontex Regulation provides that the Frontex programme of work 'shall be adopted according to ... the Community legislative programme in relevant areas of the management of the external

---

[1] Council Regulation (EC) 2007/2004 of 26 October 2004 establishing a European agency for the management of operational cooperation at the external borders of the Member States of the European Union OJ 2004 No. L349, p. 1 as amended by Regulation (EC) 863/2007 of the European Parliament and the Council of 11 July 2007 establishing a mechanism for the creation of Rapid Border Intervention Teams and amending Council Regulation (EC) 2007/2004 as regards that mechanism and regulating the tasks and powers of guest officers OJ 2007 No. L199, p. 30 and by Regulation (EU) 1168/2011 of the European Parliament and the Council of 25 October 2011 amending Council Regulation (EC) 2007/2004 establishing a European agency for the management of operational cooperation at the external borders of the Member States of the European Union OJ 2011 No. L304, p. 1 (hereinafter the Frontex Regulation), Recital (7).
[2] Frontex Regulation, Articles 2a–7, 9, 11–11d, 13, 14 and 26a.
[3] For a detailed reasoning, see my Chapter 2, Section 2.2.2.1.

borders'. Therefore, the Regulation states that Frontex is an instrument to contribute to the establishment of the policy area of external border control. One aspect of Frontex's mandate is especially relevant in this respect. When, in 2004, the Frontex Regulation was adopted, it established that Frontex's mandate consisted of 'facilitat[ing] the application of existing and future Community measures relating to the management of external borders by ensuring the coordination of Member States' actions in the implementation of those measures'.[4] Frontex's main task was to 'coordinate operational cooperation between Member States in the field of management of external borders'.[5] The 2011 amended Frontex Regulation has retained the same wording in stating Frontex's main task. However, Frontex has now also been entrusted with *increased coordination* of the operational cooperation between the Member States'.[6]

Two aspects of Frontex's increasing role demand further scrutiny: (i) joint operations and pilot projects at the external borders; and (ii) European Border Guard Teams. These features have received increased attention from lawmakers. The European Council's Stockholm Programme, a multi-annual programme for the period 2010–2014, stated that there should be further enhancement of the role of Frontex which takes into account the role and responsibilities of Member States in the area of border control.[7] For this purpose the lawmakers have inserted two new provisions in the Frontex Regulation on joint operations and pilot projects, and two new provisions on European Border Guard Teams.[8] Additionally, Council negotiations show that joint operations and pilot projects and the European Border Guard Teams were the focus of discussions on the amendment of the Frontex Regulation. The prominence of Frontex's operational activities in its mandate is shown by its tasks of risk analysis and technical assistance.[9]

---

[4] Council Regulation (EC) 2007/2004 of 26 October 2004 establishing a European Agency for the management of operational cooperation at the external borders of the Member States of the European Union OJ 2004 No. L349, p. 1, Recital (4).

[5] Article 2(1)(a) of the Frontex Regulation.

[6] Recital (3) of the Frontex Regulation, emphasis added.

[7] European Council, 'The Stockholm Programme – An Open and Secure Europe Serving and Protecting the Citizens', 2 December 2009, OJ 2010 No. C115, p. 1, para 7.

[8] Articles 3 and 3a of the Frontex Regulation.

[9] See H. Jorry, 'Construction of a European Institutional Model for Managing Operational Cooperation at the EU's External Borders: Is the Frontex Agency a Decisive Step Forward?' *CEPS Paper in Liberty and Security in Europe* No. 6/March 2007; A. W. Neal, 'Securitization and Risk at the EU Border: The Origins of Frontex' (2009) 47 *Journal of Common Market Studies* 333, 347; J. Pollak and P. Slominski, 'Experimentalist but not Accountable Governance? The Role of Frontex in Managing the EU's External Borders' (2009) 32 *West European Politics* 904, 910; J. Rijpma, 'Hybrid Agencification in the Area of

In the ensuing sections, I will analyse Frontex's structure (Section 3.2) and then proceed to examine those aspects of joint operations and pilot projects at the external borders that are most relevant to my analysis (Section 3.3). Building upon this, I will consider the composition and secondment of the European Border Guard Teams and discuss the feasibility of having a European system of border guards as part of Frontex's long-term development (Section 3.4). In conclusion, I will present my findings (Section 3.5).

3.2   Preliminary Observations on Frontex's Structure

Frontex is an EU body with legal personality, which acts in full autonomy and independence and has an autonomous budget stemming from the EU.[10] Yet as we have begun to establish, the network of responsibilities that the Agency is situated within has interdependencies and complexities that tend to defy the neatness of such categories. We have seen, for instance, the manner in which the Agency is considerably dependent on the contributions by the Member States. Any lack of interest in intervening in a Frontex's joint operation by Member States – which contend, after all, with political influences regarding border control that are scarcely noted for their stability, consistency or long-sighted calmness – may jeopardise setting up and conducting joint operations that achieve a positive outcome.

As for Frontex's legal personality, the Frontex Regulation states that, in each of the Member States, Frontex enjoys the most extensive legal capacity accorded to legal persons under each Member State's law. In particular, Frontex may acquire or dispose of movable or immovable property and may be party to legal proceedings in each Member State.[11] Further, the Frontex Regulation provides for Frontex's contractual and non-contractual liability.[12] Conversely, the Frontex Regulation does not specify whether Frontex also has international legal personality (i.e. whether it can have international rights and duties enforceable by law).[13] An analysis of whether Frontex has international legal personality

---

Freedom, Security and Justice and Its Inherent Tensions: The Case of Frontex' in M. Busuioc, M. Groenleer and J. Trondal (eds.), *The Agency Phenomenon in the European Union – Emergence, Institutionalization and Everyday Decision-making* (Manchester University Press, 2012), 92.

[10] Article 15 of the Frontex Regulation.   [11] *Ibid.*
[12] Article 19 of the Frontex Regulation.
[13] M. N. Shaw, *International Law* (Cambridge University Press, 2008), 195.

falls outside the scope of this book and is a separate problem. However, the following can be briefly observed. If it were to be found that Frontex has international legal personality, including capacity to conclude international agreements, this would imply that the EU has delegated its international legal personality, which is improbable. This way of thinking seems to be shared by Frontex. According to Article 14(2) of the Frontex Regulation, Frontex can enter into working arrangements with the authorities of third countries for operational cooperation at the external borders of the EU. These working arrangements are aimed at facilitating cooperation with the authorities of third countries by promoting developments in the areas of information exchange, risk analysis and training. Additional aims include coordinating certain joint operational measures and promoting active discussion of the development of border procedures at the technical level. The texts of the working arrangements concluded by Frontex so far clearly state that they are not international treaties and that their practical implementation must not be regarded as fulfilling international obligations of the EU and the third country that is party to the working arrangement.[14] Should a further examination of this issue establish that Frontex enjoys international legal personality, the approach of this book to the EU's responsibilities and legal standing regarding non-refoulement may need to be adjusted accordingly.

For now, however, it must suffice to examine the autonomy and independence of Frontex. In structural terms, Frontex is represented by an Executive Director appointed by the Management Board on a proposal from the Commission.[15] The Executive Director 'shall be completely independent in the performance of his/her duties' and '[W]ithout prejudice to the respective competencies of the Commission' he/she 'shall neither seek nor take instruction from any government or from any other body'.[16] The Management Board is composed of one representative from each Member State, who must be an expert in the field of operational cooperation on border management, and two representatives of the

---

[14] See e.g. the Working Arrangement on the establishment of Operational Cooperation between the European Agency for the Management of Operational Cooperation at the External Borders of the Member States of the European Union (Frontex) and the Ministry of Internal Affairs of Georgia.

[15] Article 20(a) of the Frontex Regulation. The link between Frontex and the Commission is weaker than that of other agencies, since the Commission suggests a list of candidates after an advertised open competition, Article 26(1) of the Frontex Regulation. See E. Chiti, 'An Important Part of the EU's Institutional Machinery: Features, Problems and Perspectives of European Agencies' (2009) 46 *Common Market Law Review* 1395, 1419.

[16] Article 25 of the Frontex Regulation, emphasis added.

Commission.[17] Concerning planning and a framework for action, the Management Board '*after receiving the opinion of the Commission*, [shall] adopt ... the Agency's programme of work for the coming year and forward it to the European Parliament, the Council and the Commission'.[18] As will be apparent from this presentation of Frontex's structure and of the procedure for the adoption of Frontex's programme of work, the programmatic statement of Frontex's autonomy and independence does not hold true in practice. Frontex depends on the Commission, even though it is not part of any Directorate-General of the Commission.[19] Specifically, the Commission's Directorate-General for Home Affairs is responsible for Frontex's activities. In sum, Frontex's structure shows that the Commission has a material influence on its work.

Regarding the political link between the Commission and Frontex, Sergio Carrera[20] has pointed out that the Commission 'guides Frontex on the state of affairs of the Council and informal bilateral relations with member states' representatives ... While it may be true that the Commission always keeps in mind the independence of Frontex, it seems clear that its influence over the actual activities of the agency is rather substantial'.[21] Moreover, on the relationship between the Commission and the EU agencies generally, Madalina Busuioc[22] has reported that the Commission exercises 'ongoing control' and 'informal influence' on the decisions of Frontex's Management Board.[23]

---

[17] Article 21(1) of the Frontex Regulation.

[18] Article 20(2)(c) of the Frontex Regulation, emphasis added.

[19] On the role of the EU agencies, see M. Shapiro, 'Independent Agencies' in P. P. Craig and G. de Burca (eds.), *The Evolution of EU Law* (Oxford University Press, 2011), 111; A. Wonka and B. Rittberger, 'Credibility, Complexity and Uncertainty: Explaining the Institutional Independence of 29 EU Agencies' (2010) 33 *West European Politics* 730; J. Gronnegaard Christensen, 'Administrative Capacity, Structural Choice and the Creation of EU Agencies' (2010) 17 *Journal of European Public Policy* 176; M. Busuioc, 'Accountability, Control and Independence: The Case of European Agencies' (2009) 15 *European Law Journal* 599; E. Vos, 'Reforming the European Commission: What Role to Play for EU Agencies?' (2000) 37 *Common Market Law Review* 1113. See also the political and judicial controls to which Frontex may be subject: Article 25(2) of the Frontex Regulation and Article 263 of the Treaty on the Functioning of the European Union (TFEU).

[20] Researcher at the Centre for European Policy Studies, Brussels.

[21] S. Carrera, 'The EU Border Management Strategy – Frontex and the Challenges of Irregular Migration in the Canary Islands', *CEPS Working Document* No. 261/March 2007, 13.

[22] Researcher at the London School of Economics and Political Science.

[23] Busuioc, 'Accountability, Control and Independence', 610.

3.3   Joint Operations and Pilot Projects at the External Borders

We turn now to joint operations and pilot projects which are the implementation of operational aspects of external border management at land,
air and sea borders. For our purposes, in the context of joint operations,
four aspects are relevant: (a) the initiation of a joint operation; (b) the
adoption of the operational plan; (c) the role of the coordinating officer;
and (d) the suspension or termination of joint operations.

Initiating an operation starts with a proposal from a Member State,
which is then scrutinised by Frontex: 'the Agency shall evaluate, approve
and coordinate proposals for joint operations and pilot projects made by
Member States'.[24] However, the initiative with regard to the start of the
operations may also come from Frontex itself. Article 3(1) of the Frontex
Regulation states: 'the Agency may itself initiate and carry out joint
operations and pilot projects in cooperation with the Member States
concerned and in agreement with the host Member States'.[25] The host
Member State is the 'Member State in which a joint operation, a pilot
project or a rapid intervention takes place or from which it is launched'.[26]
In Council negotiations on the text of Article 3(1) of the Frontex
Regulation, Malta initially opposed giving Frontex the power to initiate
operations. Malta suggested that Frontex should be limited to having the
task of 'proposing' the start of an operation rather than directly 'initiating' one.[27] Malta's suggestion was not endorsed in the final version of the
provision. In addition, Member States' involvement in Frontex-initiated
operations was also addressed in the negotiations on Article 3(1) of the
Frontex Regulation. On the one hand, the Commission, supported by
Cyprus, Greece, Italy and Malta, wanted to give exclusive prominence in
the provision to the role of the host Member State. Specifically, only the
host Member State would have to agree to Frontex's initiative. On the
other hand, Sweden and France favoured including a cooperative role for
the other Member States participating in an operation.[28] As shown
above, a compromise text was adopted. Also, before initiating an operation, Frontex carries out a risk analysis, taking into consideration the

---

[24] Article 3(1) of the Frontex Regulation.
[25] *Ibid.* Jorrit Rijpma has pointed out how Frontex's task of launching initiatives for
operations shows its 'too wide discretion to make political choices': see J. Rijpma,
'Hybrid Agencification', 93.
[26] Article 1a(2) of the Frontex Regulation.
[27] Doc. 7497/10 FRONT 35 CODEC 224 COMIX 212.
[28] Doc. 9390/10 FRONT 64 CODEC 388 COMIX 339 and doc. 11843/10 FRONT 101
CODEC 658 COMIX 471.

capacity of the Member States 'to face upcoming challenges, including present and future threats and pressures at the external borders'.[29]

The organisational aspects of joint operations are laid down in an operational plan, drawn up by Frontex's Executive Director and the host Member State pursuant to Article 3a(1) of the Frontex Regulation. During the negotiations on this provision, France – supported by Hungary, Luxembourg, the Netherlands and Sweden – suggested including more detailed provisions on the involvement of the other Member States participating in an operation in drawing up the operational plan, but the Commission argued that the final decisions should be taken only by Frontex and the host Member State. The final text gives the Member States participating in a joint operation only a consultative role in drawing up the operational plan.[30] The operational plan is a very detailed description of a single operation. The Executive Director draws up the operational plan in accordance with Frontex's annual programme of work.[31] Importantly, this programme of work includes an annex, called the 'operational portfolio', which gives details of future operations.[32] As we have just seen, the annual programme of work is adopted by the Management Board after the Commission has expressed its opinion. The Commission is also a member of the Management Board with two votes. Therefore, one could argue that the Commission is to some extent involved in the planning of operations, though it does not take part in the detailed execution of the operational plan, which is a matter for Frontex and the Member States participating in the operation. Against this insistence, it might be argued that the Commission only has two votes in Frontex's Management Board (compared with the 28 votes of the Member States; each Member State has one vote) and that its influence on the work of Frontex remains limited. However, we have also recently noted that the Commission can exercise substantial informal influence on some EU agencies and, in particular, on Frontex. Therefore, 'limited' does not adequately describe the involvement of the Commission in Frontex's activities once we open the process to close scrutiny.

---

[29] Article 4 of the Frontex Regulation.
[30] Doc. 7497/10 FRONT 35 CODEC 224 COMIX 212 and doc. 9390/10 FRONT 64 CODEC 388 COMIX 339.
[31] Sakari Vuorensola, head of the Legal Division (now director of the Administration Division) at Frontex: interview at Frontex's Headquarters, 8 November 2012.
[32] Vuorensola, Interview at Frontex's Headquarters, 8 November 2012.

European Border Guard Teams, composed of guest officers, are deployed in joint operations.[33] The host Member State is required to instruct the European Border Guard Teams in accordance with the operational plan.[34] According to Article 3c(2) of the Frontex Regulation, Frontex communicates its views on the instructions given by the host Member State in compliance with the operational plan, and the host Member State is obliged to take the Agency's view into consideration. During the Council negotiations on this last provision, the Member States debated the role of Frontex in giving its views on the instructions. Malta, supported by Portugal and Romania, suggested weakening Frontex's role by not obliging the host Member State to take Frontex's views into consideration. Conversely, France, Luxembourg and the Netherlands asked to replace the term 'into consideration' with wording which would give greater prominence to Frontex's views. None of these suggestions were endorsed in the final text of Article 3c(2) of the Frontex Regulation.[35] The interface between Frontex and the host Member State and between Frontex and the members of the European Border Guard Teams is the coordinating officer,[36] an expert from the staff of Frontex, who acts on behalf of Frontex during the operations. Among other tasks, the coordinating officer is required to 'monitor the correct implementation of the operational plan'.[37]

Article 3(1a) of the Frontex Regulation sets out the circumstances in which a joint operation may/must be terminated or suspended. Frontex 'may terminate' an operation if the conditions for conducting it are no longer fulfilled, after informing the Member States concerned.[38] During the Council negotiations, Greece, Italy, Malta and Romania suggested requiring Frontex to consult the host Member State before terminating an operation. The Commission opposed this suggestion as the termination of an operation by Frontex is connected to a change in the conditions of the operation. The Commission argued that in such a case the involvement of

---

[33] Articles 1a(1a) and 3a of the Frontex Regulation. I discuss the composition and secondment of European Border Guard Teams in Section 3.4.2 below.

[34] Articles 1a(1a), Articles 3a(1)(d) and 3c(1) of the Frontex Regulation.

[35] Doc. 8244/10 FRONT 47 CODEC 274 COMIX 269.

[36] Articles 8g(2)(a) and 8g(b) of the Frontex Regulation.

[37] Council Regulation (EC) 863/2007 of the European Parliament and the Council of 11 July 2007 establishing a mechanism for the creation of Rapid Border Intervention Teams and amending Council Regulation (EC) 2007/2004 as regards that mechanism and regulating the tasks and powers of guest officers OJ 2007 No. L199, p. 30, Article 8g.

[38] Council Regulation (EC) 863/2007 of the European Parliament and the Council of 11 July 2007.

the host Member State in a decision to terminate an operation was obvious and it was not necessary to make it more explicit in the legislation.[39] Furthermore, Article 3(1a) of the Frontex Regulation states that EU Member States may ask Frontex to terminate an operation. Notably, the same provision states that in cases in which the Executive Director determines the occurrence of violations of fundamental rights or of international protection obligations which are of a serious nature or are likely to persist, he or she is obliged to suspend or terminate the operation. Article 3(1a) of the Frontex Regulation does not specify the circumstances under which operations may be terminated or suspended. In March 2012, the European Ombudsman (who is empowered to conduct enquiries into instances of maladministration by the EU's institutions, bodies, offices and agencies) conducted an enquiry by his own initiative into Frontex's implementation of its fundamental rights obligations.[40] In this enquiry, the Ombudsman sought to clarify how Frontex implements the provisions of the Frontex Regulation by its use of certain administrative mechanisms, the intent of which is for Frontex to self-monitor compliance with its obligations to respect fundamental rights. It is noteworthy that the mechanism for terminating or suspending operations is part of this administrative mechanism. The European Ombudsman noted that, in Article 3(1a) of the Frontex Regulation, the 'possibilities of suspending or terminating operations involve a considerable degree of discretion and rest on a legal appraisal of what, in most instances, will amount to complex factual circumstances'.[41] He recommended that Frontex should provide 'concrete guidance' on the specific circumstances under which operations may be terminated or suspended, and establish procedural safeguards with reference to the European Charter of Fundamental Rights.[42] He also recommended that Frontex modifies its position, as explained in Frontex's submission to the Ombudsman's enquiry, according to which 'violations of fundamental rights cannot be predicted before they actually happen and cannot be systematised ... These can only be assessed on a case by case basis'.[43] These concerns of the European Ombudsman are

---

[39] Doc. 7497/10 FRONT 35 CODEC 224 COMIX 212 and doc. 9390/10 FRONT 64 CODEC 388 COMIX 339.

[40] OI/5/2012/BEH-MHZ.

[41] Draft recommendation of the European Ombudsman in his own-initiative enquiry OI/5/2012/BEH-MHZ, point 74.

[42] *Ibid.*, point 76.

[43] Opinion from Frontex on the European Ombudsman's own-initiative enquiry OI/5/2012/ BEH-MHZ, www.ombudsman.europa.eu (accessed 13 November 2015), point 5. Following Frontex's opinion, the European Ombudsman disagreed and submitted a Special Report to

shared by the Parliamentary Assembly of the Council of Europe and by fundamental rights organisations.[44] The lack of procedural safeguards on the circumstances in which the operations should be suspended or terminated, framed within the mechanism of self-monitoring compliance with obligations concerning fundamental rights, constitutes a major problem in Frontex's work. Violations of fundamental rights or of international protection obligations may occur in the context of a joint operation. Surveillance and border control activities carry with them a high risk of violating the rights of the individuals who cross the Member States' borders or who are intercepted outside such borders. This may arise due to inexperience on the part of the personnel working at the borders, the exercise of authority by Member States participating in an operation or the factual conditions under which an operation is carried out. It is therefore crucial that the Ombudsman's concerns in this respect are addressed. The 'Frontex standard operating procedure to ensure respect of fundamental rights in Frontex joint operations and pilot projects' (hereinafter the Procedure), adopted by a Decision of Frontex's Executive Director in July 2012, does not seem to be an adequate reply to the Ombudsman's concerns.[45] The Procedure does not establish clear criteria determining when an operation should be suspended or terminated. It consists of an assessment of fundamental right–related risks which may challenge the successful conduct of each proposed operation. Despite the promise by Frontex to the Ombudsman that the Procedure would be publicly available, an application for public access to documents proved necessary in order to access the document. This resulted in part of the document being categorised under 'exceptions to public access' and being classified.[46]

Notwithstanding Member State participation in all phases of the planning of the operations, the EU legal bases governing operations

---

the European Parliament: 'Special Report of the European Ombudsman in own-initiative enquiry OI/5/2012/BEH-MHZ concerning Frontex', www.ombudsman.europa.eu (accessed 13 November 2015).

[44] Parliamentary Assembly of the Council of Europe, 'Frontex: Human Rights Responsibilities', Resolution 1932(2013), point 7.4. Among the responses of the fundamental rights organisations to the invitation of the Ombudsman to interested parties to submit observations to his enquiry OI/5/2012/BEH-MHZ, see, e.g. the contribution of Statewatch and Migreurop, www.ombudsman.europa.eu (accessed 13 November 2015).

[45] Decision of Frontex's Executive Director No. 2012/87 on the adoption of the Frontex standard operating procedure to ensure respect of fundamental rights in Frontex joint operations and pilot projects of 19 July 2012.

[46] Regulation (EC) No 1049/2001 of 30 May 2001 of the European Parliament and of the Council regarding public access to European Parliament, Council and Commission documents OJ 2001 No. L145, p. 43.

give Frontex a leading role. Frontex is empowered by the Frontex Regulation to initiate an operation and to conduct the risk assessment on which the launching of the operation depends; the operational plan is drafted and amended by Frontex's Executive Director together with the Member States; Frontex contributes to the operation by communicating its views and through its coordinating officer; and Frontex's Executive Director can suspend or terminate the operation. A frank assessment of the four aspects above shows that the role of Frontex is not only a coordinating one. Coordinating operations consists of assisting and supporting the Member States only in cases in which technical and operational assistance is required by the latter. Instead, the role of Frontex tends towards a form of directing operations (i.e. the 'increased coordination' with which Frontex is entrusted by the Frontex Regulation).

Two aspects emerging from this analysis are of particular importance: (i) the Commission is involved in the planning of Frontex's operations, though it is not involved in the execution of the operational plan; and (ii) Frontex not only supports Member States' activities but also to some extent directs operations.

3.4   European Border Guard Teams (EBGTs)

3.4.1   Current Relevant Features and Future Achievements

The EBGTs are pools of border guards deployed in joint operations, pilot projects and rapid interventions.[47] Rapid interventions are triggered by 'a situation of urgent and exceptional pressure, especially the arrival at points on the external borders of large numbers of third-country nationals trying to enter the territory of that Member State illegally'.[48]

Article 33(2a) of the Frontex Regulation states that the next external evaluation of the implementation of the Frontex Regulation 'shall also analyse the needs for further increased coordination of the management of the external borders of the Member States, including *the feasibility of the creation of a European system of border guards*'.[49] In this respect, in its 2002 communication 'Towards Integrated Management of the External Borders of the Member States of the European Union', the Commission

---

[47] Articles 3b and 8a of the Frontex Regulation.   [48] Article 8a of the Frontex Regulation.
[49] The first evaluation was made in 2009. See Frontex, External Evaluation of the European Agency for the Management of Operational Cooperation at the External Borders of the Member States of the European Union, Final Report 2009 (COWI Report).

foresaw the establishment of a European Corps of Border Guards.[50] Furthermore, by looking at the long-term development of Frontex, the Stockholm Programme reiterated the importance of studying the feasibility of creating a European system of border guards.[51] The setting up of EBGTs can be seen as anticipation of and preparation for the establishment of a European system of border guards[52] as a further step towards supranationalisation and a further implementation of a common policy on external border control.[53] Such a move would also have to take into account the fact that a European system of border guards to take over the prerogatives of the border guards of the Member States cannot be established, since it would be in violation of Article 72 TFEU concerning the division of competence between the EU and its Member States.

3.4.2   The Composition and Secondment of EBGTs

Article 3b of the Frontex Regulation states that the Member States are required to contribute to the EBGTs.[54] The contribution by the Member States is planned on the basis of annual bilateral negotiations and agreements between Frontex and the Member States.[55] The secondment of border guards decided on the basis of those agreements is compulsory for Member States, unless the latter 'are faced with an exceptional situation substantially affecting the discharge of national tasks'.[56] The extent to which the secondment of border guards to the EBGTs is obligatory for Member States was clarified by the Commission during Council negotiations regarding Article 3b of the Frontex Regulation. Following a request from France, Lithuania, Malta, the Netherlands and Sweden, the Commission explained that the Frontex Regulation prescribes the obligation of secondment for Member States and that the profiles and the overall number of border guards to be seconded by each Member State are decided by Frontex's Management Board.[57] The assessment of their capacity to second border guards is left to the Member States, which are also autonomous in selecting staff and deciding on the duration of

---

[50] COM(2002) 233 final, para 20.

[51] European Council, The Stockholm Programme, para 5.1. The Commission has issued a study on the feasibility of having a European system of border guards: DG Home, 'Study on the Feasibility of the Creation of a European System of Border Guards to Control the External Borders of the Union – ESBG', Final Report, 16 June 2014. This matter will be also addressed in the first evaluation following the entry into force of Regulation 1168/2011.

[52] See likewise Rijpma, 'Hybrid Agencification', 94.   [53] See Chapter 2, Section 2.1.

[54] Article 3b(1) of the Frontex Regulation.   [55] Article 3b(2) of the Frontex Regulation.

[56] Ibid.   [57] Doc. 7497/10 FRONT 35 CODEC 224 COMIX 212.

secondment.[58] A further contribution to the EBGTs comes from Frontex, which is required by the Frontex Regulation to deploy the border guards temporarily deployed by the Member States as national experts.[59] Notably, Frontex is not required to contribute to the EBGTs with its own personnel but with personnel seconded to Frontex by the Member States.

In summary, then, the EBGTs are composed of border guards seconded by the Member States, of border guards of the Member State hosting an operation and of border guards seconded by the Member States and temporarily put at Frontex's disposal. No Frontex personnel are part of the EBGTs.

As noted, the division of competence between the EU and its Member States prevents the establishment of a European system of border guard which, if present, would work as a body at the disposition of Frontex in the execution of joint operations. Accordingly, Frontex currently has to rely on the contribution of the Member States in terms of personnel. The secondment of border guards is mandatory for Member States once they decide to take part into a joint operation. This means that the Agency's capability and effectiveness in the management of the external borders is highly dependent on Member States' willingness and strategic interest to participate in the operations. A telling illustration of this occurred in 2010 and 2011 when Malta decided not to take part in joint operation Chronos and hence no longer commit resources to this joint operation that it had been hosting since 2008. The reason offered by the Maltese government was that the problem of irregular migration had been contained thanks to an agreement of joint patrols between Italy and Libya.[60]

In short, border guards seconded by the Member States, whether for a single operation or as national experts seconded to Frontex, are 'guest officers'. The Member State seconding the border guards is the 'home' Member State. The Member State hosting an operation is the 'host' Member State. The mechanism of deployment of the EBGTs can be defined as 'on call', since the Frontex Regulation provides that the Member States are required to second border guards at Frontex's request and not on a permanent basis.[61]

---

[58] *Ibid.*   [59] Article 3b(3) of the Frontex Regulation.
[60] On the decision of Malta not to take part in joint operation Chronos, www.timesofmalta .com (accessed 13 November 2015).
[61] Rijpma, 'Hybrid Agencification', 94.

Building upon this, it is important to develop an analysis of the provisions establishing the tasks and powers of 'guest officers' in order to examine what the prerogatives of the guest officers are.[62] Article 10 of the Frontex Regulation establishes the tasks and powers of guest officers. Article 10(1) of the Frontex Regulation provides: 'guest officers shall have the capacity to perform all tasks and exercise all powers for border checks and border surveillance' in accordance with the Schengen Borders Code (SBC).[63] Such tasks and powers are 'necessary for the realisation of the objectives' of the SBC.[64] The SBC sets out the common rules for all Member States governing the movement of persons across borders. Therefore, the tasks and powers of the guest officers are based on EU law and not on national law. In this respect, Sakari Vuorensola, the head of the Legal Division (now director of the Administration Division) at Frontex, has affirmed that the guest officers of the EBGTs are provided by EU law, that is, the Frontex Regulation, with executive powers to exercise, with certain limitations, their border management tasks. For this reason, according to the head of the Legal Division, the guest officers have a more developed role than that of being organs of their own Member States since, to a certain extent, they can be considered 'European federalist resources'.[65] This view, according to which the provisions regarding tasks and powers of the guest officers in the Frontex Regulation may point towards more supranationalisation in EU external border control, may be broadly shared. Nevertheless, it needs to be qualified by examining the limitations on the exercise of executive powers by guest officers. First, the operational execution of the provisions of the SBC is still the prerogative of the authorities of the Member States in accordance with their national law, in compliance with Article 72 TFEU.[66] When the guest officers perform their tasks and exercise their powers (i.e. give operational execution to the provisions of the SBC), they are operating in the territory of a Member State other than their own.[67] In so doing, they are required to comply with EU law, international law in accordance with fundamental rights and the national law of the host Member State.[68] Second,

---

[62] On the exercise of tasks and powers by the guest officers, see also Articles 2a and 5 of the Frontex Regulation.

[63] Article 10(1) of the Frontex Regulation.   [64] *Ibid.*

[65] Sakari Vuorensola, head of the Legal Division (now director of the Administration Division) at Frontex: interview at Frontex's Headquarters, 8 November 2012.

[66] See my analysis of Article 72 TFEU in Chapter 2, Section 2.2.3.2.

[67] Commission Communication 'Towards Integrated Management of the External Borders of the Member States of the European Union' envisaged that this could constitute a fundamental question on constitutional grounds; see note 48, 21.

[68] Article 10(2) of the Frontex Regulation.

'guest officers may only perform tasks and exercise powers under instructions from and, as a general rule, in the presence of border guards of the host Member State'.[69] Third, the national law of the home Member State applies (instead of the national law of the host Member State) when guest officers are authorised to carry weapons, ammunition and equipment. However, the host Member State can prohibit the carrying of weapons, ammunition and equipment if the same prohibition applies to its own border guards.[70] Fourth, 'guest officers shall be authorised to use force, including service weapons, ammunition and equipment, with the consent of the home Member State and the host Member State, in the presence of border guards of the host Member State and in accordance with the national laws of the host Member State'.[71] These four conditions are cumulative; but weapons, ammunition and equipment can be used for legitimate self-defence and defence of guest officers without previous authorisation and 'in accordance with the national law of the host Member State'.[72] Fifth, another limitation on the use of executive power by a guest officer in the territory of the host Member States is expressly stated in Article 10(10) of the Frontex Regulation, which constitutes an exception to the prerogatives of guest officers provided for in Article 10(1) of the Regulation: 'Decisions to refuse entry in accordance with Article 13 of [the SBC] shall be taken *only* by border guards of the host Member State.'[73] Article 13 of the SBC establishes the conditions under which a third-country national is refused entry to the territories of the Member States. Refusal of entry is 'without prejudice to the application of special provisions concerning the right to asylum and to international protection or the issue of long-stay visas'.[74] According to Article 10(1) of the Frontex Regulation, refusal of entry is the exclusive prerogative of the border guards of the host Member State. On the strength of all this, it appears that the limitations under EU law, international law, national law and the operational instructions of the host Member State restrict the executive powers which the guest officers are entitled to exercise according to the SBC.

3.5   Conclusions

In this chapter I have analysed the role presently played by Frontex Border Agency in the management of the external borders of the EU.

---

[69] Article 10(3) of the Frontex Regulation.   [70] Article 10(5) of the Frontex Regulation.
[71] Article 10(6) of the Frontex Regulation.   [72] Article 10(7) of the Frontex Regulation.
[73] Emphasis added.   [74] Article 13(1) of the Frontex Regulation.

The division of competence between the EU and its Member States in setting up a common policy on external border control is reflected in the way Frontex's joint operations are structured. In this connection, Frontex is tasked with an increased coordination of the Member States in the control of the EU's external borders, the extent of which is shown by my analysis of the structure of joint operations and of the EBGTs. In summing up the legal picture of 'who does what' in Frontex's joint operations, it is possible to draw the following conclusions. First, the Commission participates to some extent in the planning of Frontex's operations, and Frontex carries out what the Frontex Regulation calls 'increased coordination' of Member States' border control activities. In fact, Frontex is not limited to providing technical and operational assistance but takes a more leading role. Second, the EBGTs are deployed at Frontex's request. This means that: (i) the Member States make border guards available when requested; (ii) Frontex does not have personnel to deploy at its permanent disposal; and (iii) the secondment of border guards is mandatory for the Member States. Third, the tasks and the powers of guest officers are established by Article 10 of the Frontex Regulation referring to the SBC. However, the exercise of executive powers by the guest officers is restricted by several limitations of international law, EU law and national law. Finally, guest officers taking part in Frontex's joint operations support the national border guards of the host Member State, but the former do not take over the latter's prerogatives.

The International Responsibility of the EU and Its Member States in Frontex's Joint Operations

4.1 Objectives and Structure

I should recall that the arguments which animate this book are not a prosecutorial search for specific, operative violations of non-refoulement or other fundamental rights. Instead, the intentions of the close scrutiny that I present might be considered more preventative than punitive: by identifying specific areas in which the EU and Frontex are eager to gather coordinative influence but remain inter-dependent and potentially legally ill-equipped to do so, I aim to shed light on the problematic areas of law most likely to give rise to violations. Scholarship of this nature, therefore, hopes to contribute to a reduction of this likelihood. The point of the legal problem zones explicated in my discussion is that they leave *all* protagonists more exposed than they ought to be; or need to be. Those seeking refuge require assurance regarding non-refoulement; those patrolling require not merely an assurance that they have complied 'operationally' but that the whole legal setting of their actions is sufficiently established, supported and understood. It is in the light of this context that we turn to our detail: entering and examining the circumstances in which the EU and its Member States may incur responsibility for internationally wrongful acts in the context of Frontex's joint operations. In this chapter, I will begin by examining different approaches to establishing and assessing the responsibility of the EU and its Member States under international law (Section 4.2). The discussion will proceed to the constitutive elements of an internationally wrongful act and, in particular, an examination of the extent to which the conduct of a border guard of a Member State is attributable to the EU and/or to its Member States (Section 4.3). I will then analyse the extent to which the EU or a Member State might be deemed derivatively responsible for an internationally wrongful act committed by a border guard of another Member State (Section 4.4). A summary of my findings will conclude the chapter (Section 4.5).

4.2 Background to the International Responsibility of the EU and Its Member States

4.2.1 The EU's Legal Personality

Legal consequences and evaluations remain intricate; but the abiding, animating issue in this context can be plainly stated: the activities of Frontex and the Member States in the context of joint operations at the external borders of the EU may trigger the international responsibility of the EU and its Member States.

The international responsibility of the EU (i.e. the fact that the EU is subject to international law) can be assessed if it is proved that the EU has international legal personality, which is the capacity of an entity to have international rights and duties that are enforceable by law.[1] Article 47 Treaty on European Union (TEU), which is one of the 'final provisions' of the TEU, states that the EU has legal personality. There are also provisions of the Treaty on the Functioning of the European Union (TFEU) which establish the legal capacity of the EU in each Member State and the EU's contractual and non-contractual liability.[2] The question is whether Article 47 TEU can be interpreted to mean that the EU also has international legal personality.

Together with several rulings in which it is stated that the EU (in some cases the European Economic Community) is subject to international law,[3] the European Court of Justice addressed the issue of the international legal personality in the *European Agreement on Road Transport* case (the *AETR* case).[4] The *AETR* judgment was the first case in which the European Court of Justice ruled on implied powers in the external action of the European Economic Community (EEC). The case concerned a European agreement in 1962 regarding the work of crews of vehicles engaged in international

---

[1] A. Giannelli, 'Customary International Law in the European Union' in E. Cannizzaro, P. Palchetti and R. Wessel (eds.), *International Law as Law of the European Union* (Brill Nijhoff, 2011), 94. See Chapter 3, Section 3.2 with regard to the international legal personality of Frontex and Chapter 5, Section 5.2.1 on how breaches of international obligations engage the international responsibility of the EU and/or its Member States.

[2] Articles 335 and 340 TFEU.

[3] Case C-286/90 *Anklagemyndighenden* v. *Peter Michael Poulse and Diva Navigation Corp.* [1992] ECR I-6019, para 9; Case C-162/96 *Racke* [1998] ECR I-3655; [1998] 3 CMLR 219, para 45; Joined Cases C-402/05 P and C-415/05 P *Kadi and Al Barakaat International Foundation* v. *Council and Commission* [2008] ECR I-6351, para 291; Case C-366/10 *The Air Transport Association of America* [2011] I-13755; [2012] 2 CMLR 4, para 101.

[4] Case 22/70 *Commission* v. *Council (European Agreement on Road Transport)* [1971] ECR 263.

road transport. The agreement was entered into by the Member States of the EEC as it was then constituted and by other European states under the auspices of the United Nations Economic Commission for Europe. The EEC Member States concluded negotiations over the agreement by passing a resolution in the Council of the European Communities. The resolution was challenged by the Commission of the European Communities on the basis that the EEC and not the Member States should have concluded the agreement. The Commission claimed that since the adoption of Regulation (EEC) 543/69 on the harmonisation of certain social legislation relating to road transport, the EEC and not the Member States had competence in the policy area of road transport.[5]

The *AETR* judgment is relevant to this book's core considerations because the European Court of Justice addressed the issue of the EEC's legal personality in this judgment. The Court of Justice interpreted Article 210 of the EEC Treaty, which stated, 'The Community shall have legal personality', to the extent that 'in its external relations the Community enjoys the capacity to establish contractual links with third countries'.[6] The EEC's capability to negotiate and conclude international agreements with third countries requires the exercise by the EU of international legal personality. Therefore, Article 210 was interpreted as granting international legal personality to the EEC. As Marise Cremona has observed, 'there is every reason to suppose that Article 47 TFEU revised would be interpreted to this effect by the ECJ, following the reasoning in *AETR*'.[7] A further argument in favour of the international legal personality of the EU is that Articles 3(5) and 21 TEU require the EU to respect international law when it acts on the international scene.[8]

---

[5] OJ 1969 No. L77, p. 49.

[6] *Commission* v. *Council (European Agreement on Road Transport)*, paras 13–14.

[7] See M. Cremona, 'Defining Competence in EU External Relations: Lessons from the Treaty Reform Process' in A. Dashwood and M. Maresceau (eds.), *Law and Practice of EU External Relations: Salient Features of a Changing Landscape* (Cambridge University Press, 2008), 38. See also M. Cremona, 'The European Union as an International Actor: The Issues of Flexibility and Linkage' (1998) 3 *European Foreign Affairs Review* 67, 67–68; C. Tomuschat, 'The International Responsibility of the European Union' in E. Cannizzaro (ed.), *The European Union as an Actor in International Relations* (Kluwer Law International, 2002), 181–182; P. de Schoutheete and S. Andoura, 'The Legal Personality of the European Union' (2007) *LX* Studia Diplomatica, EGMONT, Brussels, 5.

[8] A. Sari and R. A. Wessel, 'International Responsibility for EU Military Operations: Finding the EU's Place in the Global Accountability Regime' in B. van Vooren, S. Blockmans and J. Wouters (eds.), *The EU's Role in Global Governance: The Legal Dimension* (Oxford University Press, 2012), 4. See also F. Hoffmeister, 'Litigating against the European Union and Its Member States – Who Responds under the ILC's Draft Articles on International

Frontex is an EU body and its activities are closely connected with the activities of EU institutions, in particular the European Commission. This is confirmed by the political and judicial controls to which Frontex is subject.[9] In earlier chapters, we have also substantiated the ways in which the EU uses operational cooperation under Frontex's auspices to develop a common policy on external border control.[10] Thus, the EU's international responsibility may be triggered by Frontex's action.[11]

4.2.2   The 'Organic Model' and the 'Competence Model'

Prior to examining the circumstances under which the EU and its Member States may incur responsibility for internationally wrongful acts in Frontex's joint operations, it is vital to identify the most suitable approach for establishing such responsibility. In evaluating this, I will focus on the element of attribution which is one of the elements necessary for establishing responsibility for an internationally wrongful act. The element of attribution is prominent in assessments of the international responsibility of the EU. This is due to the fact that a legal and political entity acts by virtue of its organs, and it is therefore necessary to ascertain when the acts of its organs are attributable to the entity itself.

Pieter Jan Kuijper and Esa Paasivirta have identified various models of attribution which can be used to establish the international responsibility of the EU.[12] These models take into consideration the 'different operational modes' and 'the essential features of EU action'.[13] For the purposes of the ensuing analysis I will take into consideration the 'organic model' and the 'competence model'.

Kuijper and Paasivirta define the 'organic model' as follows:

> By 'organic model' it is meant simply that the organization can be shown to have been acting by its organs. In other words, the acts giving rise to

---

Responsibility of International Organizations?' (2010) 21 *European Journal of International Law* 723, 724; A. Giannelli, 'Customary International Law', 93.

[9] Article 25(2) of the Frontex Regulation and Article 263 TFEU.   [10] See Chapter 3.

[11] In Chapter 3, Section 3.2, I have excluded that Frontex itself has international legal personality, and, accordingly, it cannot be responsible for violations under international law.

[12] P. J. Kuijper and E. Paasivirta, 'EU International Responsibility and Its Attribution: From the Inside Looking Out' in M. Evans and P. Koutrakos (eds.), *The International Responsibility of the European Union: European and International Perspectives* (Hart Publishing, 2013). Cfr. the analysis of Tomuschat, 'The International Responsibility', 181–189.

[13] Kuijper and Paasivirta, 'EU International Responsibility', 48.

claims of responsibility can be attributed to the organs of the organization or its personnel. If this condition can be satisfied, it points in the direction of the responsibility of the organization under international law provided other conditions for responsibility are fulfilled.[14]

In identifying this model of attribution, Kuijper and Paasivirta expressly refer to the rules 'in place to determine how and under which conditions certain acts performed by such organs and individuals can be attributed to the corporate body'.[15] Such rules are reflected in the Articles on State Responsibility (ASR)[16] and the Articles on the Responsibility of International Organizations (ARIO)[17] issued by the International Law Commission. Kuijper and Paasivirta point out that according to the 'organic model' responsibility is not established only by identifying 'a formal organic link with the organization of the state', but also by looking at complementary rules of attribution, for instance when attribution to the state or the international organisation derives from the conduct of organs placed at the disposal of the state (or international organisation) by another state.[18] According to Kuijper and Paasivirta, the 'organic model' is appropriate for establishing the responsibility of the EU in the framework of common security and defence policy (CSDP) missions.[19] In such missions, the EU does not have military personnel at its disposal and must rely on the personnel seconded by its Member States for the setting up of the mission. In this respect, the structure of CSDP missions is not different from the structure of UN peacekeeping operations to which the 'organic model' is normally applied. As with UN peacekeeping operations, the structure of CSDP missions raises the issue of whether resultant acts are attributable to the EU or to the Member States seconding the personnel. Attribution to the EU seems to be justified by the fact that CSDP missions are operationally managed at EU level and not at Member State level.[20]

Alternatively, the 'competence model' can be applied in efforts to establish the respective responsibilities of the EU and its Member States. The 'competence model' reflects the common EU situation whereby decisions taken at EU level are implemented by the Member States. Under the

---

[14] *Ibid.*, 49.   [15] *Ibid.*   [16] UN Doc. A/Res/ 56/83 (12 December 2001).
[17] UN Doc. A/64/10 (2009); A/CN.4/L.778 (12 August 2011).   [18] *Ibid.*
[19] See also Sari and Wessel, 'International Responsibility for EU Military Operations', 6; N. D. White and S. MacLeod, 'EU Operations and Private Military Contractors: Issues of Corporate and Institutional Responsibility' (2008) 19 *European Journal of International Law* 965, 973.
[20] Kuijper and Paasivirta, 'International Responsibility', 54.

'competence model', the responsibility stays where the competence is. By way of illustration: if the EU has exclusive competence in a policy area, the responsibility stays with the EU even though a decision taken at the EU level is implemented by a Member State. The 'competence model' covers breaches committed by the Member States when they implement EU legislation. Accordingly, a breach is attributed either to the EU or to the Member States, depending on how competence is allocated.[21]

The 'competence model', which focuses on preserving the division of power between the EU and its Member States, has been supported by the European Commission in the drafting of the International Law Commission's ARIO.[22] The European Commission has pointed out that the 'specificities of the European Union' derive from the fact that 'the European Union acts and implements its international obligations to a large extent through its member States and their authorities, and not necessarily through "organs" and "agents" of its own.'[23]

The Commission's defence of the *sui generis* nature of the EU as an international organisation has not satisfied the International Law Commission. The International Law Commission has preferred the 'organic model' in the drafting of the ARIO without allowing prominence to the specificities of the EU. According to some legal writers, the ARIO 'do not sufficiently take into account the specific traits of the EU structure and its functioning'.[24] Hence, it has been argued that the rules in the ARIO may be replaced by special rules for the attribution to the EU of its Member States' conduct when binding EU legislation is implemented (i.e. the 'competence

---

[21] *Ibid.*, 54, 59. On the responsibility of international organisations for conduct of member States implementing their normative acts, see N. Nedeski and A. Nollkaemper, 'Responsibility of International Organizations in Connection with Acts of States' (2012) 9 *International Organizations Law Review* 33. For a discussion on the application of the competence model in the field of human rights protection see A. von Bogdandy and M. Steinbruck Platise, 'ARIO and Human Rights Protection: Leaving the Individual in the Cold' (2012) 9 *International Organizations Law Review* 67, 70–72. An application of the 'competence model' can be found in the document on the, by now unaccomplished, accession of the EU to the European Convention on Human Rights (ECHR): Document 47+I(2013)008, para 37. See Kuijper and Paasivirta, 'International Responsibility', 64. On the consequences of the accession of the EU to the ECHR see T. Lock, 'The ECJ and the ECtHR: The Future Relationship between the Two European Courts' (2009) 8 *Law and Practice of International Courts and Tribunals* 375.

[22] For the latest comments of the European Commission on the draft Articles on the Responsibility of International Organizations, see UN doc A/CN.4/637.

[23] UN doc A/CN.4/637, 7.

[24] Kuijper and Paasivirta, 'International Responsibility', 69. See also Hoffmeister, 'Litigating against the European Union', 727.

model' may be applied). This would be made possible by invoking Article 64 ARIO, which establishes a *lex specialis* in this respect.[25]

4.2.3   Potential Breaches of the Principle of Non-Refoulement in Frontex's Joint Operations: Applying the Two Models

As will be substantiated in later chapters,[26] both the Schengen Borders Code[27] (SBC) and the Frontex Regulation,[28] which are the EU's legal instruments regulating operational cooperation at the EU's external borders, prohibit refoulement in border control activities. For instance, Article 3(b) SBC states that the Code applies to any person crossing the EU's external borders: 'without prejudice to . . . the rights of refugees and persons requesting international protection, *in particular as regard non-refoulement*'.[29] Importantly, the 2011 amendments to the Frontex Regulation have strengthened safeguards for protecting human rights

---

[25]   Kuijper and Paasivirta, 'International Responsibility', 69; Hoffmeister, 'Litigating against the European Union', 745; E. Cannizzaro, 'Beyond the Either/Or: Dual Attribution to the European Union and to the Member State for Breach of the ECHR' in M. Evans and P. Koutrakos (eds.), *The International Responsibility of the European Union: European and International Perspectives* (Hart Publishing, 2013), 307. Kuijper and Paasivirta have also identified the 'consensus model' to establish attribution to the EU and its Member States. The 'consensus model' relates to those cases in which the EU and its Member States decide whether or not to be jointly responsible in the implementation of the obligations deriving from an agreement to which both the EU and its Member States are parties. According to Kuijper and Paasivirta, the 'consensus model' applies, for instance, in bilateral association agreements in which the EU and its Member States decide which obligations of the agreement are subject to joint responsibility of the EU and its Member States. The 'consensus model' can, to some extent, be assimilated to the 'competence model' and, given this similarity, its analysis does not add any further useful elements to my discussion: Kuijper and Paasivirta, 'International Responsibility', 63.

[26]   See Chapter 5, Section 5.3.6.

[27]   Regulation (EC) 562/2006 establishing a Community Code on the rules governing the movement of persons across borders (Schengen Borders Code) OJ 2006 No. L105, p. 1.

[28]   Council Regulation (EC) 2007/2004 of 26 October 2004 establishing a European agency for the management of operational cooperation at the external borders of the Member States of the European Union OJ 2004 No. L349, p. 1 as amended by Regulation (EC) 863/2007 of the European Parliament and the Council of 11 July 2007 establishing a mechanism for the creation of Rapid Border Intervention Teams and amending Council Regulation (EC) 2007/2004 as regards that mechanism and regulating the tasks and powers of guest officers OJ 2007 No. L199, p. 30 and by Regulation (EU) 1168/2011 of the European Parliament and the Council of 25 October 2011 amending Council Regulation (EC) 2007/2004 establishing a European agency for the management of operational cooperation at the external borders of the Member States of the European Union OJ 2011 No. L304, p. 1 (hereinafter the Frontex Regulation).

[29]   Emphasis added.

which consist of Frontex's obligation to develop a Fundamental Rights Strategy and a Code of Conduct; the appointment of a Fundamental Rights Officer; and the creation of a Consultative Forum on Fundamental Rights.[30] In scrutinising joint operations and pilot projects at the EU external borders,[31] I noted that the European Ombudsman criticised the wording of Article 3(1a) of the Frontex Regulation which concerns the termination or suspension of the joint operations. According to the European Ombudsman, such a provision leaves a considerable degree of discretion to Frontex regarding the termination or suspension of the operations. At first sight, this may appear a case in which an internationally wrongful act may occur as a consequence of the implementation of EU legislation. However, in this case, breaches may occur in connection with the operationalisation of Article 3(1a) of the Frontex Regulation and not because this legislation has not been accurately drafted. In fact, the European Ombudsman, seeking to ensure the effectiveness of such provision, suggested Frontex needed to establish procedural safeguards at the operational level.

On this point, Guy S. Goodwin-Gill has analysed the legislation on Frontex-led operations as follows:

> 'The [Decision's] formulation of the applicable law in the matter of protection, however, is unremarkable, restating the principle of non-refoulement and the need to avoid indirect breach, but also providing for those intercepted an opportunity to set out reasons why they might be at risk of such a violation of their rights' ... 'The problem, though, lies not in formal recognition of protection principles but, as ever, in *operationalizing the rules* – in making protection a reality *at the point of enforcement*'.[32]

---

[30] Articles 2a and 26a of the Frontex Regulation.   [31] Chapter 3, Section 3.3.

[32] G. S. Goodwin-Gill, 'The Right to Seek Asylum: Interception at Sea and the Principle of Non-refoulement' (2011) 23 *International Journal of Refugee Law* 443, 448–449. In this quoted passage, Goodwin-Gill refers specifically to the formulation of General principle 1.2 of the Sea External Borders Decision – Council Decision 2010/252/EU of 26 April 2010 supplementing the Schengen Borders Code as regards the surveillance of the sea external borders in the context of operational cooperation coordinated by the European Agency for the Management of Operational Cooperation at the External Borders of the Member States of the European Union OJ 2010 No. L111, p. 20. The Decision has been replaced by Regulation (EU) 656/2014 of 15 May 2014 of the European Parliament and of the Council establishing rules for the surveillance of the external sea borders in the context of operational cooperation coordinated by the European agency for the management of operational cooperation at the external borders of the Member States of the European Union OJ 2014 No. L189, p. 93. For an analysis of the Regulation, see Chapter 5, Section 5.3.6.

Goodwin-Gill recognises that the EU law on Frontex-led operations provides sufficient protection against refoulement. Moreover, he emphasises that breaches of the principle of non-refoulement are most likely to occur when the rules are operationalised (i.e. when EU legislation is implemented at the operational level).

Thus, any breaches of the principle of non-refoulement committed by Member States' border guards in the exercise of their law-enforcement power are most likely to be generated by decisions made at the operational level. (Explicitly, legal infractions are more likely to stem from the point at which an operational plan is drawn up, rather than arise as a consequence of the implementation of EU legislation.)

In the light of this, there are at least two reasons why the 'organic model' is the more appropriate model for assessing the responsibility of the EU and its Member States concerning potential breaches of the principle of non-refoulement in the context of joint operations under Frontex's auspices. Firstly, operational cooperation has a structure similar to the common security and defence policy (CSDP) missions and UN peacekeeping operations to the extent that neither the EU (in operational cooperation or CSDP missions) nor the UN has its own personnel and that both the EU and the UN depend on personnel seconded by their members. As we have seen in the course of examining Kuijper and Paasivirta's work, the 'organic model' is suitable for assessing the responsibility of the EU in the context of CSDP missions. Given their similar structure, the application of the 'organic model' may also be extended to the assessment of the responsibility of the EU in joint operations coordinated by Frontex.[33]

A second factor in support of applying the 'organic model' here relates to unwarranted limitation: applying the 'competence model' rather than the 'organic model' to joint operations might result in an unsatisfactory outcome of the assessment of EU's responsibility in joint operations.

---

[33] A counterargument might be that the structure of Frontex's joint operations and CSDP missions are not the same; the extent of authority transferred to the EU in Frontex's joint operations is not as extensive as the extent of authority transferred to the EU in CSDP missions. I have explained that Frontex is responsible for increased coordination of joint operations, but this cannot be equated with a transfer of authority to the EU. However, this aspect is not relevant when deciding which model ('competence' or 'organic') to apply. This aspect will become relevant for assessing the extent of EU authority in the context of Frontex's joint operations once we proceed to examining the circumstances in which the EU and its Member States may incur responsibility for internationally wrongful acts in the context of Frontex-led operations. I will deal with this issue in Section 4.3.1.4.

The 'competence model' identifies responsibility where competence is. The exercise of law-enforcement power falls within the competence of the Member States and can never be exercised by the EU. Since it is in the exercise of law-enforcement power that possible breaches of the principle of non-refoulement occur, accordingly, in the context of joint operations, the responsibility of the EU in relation to these breaches would always be excluded. Conversely, the application of the 'organic model' allows an assessment of the extent of the EU's responsibility when Member State's border guards exercise law-enforcement power by looking at the 'derivative responsibility' of the EU. Importantly, this reasoning applies to possible breaches of the principle of non-refoulement generated by decisions taken at the operational level and not to breaches derived from the implementation of EU law.

In the context of Frontex's joint operations, the 'competence model' reasserts its usefulness in this parallel, distinct legal sphere of implementation. Though it is unlikely, breaches of the principle of non-refoulement in joint operations may be committed by Member States when they implement EU legislation (i.e. the SBC and the Frontex Regulation). This would mean that EU legislation on Frontex's joint operations has protection gaps which allow breaches of the principle of non-refoulement to occur. Goodwin-Gill has identified protection gaps in the lack of 'a protection mandate' which ought to be given to Frontex and assumed by the Member States to ensure 'the principle of effectiveness of obligations' under general international law and human rights law.[34] Accordingly, the conduct of a Member State's border guards should not be attributed to the Member State – as it would be with the 'organic model' – but to the EU, since a Member State's border guards act to implement EU legislation.[35] In such a situation the division of competence between the EU and its Member States is important, and the 'competence model' seems to be the most suitable solution. Conversely, if the 'organic model' of attribution were applied in the situation described – where a Member State's border guards commit breaches when implementing EU legislation – only the Member States, and not the EU, would be considered

---

[34] Goodwin-Gill, 'The Right to Seek Asylum', 456. On this point, see the Parliamentary Assembly of the Council of Europe's call on Frontex, the European Union and the Member States to address issues concerning the operational and structural level of Frontex and its activities, Resolution 1932(2013).

[35] See my discussion on the division of competence between the EU and its Member States in Frontex's joint operations in Chapter 2, Section 2.2.

responsible for the breaches, in spite of the fact that implementation of EU legislation is the crux of the matter.[36]

4.2.4   The International Law Commission's Work: A Matter of Legal Authority

The 'organic model' of attribution is reflected in the ASR and the ARIO which were adopted by the International Law Commission in 2001 and in 2011, respectively. They 'seek to formulate, by way of codification and progressive development, the basic rules of international law concerning the responsibility of States [and international organisations] for their internationally wrongful acts'.[37] The ASR has been noted in a resolution of the United Nations General Assembly of the United Nations (the UN General Assembly), and the International Law Commission has recommended that the UN General Assembly consider convening an international conference of plenipotentiaries to conclude a convention on the international responsibility of states. Also, the ARIO has been noted in a resolution of the UN General Assembly and the International Law Commission has recommended that the UN General Assembly hold an international conference to conclude a convention on the topic.

The International Law Commission is a subsidiary organ of the UN General Assembly. It was established by the UN General Assembly in 1949 for the discharge of its responsibilities under Article 13(1) of the Charter of the United Nations which requires the UN General Assembly to 'initiate studies and make recommendations for the purpose of . . . encouraging the progressive development of international law and its codification'.[38] According to its Statute, the International Law Commission 'shall have for its object the promotion of the progressive development of international law and its codification'.[39] The function of promoting 'the progressive development of international law' means 'the

---

[36] Kuijper and Paasivirta, 'International Responsibility', 54; E. Cannizzaro, 'Postscript to Chapter 12' in M. Evans and P. Koutrakos (eds.), *The International Responsibility of the European Union: European and International Perspectives* (Hart Publishing, 2013), 300.

[37] *Yearbook of the International Law Commission*, 2001, Vol. II, Part Two, p. 31, para (1). Although the quotation is taken from the Commentaries to the ASR, the definition also applies to the ARIO since 'codification' and 'progressive development' of international law are both tasks of the International Law Commission according to its Statute.

[38] Charter of the United Nations, San Francisco, 24 October 1945, in force 24 October 1945, 1 UNTS XVI.

[39] Statute of the International Law Commission adopted by the General Assembly in Resolution 174 (II) of 21 November 1947, as amended by Resolutions 485 (V) of

preparation of draft conventions on subjects which have not yet been regulated by international law or in regard to which the law has not yet sufficiently developed in the practice of State'.[40] The function of promoting the 'codification of international law' means 'the more precise formulation and systematisation of rules of international law in fields where there already has been extensive State practice, precedent and doctrine'.[41]

Notwithstanding the distinction made between these two functions in the International Law Commission's Statute, it is common ground that in the Commission's work the two functions often overlap. The International Law Commission has noted that in its work a composite idea of 'codification and progressive development' prevails according to which already accepted principles of regulation are codified together with the development of new ideas.[42] Therefore, distinguishing between the two functions is not possible and the extent to which the work of the International Law Commission is more 'progressive development' or more 'codification' depends on the topic currently presiding in its work.[43]

As for the legal authority of the ASR and the ARIO, the Articles are legally binding to the extent that they codify existing rules of customary international law and are, therefore, widely supported by practice.[44] Case law has affirmed that several provisions of the ASR constitute customary international law.[45] With regard to the ARIO, the International Law

12 December 1950, 984 (X) of 3 December 1955, 985 (X) of 3 December 1955 and 36/39 of 18 November 1981.

[40] Statute of the International Law Commission, Article 15.   [41] *Ibid.*

[42] Report of the Working Group on review of the multilateral treaty-making process, Document A/CN.4/325, para 102; and Report of the Commission to the General Assembly on the work of its forty-eighth session, A/CN.4/SER.A/1996/Add.1 (Part 2), paras 156, 157.

[43] Report of the Commission to the General Assembly on the work of its forty-eighth session, A/CN.4/SER.A/1996/Add.1 (Part 2), para 157.

[44] For an analysis of the ASR and the ARIO as a source of international law, see C. Parry, *The Sources and Evidences of International Law* (Manchester University Press, 1965), 23–24; D. D. Caron, 'The ILC Articles on State Responsibility: The Paradoxical Relationship between Forma and Authority' (2002) 96 *The American Journal of International Law* 857, 867; M. N. Shaw, *International Law* (Cambridge University Press, 2008), 781; I. Brownlie, *Principles of Public International Law* (Oxford University Press, 2012), 43–44; M. Janmyr, *Protecting Civilians in Refugee Camps: Issues of Responsibility and Lessons from Uganda* (DPhil thesis, University of Bergen, 2012), where it is argued that 'in the absence of customary international law … a number of general principles could thus justify the inclusion of certain rules in the ARIO', 284.

[45] See e.g. Application of the Convention on the Prevention and Punishment of the Crime of Genocide (Bosnia and Herzegovina v. Serbia and Montenegro), Judgment, I.C.J Reports 2007 (hereinafter the Genocide Convention Case), paras 385, 401, 407; Rainbow Warrior Arbitration between France and New Zealand, 82 ILR, 499; Case C-63/09 Walz v. Clickair SA [2010] ECR I-4239, para 27–28.

Commission has admitted that the Articles 'are based on a limited practice' and that the ARIO does not have the same legal authority as the ASR. ARIO's legal authority depends on the extent to which it is accepted by states and international organisations.[46] The importance of ARIO is noteworthy since some of its Articles have been used by national courts and the European Court of Human Rights (ECtHR) in their judgments.[47] This shows that while ARIO's Articles are not legally binding in so far as they do not reflect customary international law, ARIO's Articles nevertheless have a legal value.[48]

4.3   The Constitutive Elements of an Internationally Wrongful Act

The legal analysis which follows gathers details in the service of a framing question. Namely, to what extent is the conduct of a border guard of a Member State attributable to the EU and/or to its Member States participating in a joint operation? Article 4 ARIO provides that:

> There is an internationally wrongful act of an international organization when conduct consisting of an action or omission:
>
> (a) is *attributable* to that organization under international law; and
> (b) constitutes a breach of an international obligation of that organization.[49]

Article 4 ARIO lists the constituent elements of an internationally wrongful act of an international organisation. Article 2 ASR makes the same provision, except with the word 'state' instead of 'international organization'.[50]

---

[46] *Yearbook of the International Law Commission*, 2011, Vol. II, Part Two, p. 3, para (5).

[47] See Section 4.3.1.2 below. For the decisions of national courts, see the UK House of Lords *R (Al-Jedda)* v. *Secretary of State for Defence* [2007] UKHL 58, [2008] 1 AC 332; and the District Court of Appeal of the Hague *Mustafic et al.* v. *the Netherlands*, LJN: BR0132, 5 July 2011; for the ECtHR, *Behrami and Behrami and Saramati* v. *France, Germany and Norway* App No. 71412/01 and 78166/01 (ECtHR, 02 May 2007) and *Al-Jedda* v. *the United Kingdom* App No. 27021/08 (ECtHR, 7 July 2011).

[48] The practical importance of ARIO has also been pointed out by J. Alvarez, 'Misadventures in Subjecthood' (2010), EJIL: Talk! www.ejiltalk.org (accessed 13 November 2015).

[49] Emphasis added.

[50] For an analysis of the consequences of the transposition of the wording of the ASR to the responsibility of international organisations see J. d'Aspremont 'The Articles on the Responsibility of International Organizations: Magnifying the Fissures in the Law of International Responsibility' (2012) 9 *International Organizations Law Review* 15.

4.3.1 Responsibility of the EU

4.3.1.1 Attribution of Conduct to Frontex

The attribution of conduct to Frontex is elucidated by looking at Article 4 ASR and Article 7 ARIO. According to Article 4 ASR, 'the conduct of any State organ shall be considered an act of that State under international law.' Article 7 ARIO states: 'The conduct of an organ of a State ... that is placed at the disposal of [another] an international organization shall be considered under international law an act of the latter organization if the organization exercises effective control over that conduct.' Article 4 ASR affirms the principle of the unity of the State, whereby the conduct of an organ of a State is attributable to that State.[51] The definition of a State organ given in Article 4 ASR is very broad: 'whether the organ exercises legislative, executive, judicial or any other functions, whatever position it holds in the organization of the State, and whatever its character as an organ of the central Government or of a territorial unit of the State'. No distinction is made between the conduct of superior or subordinate officials and it is the internal law of the State that determines the status of a State organ: 'An organ includes any person or entity which has that status in accordance with the internal law of the State.'[52] As addressed in Chapter 3,[53] the border guards of Member States operating in Frontex's joint operations exercise governmental functions. Usually, law-enforcement authorities (such as the police or bodies with a military status such as Guardia di Finanza in Italy and Koninglijke Marechaussee in The Netherlands) are responsible for border controls. Therefore, the border guards of a Member State fall within the definition in Article 4 ASR and under international law, as organs of the Member State, their conduct must be considered acts of the Member State. However, Member States participating in operations are required to make their border guards available to contribute to the European Border Guard Teams (EBGTs) at the request of Frontex. Article 7 ARIO is thus relevant.

In the Commentaries to the ARIO, the International Law Commission explains that Article 7 ARIO applies where the personnel seconded by a state to an international organisation act to a certain extent as an organ of the seconding state.[54] The Commentaries to both the ASR and the

---

[51] *Yearbook*, 2001, p. 40, paras (1) and (6).
[52] Article 4(2) RAS. See *Yearbook*, 2001, p. 41.   [53] Chapter 3, Section 3.4.2.
[54] *Yearbook*, 2011, p. 19, para (1). Article 7 ARIO, para (1). If the organ of a State is placed fully at the disposal of an international organisation, then the conduct of the seconded

ARIO are issued by the International Law Commission and are official. In this respect, according to Article 20 of the Statute of the International Law Commission,[55] the International Law Commission is required 'to prepare its drafts in the form of articles and shall submit them to the General Assembly together with a commentary containing ... adequate presentation of precedents and other relevant data, including treaties, judicial decisions and doctrine'. The Commentaries give the example of military contingents put at the disposal of the UN for its peacekeeping operations.[56] In this case, the seconding state still has disciplinary powers and criminal jurisdiction over the seconded personnel.[57] The Commentaries note that in this situation it is not clear whether the conduct of the seconded organ is attributable to the seconding state or to the receiving organisation.[58] This problem is resolved by looking at who has effective control over the conduct of the seconded organ.

In Frontex's joint operations the Member State hosting the operation has civil liability for damage and criminal jurisdiction for criminal offences committed by guest officers, whereas disciplinary powers over border guards remain with the home Member State.[59] In order to understand whether the conduct of border guards in Frontex's operations is attributable to the Member States or to the EU, it is necessary to assess whether Frontex exercises effective control over the conduct of the border guards.[60] To make this assessment, it is first necessary to understand when there is 'effective control'.

---

organ is without doubt attributable to the international organisation. In this case Article 6 ARIO applies: '1.The conduct of an organ or agent of an international organization in the performance of functions of that organ or agent shall be considered an act of that organization under international law, whatever position the organ or agent holds in respect of the organization. 2. The rules of the organization shall apply in the determination of the functions of its organs and agents.'

[55] UN Doc. A/CN.4/4.   [56] *Yearbook*, 2011, p. 19, para (1).   [57] *Ibid.*   [58] *Ibid.*

[59] Chapter 3, Section 3.4.2.

[60] This is not necessarily an either/or question since in principle it may be possible to attribute the wrongful conduct of border guards under Frontex's joint operations both to the Member State seconding the border guards and to the EU acting through Frontex, see e.g. A. Nolkaemper and D. Jacobs, 'Shared Responsibility in International Law: A Conceptual Framework' (2013) 34 *Michigan Journal of International Law* 359; F. Messineo, 'Multiple Attribution of Conduct', *SHARES Research Paper* No. 2012–11; O. F. Direk, 'Responsibility in Peace Support Operations: Revisiting the Proper Test for Attribution Conduct and the Meaning of the "Effective Control" Standard' (2014) 61 *Netherlands International Law Review* 1, 9. In my book, I do not examine this case of multiple attribution since neither the text of Article 7 ARIO nor the Commentaries to the Article 7 ARIO seem to recognise it.

4.3.1.2 Interpretation of the Concept of 'Effective Control' by the Courts

The ECtHR dealt with the concept of 'effective control' in the *Behrami* and *Saramati* cases.[61] The cases concerned NATO's intervention in Yugoslavia in 1999; UN Security Council Resolution 1244 (1999) which gave a mandate to the UN Mission in Kosovo (UNMIK); and the military forces led by NATO to maintain security and manage the civil administration of Kosovo. The *Behrami* case was concerned with the killing and injuring of two boys due to the belated explosion of a NATO mine. Mr Behrami, father of the two boys, claimed that the French forces seconded to the Kosovo Force (KFOR), a NATO-led international peacekeeping force responsible for establishing security in Kosovo, were responsible because they had not de-mined the area. The *Saramati* case concerned the internment of Mr Saramati on the charge of attempted murder by order of KFOR officials belonging to the French and Norwegian military forces.[62] UNMIK was involved in the operations in both cases. In these two cases the applicants claimed that there had been breaches of Article 2 ECHR and Articles 5 and 13 ECHR, respectively. The two applications were jointly declared inadmissible *ratione personae* by the ECtHR, which established that the alleged breaches were attributable to the United Nations. The ECtHR stated that '[the United Nations Security Council] relies on States to provide the necessary military means ... the multilateral and complex nature of such security mission renders necessary some delegation of command ... the Court considers that the key question is whether the United Nations Security Council retained ultimate authority and control so that operational command only was delegated'.[63] While affirming the 'effectiveness or unity of NATO command in operational matters',[64] by applying the 'ultimate authority and control test', the ECtHR found that 'KFOR was exercising lawfully delegated Chapter VII powers of the [United Nations Security Council] so that the impugned action was, in principle, attributable to the [United Nations]'.[65] The ECtHR also found that UNMIK was a subsidiary organ of the United Nations created under Chapter VII of the UN Charter.[66] Accordingly, the ECtHR found that 'authority and

---

[61] *Behrami and Saramati.*

[62] The application was initially also made against Germany, which was removed from the list of defendants as the applicant was unable to prove its involvement in his detention, see *Behrami and Saramati*, paras 64, 65.

[63] *Behrami and Saramati*, paras 132–133.   [64] *Ibid.*, para 139.   [65] *Ibid.*, para 141.

[66] *Ibid.*, para 142–143.

control' was retained by the UN Security Council when it delegated its security powers by Security Council Resolution 1244 to KFOR and UNMIK, and that the impugned actions of KFOR and UNMIK were attributable to the UN.[67] Given this attribution to the UN, the ECtHR declared it lacked jurisdiction *ratione personae* to examine the case.[68]

Thus, the test of attribution adopted by the ECtHR is one of 'ultimate authority and control' by delegation of powers. This is not a test which looks at the factual elements as it would have been if, as in the *Behrami* and *Saramati* decision, the ECtHR had considered who had 'operational command' (i.e. who retains command and control over the operations). In order to examine the choice of the ECtHR with regard to the applied test of attribution, a distinction needs to be drawn between rules of attribution and rules of delegation. The rules of attribution establish whether a state or international organisation is responsible under international law. The rules of delegation establish whether an organ of an international organisation can lawfully delegate its powers to another entity under the internal rules of the organisation.[69] On this point, Marko Milanovic and Tatjana Papic have put forward the view that 'an authorisation by the Security Council may preclude the wrongfulness of an act by a state, but it cannot have an impact on attribution', as the ECtHR maintained in its decision in *Behrami* and *Saramati*.[70] The test of attribution applied by the ECtHR in this decision fails to distinguish between the rules of attribution and the rules of delegation.[71]

---

[67] *Ibid.*, paras 134, 144.   [68] *Ibid.*, paras 151–152.

[69] See likewise M. Milanovic and T. Papic, 'As Bad as It Gets: The European Court of Human Rights' Behrami and Saramati Decision and General International Law' (2009) 58 *International and Comparative Law Quarterly* 267, 281; K. M. Larsen, 'Attribution of Conduct in Peace Operations: The Ultimate Authority and Control Test' (2008) 19 *European Journal of International Law* 509, 516–517.

[70] Milanovic and Papic, 'As Bad as It Gets', 281.

[71] See Larsen, 'Attribution of Conduct', 522; A. Orakhelashvili, 'R 'R(on the Application of Al-Jedda) (FC) v. Secretary of State for Defence [2007] UKHL 58' (note) (2008) 102 *The American Journal of International Law* 337, 341. The ECtHR adopted the approach of some legal scholars who affirmed the legality of delegation of power by the Security Council as long as the Security Council retains the overall authority and control over the exercise of such power. Other legal scholars maintain that responsibility cannot be delegated but stays with the delegating organ: see D. Sarooshi, *The United Nations and the Development of Collective Security* (Oxford University Press, 2000); E. de Wet, *The* Chapter VII *Powers of the United Nations Security Council* (Hart Publishing, 2004). Christian Tomuschat justifies 'opting for the looser criterion of "ultimate authority and control" if an authorisation to use force is surrounded by a tight network of supervision and control': C. Tomuschat, 'Attribution of International Responsibility: Direction and

The 'ultimate authority and control' test has been applied by the ECtHR in several cases since the *Behrami* and *Saramati* cases.[72] In 2007, the ECtHR made a partial twist in its interpretation of the concept of 'effective control' in the *Al-Jedda* cases. In *R (Al-Jedda) v. Secretary of State for Defence*,[73] the United Kingdom House of Lords ruled on the application of Mr Al-Jedda, who had been subject to preventive detention in Iraq by British troops between 2004 and 2007 without charge or trial. Mr Al-Jedda claimed that his detention breached Article 5 ECHR. The presence of a multinational force in Iraq was authorised by Security Council Resolution 1546 (2004). The House of Lords was not requested to overrule the *Behrami* and *Saramati* case, but to decide whether the facts in *Al-Jedda* were the same as the facts in *Behrami* and *Saramati*.[74] The majority of the Law Lords ruled that the facts in the two cases were different, since in Iraq there was no delegation of powers by the United Nations which was the basis of attribution of the impugned action in *Behrami* and *Saramati*.[75] Accordingly, the 'ultimate control' test did not apply. The House of Lords ruled that the 'effective command and control' test was the test of attribution to be applied in the *Al-Jedda* case.[76] According to this test, the multinational force was found to have effective command and control. Thus, the British troops, as members of the multinational force, were found responsible for the detention of Mr Al-Jedda. In this process, a majority of the House of Lords applied the attribution test based on who exercises effective control of the operation, but without dismissing the 'ultimate control' test. The decision was based on the distinction between the facts of the two cases.

The approach of the House of Lords in the *Al-Jedda* case was followed by the ECtHR in the *Al-Jedda v. United Kingdom* case.[77] The ECtHR concurred with the majority of the House of Lords. By agreeing with the distinction between the facts in the *Al-Jedda* case and the facts in the

---

Control' in M. Evans and P. Koutrakos (eds.), *The International Responsibility of the European Union: European and International Perspectives* (Hart Publishing, 2013), 30.

[72] *Kasumaj v. Greece* App No. 6974/05 (ECtHR, 5 July 2007); *Gajic' v. Germany* App No. 31446/02 (ECtHR, 28 August 2007); and *Beric 'and Others v. Bosnia and Herzegovina* App No. 36357/04 (ECtHR, 16 October 2007).

[73] R (*Al-Jedda*).

[74] See F. Messineo, 'The House of Lords in *Al-Jedda* and Public International Law: Attribution of Conduct to Unauthorised Forces and the Power of the Security Council to Displace Human Rights' (2009) 56 *Netherlands International Law Review* 35, 46; Orakhelashvili, 'R 'R(on the Application of Al-Jedda)', 340.

[75] *R (Al-Jedda) v. Secretary of State for Defence*, para 24. [76] *Ibid.*

[77] *Al-Jedda v. the United Kingdom.*

Behrami and *Saramati* cases, it ruled that 'the United Nations Security Council had neither effective control nor ultimate authority and control over the acts and omissions of troops within the Multinational Force'.[78] Mr Al-Jedda's detention was attributed to the United Kingdom rather than to the UN. In the *Al-Jedda* case, the test of attribution of conduct applied by both the United Kingdom House of Lords and the ECtHR was 'effective control'. Subsequently, the effective control test of attribution was applied by the District Court of Appeal of The Hague in a case concerning the killing of three Bosnian Muslim men in the context of the Srebrenica massacre after the men had been removed from the compound of the Dutch military forces contributing to the UN Protection Force.[79] The District Court of Appeal found that the conduct was attributable to the State of the Netherlands rather than to the UN. Cumulatively, what such cases show is that the 'effective control' test, which answers the question of who retains command and control over operations, seems to be the one which finds application.

4.3.1.3   When 'Effective Control' Exists According to the Commentaries to ARIO

The concept of 'effective control' is defined in the Commentaries to Article 7 ARIO as: 'the factual control that is exercised over the specific conduct taken by the organ or agent placed at the receiving organization's disposal'.[80] The definition does not clarify what effective or factual control means, or the criteria for assessing whether an international organisation exercises effective control. The Commentaries to the Article add several comments to explain the concept of 'effective control'. Firstly, the Commentaries specify that there is not effective control when a State sending personnel retains disciplinary powers and criminal

---

[78] *Ibid.*, para 84.
[79] *Mustafic et al.* v. *the Netherlands*, LJN BW9014, 26 June 2012. The judgment of the District Court of Appeal reversed the judgment of the District Court which applied the 'ultimate control' test. See also the case *Nuhanovic* v. *the Netherlands*, LJN BW 9015, 26 June 2012, which was considered in parallel with the previous one. Notably, in 2013, in relation to the same facts, the ECtHR has declared inadmissible the application of relatives of victims of the Srebrenica massacre and an NGO representing relatives of the victims. The application was against the decision of the Netherlands' courts to declare the applicants' case against the United Nations inadmissible on the ground that the United Nations are immune from the jurisdiction of the national courts: *Stichting Mothers of Srebrenica and Others* v. *the Netherlands* App. No. 6554212/12 (ECtHR, 11 June 2013). For a commentary of the case see J. K. Cogan, 'Stichting Mothers of Srebrenica v. Netherlands' (2013) 107 *The American Journal of International Law* 884.
[80] *Yearbook*, 2011, p. 20, para (4).

jurisdiction over the personnel, since the control stays with the State sending the personnel.[81] The Commentaries further explain that 'attribution of conduct to the contributing State is clearly linked with the retention of some powers by that State over its national contingent.'[82] In this author's opinion, this explanation is problematic because of the way it takes a specific, difficult area of legal imprecision and proffers it unaltered as a solution. We encounter, here, a troubling circularity. The Commentaries to Article 7 ARIO explain the rationale of this provision by pointing out that Article 7 ARIO covers those situations in which there is not full secondment of personnel from a state to an international organisation *because* the sending state still retains disciplinary powers and criminal jurisdiction over the personnel.[83] Accordingly, the Commentaries say it is necessary to establish who exercises effective control (i.e. the State or the international organisation). However, by saying that effective control by the international organisation is excluded when the sending State retains disciplinary powers and criminal jurisdiction, the Commentaries seem to be discussing the very necessity of having Article 7 ARIO. In other words, the fact that the sending State retains jurisdiction and disciplinary power is the source of the problem rather than its solution. This argument is supported by the ECtHR's ruling in *Behrami* and *Saramati*. As I have shown earlier, this ruling has been – at least in part – superseded by subsequent rulings and has been criticised by many legal writers.[84] However, in this ruling, the ECtHR, correctly it is submitted, stated that the effective operational control exercised by NATO in an operation authorised by the UN is not undermined by the fact that States sending troops have exclusive jurisdiction in disciplinary and criminal matters.[85] In the Commentaries to Article 7 ARIO, the International Law Commission pointed to the correctness of this finding of the ECtHR.[86] Thus, effective control cannot be excluded by the fact that the sending State retains disciplinary powers and civil and criminal jurisdiction; but the retention of some powers by the sending State may be an element in favour of such exclusion. A second aspect of the Commentaries needs only to be stated here rather than submitted to longer exegesis. The Commentaries explain that the International Law Commission identifies the entity which exercises

---

[81] *Ibid.*, p. 21, para (7). [82] *Ibid.* [83] *Ibid.*, p. 20, para (1).

[84] See Section 4.3.1.2. See e.g. Larsen, 'Attribution of Conduct', 512–525; Messineo 'The House of Lords', 39–47; Milanovic and Papic 'As Bad as It Gets', 281–286; Orakhelashvili, 'R 'R(on the Application of Al-Jedda), 341–342.

[85] *Behrami and Saramati*, para 139. [86] *Yearbook*, 2011, p. 23, para (10).

effective control as the one which gives the orders. Thirdly – and importantly in relation to joint operations – the International Law Commission has referred to what the UN Secretary General stated regarding combat-related activities: 'international responsibility for the conduct of the troops lies where operational command and control is vested according to the arrangements establishing the modalities of cooperation between the State or States providing the troops and the United Nations'.[87] Although the UN has claimed exclusive command and control over peacekeeping forces, the International Law Commission has specified that the conduct of the members of such forces is to be attributed on the basis of factual criteria.[88] Fourthly, Article 6 ASR, which corresponds to Article 7 ARIO, states that the attribution of conduct to the State to which personnel are seconded by a sending State occurs when 'the organ is acting in the exercise of elements of the governmental authority of the State'. The wording of Article 6 ASR is different and not applicable to international organisations.[89] However, the Commentaries to Article 7 ARIO reflect the Commentaries to Article 6 ASR when they state that the conduct of the deployed organ must be 'under its exclusive direction and control, rather than on instructions from the sending State'.[90]

In summary, the assessment of 'effective control' requires an examination of variable factual elements and scrutiny of who gives the orders to the deployed personnel. In joint operations it is necessary to consider who has operational command and control. The retention of some powers by the sending State does not exclude the exercise of effective control by the international organisation. However, instructions from the sending State may preclude the exercise of exclusive control by the international organisation.

4.3.1.4   Does Frontex Exercise Effective Control over the Conduct of Border Guards?

We turn now to the more specific question of whether the conduct of border guards seconded by Member States to EBGTs can be attributed to Frontex. A legally productive way to pose this question is by examining whether Frontex exercises effective control over their conduct (keeping in mind that a final assessment can be conducted only by examining the specific and concrete circumstances of each Frontex's joint operation,

---

[87] A/51/389, paras 17–18, 6. *Yearbook*, 2011, p. 22, para (9).
[88] *Yearbook*, 2011, p. 22, para (9).   [89] *Ibid.*, p. 20, para (4).
[90] *Yearbook*, 2001, p. 44, para (2).

which this book does not undertake to do). Legislative evidence supporting this would point to areas where the EU may incur responsibility, since
Frontex is an EU body.

In this context 'effective control' refers to who has the operational
command and control. The relevant features of Frontex's joint operations described previously show that the non-host Member State's border
guards perform their tasks and exercise their powers only under instructions from (and in the presence of) border guards of the host Member
State. The instructions given by the host Member State must be in
accordance with the operational plan adopted by Frontex's Executive
Director and the Member States participating in the operation. Thus, the
instructions are issued by the host Member State but their content
reproduces a decision made at EU level.[91] Complexity arises because
(despite the origin of the content of the order) the ARIO seems to require
the international organisation to be the only body to exercise direction
and control, with no instructions being issued by the sending State, in
order for conduct by the deployed organ to be attributed to an international organisation.

The same applies to the role of the coordinating officer – a Frontex staff
member – during operations. It is true that the coordinating officer has
full access to the EBGTs and that Frontex communicates its views via the
coordinating officer to the host Member State on the instructions the host
Member State has issued in accordance with the operational plan.
However, it is the host Member State that has command and control of
the conduct of the border guards. In fact, when Frontex sends its views
via the coordinating officer, these views must be *taken into consideration*.
This means that these views are not instructions which the border guards
must follow.[92]

Effective control is not excluded by the sending State retaining civil
and criminal jurisdiction and disciplinary powers. However, the retention of some power by a sending State, in conjunction with other
elements, may signify the lack of effective control by the international
organisation. In the case of Member States' border guards contributing to
EBGTs, the Frontex Regulation establishes that the host Member State
has civil and criminal jurisdiction and that the home Member State has
disciplinary powers.

---

[91] See Chapter 3, Section 3.3.
[92] On the actions by executive officers and the international responsibility of the European
Union, see Tomuschat, 'The International Responsibility', 186.

The obligation of Frontex's Executive Director to suspend or terminate operations in case of violations of a serious nature, or violations that are likely to persist, is not sufficient to establish that Frontex has effective control of the operations if the other requirements of the 'effective control' test are not met. Since this is not the case, this author's view is that Frontex does not exercise effective control over the conduct of the border guards deployed to EBGTs; and thus the EU cannot incur responsibility for the conduct of the border guards.

According to Article 4 ARIO, attribution of conduct to an international organisation is the first element of an internationally wrongful act. I have concluded that this first element is not present in the case of joint operations coordinated by Frontex. This means that it is not necessary to analyse the second element of an internationally wrongful act of an international organisation: namely, that the action or omission constitutes a breach of an obligation of the international organisation. In Chapter 5, I offer an analysis of the international legal instruments binding on the EU. A cross reference with this analysis is relevant when I proceed to examine the 'derivative responsibility' of the EU and its Member States in Section 4.4.

4.3.2   Responsibility of the Member States

It is now necessary to look at the attribution of conduct to the Member States in the context of Frontex's joint operations pursuant to Article 4 ASR. Article 4 ASR states that the conduct of a state organ is attributable to that state.[93] This provision applies to the border guards of a host Member State who act as organs of that Member State. However, as evidenced earlier in this chapter, Member States participating in Frontex's joint operations are required to second their border guards to EBGTs, which act under instructions from the Member State hosting the operation. It is enlightening to examine whether the acts of these border guards ('guest officers') are attributable to the sending Member State pursuant to Article 4 ASR or whether their secondment triggers the application of Article 6 ASR.

Article 6 ASR states: 'the conduct of an organ placed at the disposal of a State by another State shall be considered an act of the former State under international law if the organ is acting in the exercise of elements of the governmental authority of the State at whose disposal it is placed.' As noted, the border guards are organs of the Member State. To evaluate

---

[93] See Section 4.3.1.1.

whether the requirements of Article 6 ASR are met, it is now necessary to analyse: (i) whether the guest officers are placed at the disposal of the host Member State; and (ii) whether they act 'in the exercise of elements of the governmental authority' of the host Member State.

Concerning the first criterion, the International Law Commission's Commentaries to the ASR define 'placed at the disposal' as follows:

> the organ is acting with the consent, under the authority of and for the purposes of the receiving State. Not only must the organ be appointed to perform functions appertaining to the State at whose disposal it is placed, but in performing the functions entrusted to it by the beneficiary State, the organ must also act in conjunction with the machinery of that State and under its exclusive direction and control, rather than on instructions from the sending State ... what is crucial for the purposes of Article 6 is the establishment of a functional link between the organ in question and the structure or authority of the receiving State.[94]

As evidenced in Chapter 3, Section 3.4.2, when guest officers perform their tasks they act only under the instructions of the host Member State and in the presence of border guards of the host Member State (i.e. guest officers act in conjunction with the machinery of the host Member State). Only two exceptions apply to this regime. Firstly, guest officers carry weapons, ammunition and equipment, as authorised under the national law of the home Member State rather than the national law of the host Member State. However, this can be prohibited by the host Member State if the same prohibition applies to its own border guards. Secondly, when guest officers use force, they must first obtain the consent of both the home and the host Member States. Cumulatively, this shows that guest officers are under the exclusive control of the host Member State. Above all, they do not receive instructions from the home Member State; they are placed at the disposal of the host Member State.

Concerning the second criterion, it is instructive to analyse two cases decided by the ECtHR which dealt with the 'exercise of elements of governmental authority'.[95] The first case, *Drozd and Janousek v. France and Spain*, concerned the conviction by an Andorran court of a Spanish citizen and a Czechoslovak citizen for an armed robbery committed in Andorra.[96] In accordance with the Andorran legal system, the court deciding the case was composed of judges seconded by France and

---

[94] *Yearbook*, 2001, p. 44, paras (2) and (4).
[95] The two cases are referred to in the International Law Commission's Commentaries to the ASR. See *Yearbook*, 2001, p. 44.
[96] *Drozd and Janousek v. France and Spain* App No. 12747/87 (ECtHR, 26 June 1992).

Spain. The ECtHR was asked to decide whether the breach of Article 6 ECHR claimed by the appellants could be attributed to France or Spain or both. The ECtHR ruled that it lacked jurisdiction *ratione personae* and that: (i) 'judges from France and Spain sit as members of Andorran courts, they do not do so in their capacity as French or Spanish judges'; (ii) they 'exercise their functions in an autonomous manner'; (iii) 'their judgments are not subject to supervision by the authorities of France and Spain'; and (iv) 'there is nothing in the case-file which suggests that the French and the Spanish authorities attempted to interfere with the applicants' trial'.[97] The exercise of governmental authority by the receiving State appears from the fact that the judges sit as members of the Andorran court, without supervision or interference from the sending States. The second case, *X and Y* v. *Switzerland*, was decided by the European Commission of Human Rights.[98] The case concerned an agreement between Switzerland and Liechtenstein whereby the Federal Aliens' Police of Switzerland was given competence in respect to third-country nationals in Liechtenstein, acting under Swiss law. The European Commission of Human Rights found that 'acts by Swiss authorities with effect in Liechtenstein bring all those to whom they apply under Swiss jurisdiction within the meaning of Article 1 of the Convention'.[99] For our purposes, it is relevant that: (i) Swiss officers had competence to act in Liechtenstein territory under Swiss law; and (ii) they exercised public authority with the consent of Liechtenstein. Thus, in this case there was no exercise of governmental authority by Liechtenstein as the receiving State. Hence, the 'exercise of elements of governmental authority' consists of the seconded personnel exercising the public authority of the hosting State without interference from the sending State. In line with this, the International Law Commission's Commentaries to Article 6 ASR explain that this criterion is met where 'the conduct of the loaned organ involves the exercise of governmental authority of that State' which amounts to 'transferred responsibility'.[100]

This reflects, in turn, upon the secondment of guest officers from the home Member State to the host Member State in Frontex's joint operations. Recall that border guards seconded by the home Member State receive instructions only from the host Member State and only act in the presence of border guards of the host Member State. Furthermore, the

---

[97] *Ibid.*, para 96.
[98] *X and Y* v. *Switzerland* App No. 7289/75 and 7349/76 (Commission Decision, 14 July 1977).
[99] *Ibid.*, para 2.   [100] *Yearbook*, 2001, p. 44, para (5).

Frontex Regulation does not provide for instructions to be issued to its deployed personnel by a home Member State which could constitute interference in the exercise of authority by the host Member State. In short, the second requirement of Article 6 ASR appears to be met when guest officers are seconded. Indeed, overall both the criteria of Article 6 ASR appear to be met: (1) guest officers are placed at the disposal of the host Member State; and (2) they act in the exercise of the governmental authority of the host Member State. Thus, under international law the acts of a border guard placed at the disposal of a host Member State must be considered to be acts of the host Member State.[101] In sum, according to Article 2 ASR, a State commits an internationally wrongful act when conduct: (i) is attributable to that State under international law; and (ii) constitutes a breach of an international obligation of that State.

Concerning the first element, I have concluded that in the context of joint operations coordinated by Frontex, the conduct of border guards of the host Member State are attributable to the host Member State. This is because, under Article 4 ASR, the conduct of a State organ is attributable to that State. Also, I have concluded that the conduct of guest officers is attributable to the host Member State. This is because, under Article 6 ASR, the guest officers are placed at the disposal of the host Member State and act in the exercise of elements of the governmental authority of the host Member State. Concerning the second, breach-focused element, the legal setting dictates that 'there is a breach of an international obligation by a State when an act of that State is not in conformity with what is required of it by that obligation, regardless of its origin or character.'[102] In order to assess the applicability and permutations of this second criterion, we must enter into a more detailed scrutiny of the primary obligations of the Member State. Chapter 5 will analyse the obligations of the Member States to prohibit refoulement. Chapter 8 will offer an analysis of the circumstances in which such obligations may be breached.

4.4 'Derivative Responsibility' of the EU and Its Member States

4.4.1 The Principle of 'Independent Responsibility'

Previous sections have examined cases and questions which have revolved around precisely when conduct constitutes an internationally wrongful act of the EU or of a Member State. These cases fall within the

---

[101] M. den Heijer, *Europe and Extraterritorial Asylum* (Hart Publishing, 2012), 256.
[102] Article 12 ASR.

general principle stated in Article 1 ASR and Article 3 ARIO according to which: 'every internationally wrongful act of a State [international organisation] entails the international responsibility of that State [international organisation]'. The International Law Commission calls this 'the principle of independent responsibility'.[103] According to the principle of 'independent responsibility', each international organisation or State is responsible for its own internationally wrongful conduct which is attributable to it.[104] However, an internationally wrongful act may result from the conduct of an international organisation and a state acting together, or of two or more states acting together. In these cases, the international organisation and the states act independently when they commit an internationally wrongful act.

A further consideration with regard to the responsibility of States and international organisations acting together concerns the attribution of joint conduct to the State and the international organisation. 'Joint conduct' means that a State and an international organisation are together responsible for the same internationally wrongful act. The principle of 'independent responsibility' seems to exclude joint responsibility.[105] However, the International Law Commission appears to be agnostic in this respect. The ASR does not exclude the possibility that more than one State can be responsible for a single act. Article 47(1) ASR states: 'where several States are responsible for the same internationally wrongful act, the responsibility of each State may be invoked in relation to that act.'[106] The Commentaries explain that Article 47(1) ASR 'states the general principle that ... each State is separately responsible for the conduct attributable to it'.[107] It also states that Article 47(1) ASR 'neither recognises a general rule of joint and several responsibility, nor does it exclude the possibility that two or more States will be responsible for the same internationally wrongful act'.[108] Thus, according to the International Law Commission, it might be possible for two or more Member States to be responsible for the same breach of the principle of non-refoulement in the context of joint operations.

Additionally, there is an exception to the principle of independent responsibility in cases of derivative responsibility in which a State or an

---

[103] *Yearbook*, 2001, p. 64, para (1).
[104] Article 47(1) ASR and Article 48(1) ARIO. See on the principle of 'independent responsibility', Nollkaemper and Jacobs, 'Shared Responsibility', 381.
[105] Nollkaemper and Jacobs, 'Shared Responsibility', 383.
[106] See also Article 48(1) ARIO and Commentaries, *Yearbook*, 2011, p. 76, para (1).
[107] *Yearbook*, 2001, p. 124, para (1).   [108] *Ibid.*, p. 125, para (6).

international organisation aids or assists, directs and controls, or coerces another State or international organisation to commit an internationally wrongful act. In this case, the aiding State or the international organisation may be responsible. I will examine this exception in the following section.

4.4.2 'Derivative Responsibility' in the ASR and in the ARIO

Exceptional cases present a legal setting where the 'conduct of the organ of one State, not acting as an organ or agent of another State, is nonetheless chargeable to the latter State'.[109] This situation arises when an act is committed by an organ of a State and constitutes an internationally wrongful act of that State. The second State or international organisation is internationally responsible because of its aid or assistance (Article 16 ASR), direction and control (Article 17 ASR) or coercion (Article 18 ASR) in committing the internationally wrongful act. These cases are an exception to the principle of independent responsibility and have been referred to as 'derivative responsibility' by the International Law Commission.[110]

Neither Article 17 ASR nor Article 18 ASR appears to be applicable to Frontex's joint operations. Article 16 ASR appears to be the only case of derivative responsibility of relevance here. For present purposes, the following situation may be framed as a case of aid or assistance from one Member State to another in Frontex's joint operations. As explained in Section 4.3.1.4, in joint operations the home Member State seconds its border guards (guest officers) to an EBGT and the guest officers act under the instructions of the host Member State, to which their conduct is attributable. Thus, the home Member State may have derivative responsibility for an internationally wrongful act of the host Member State.

Derivative responsibility is also envisaged in the ARIO. This refers to aid or assistance (Article 14 ARIO), direction and control (Article 15 ARIO), coercion (Article 16 ARIO) and circumvention (Article 17

---

[109] Ibid., p. 64, para (5).
[110] Ibid., p. 65, para (7). The recognition of 'derivative responsibility' in the ASR and the ARIO has not been looked upon favourably by some legal writers, since the cases of shared responsibility between State and State and international organisation and State remain rare, see e.g. Nollkæmper and Jacobs 'Shared Responsibility', 387. Other legal writers use 'derivative responsibility' when assessing the responsibility of Member States acting together, see e.g. den Hejer, 'Europe and Extraterritorial Asylum', 91.

ARIO). Only Article 14 ARIO – the furnishing of aid or assistance – appears to have immediate application to Frontex's joint operations.[111]

Frontex provides aid or assistance to the Member States in many different ways. It prepares risk analysis on threats at the external borders of the Member States; it provides training at EU level for border guards composing EBGTs; it carries out scientific research for the control and surveillance of the external borders; it acquires (also in co-ownership with the Member States) technical equipment for external border control to be deployed in operations; and, finally and most importantly, Frontex coordinates operations.[112] Therefore, the EU may be derivatively responsible, via Frontex, for an internationally wrongful act of a host Member State (i.e. the Member State to which the conduct of a border guard is attributed).

Additionally, Frontex enters into working arrangements with the authorities of third countries regarding the exchange of best practice and the training of border guards; it invites observers from third countries to participate in its activities; it is empowered to launch and finance technical assistance projects in third countries; it deploys liaison officers to third countries to establish and maintain contacts 'with the competent authorities of the third country . . . with the view to contribute to the prevention of and fight against illegal immigration and the return of illegal migrants'.[113] Frontex's collaboration with the authorities of countries concerning the origin and transit of irregular migration attracts criticism.[114] It may entail supporting the border control activities of third

---

[111] The considerations of Article 18 ASR outlined above apply to the corresponding Article 16 ARIO. As for Article 15 ARIO, the Commentaries extend the concept of 'direction and control' so as to encompass those cases where 'an international organisation takes a decision binding its members . . . the adoption of a binding decision on the part of the international organisation could constitute, under certain circumstances, a form of direction and control in the commission of an internationally wrongful act', *Yearbook*, 2011, p. 38, para (4). The requirement that must be fulfilled is that the member of the international organisation is not given discretion in relation to the conduct. As evidenced in Chapter 3, in the context of Frontex's joint operations neither the EU nor Frontex adopt a decision which is binding on the Member States. The same reasoning applies to Article 17 ARIO.

[112] See further Chapter 3, Section 3.1.   [113] Article 14 of the Frontex Regulation.

[114] See V. Moreno Lax, 'Frontex as a Global Actor: External Relations with Third Countries and International Organizations' in M. Dony (ed.), *The External Dimension of the Area of Freedom, Security and Justice* (Universite Libre de Bruxelles Press, 2012); M. Fink, 'Frontex Working Arrangements: Legitimacy and Human Rights Concerns Regarding "Technical Relationships"' (2012) 75 *Merkourios – Utrecht Journal of International and European Law* 20. On Frontex's working arrangements: www.frontex.europa.eu (accessed 13 November 2015).

countries with human rights records which do not live up to the international and EU human rights standard. For instance, Frontex has concluded working arrangements with the authorities of 17 third countries and is negotiating further arrangements with another seven third countries, among them Libya and Egypt where serious violations of refugee and migrant rights are reported.[115]

Thus, there may be derivative responsibility pertaining to the EU through Frontex even for an internationally wrongful act of a third country. Yet the present study must limit its scope and scrutiny to the extent to which the EU and its Member States may incur responsibility for violations of the principle of non-refoulement in joint operations under Frontex's auspices. We must await further developments and the latitude of a separate forum to assess whether an internationally wrongful act of a third country triggers the derivative responsibility of the EU.

4.4.3 Aid or Assistance When Committing an Internationally Wrongful Act

Article 16 ASR and Article 14 ARIO expressly state that a State or an international organisation can be derivatively responsible for aid or assistance given in the commission of an internationally wrongful act. Article 16 ASR states:

> A State which aids or assists another State in the commission of an internationally wrongful act by the latter is internationally responsible for doing so if:
>
> (a) that State does so with knowledge of the circumstances of the internationally wrongful act; and
> (b) the act would be internationally wrongful if committed by that State.

Article 14 ARIO has been formulated by using the text of Article 16 ASR and replacing 'State' with 'international organization', as the entity which aids or assists. In fact, the Commentaries to the ARIO explain that 'the international responsibility that an entity may incur under international

---

[115] For an account of the violations of refugee and migrant rights in Libya see Amnesty International News: www.amnesty.org and in Egypt see Human Rights Watch News: www.hrw.org (both accessed 13 November 2015). See also the case *Hirsi Jamaa and Others* v. *Italy* before the European Court of Human Rights (App No. 27765/09, ECtHR, 23 February 2012), where Italy has been found in violation of the European Convention of Human Rights for intercepting Somali and Eritrean migrants and sending them back to Lybia, analysed in Chapter 6, Section 6.2.2.2.4 of this book.

law for aiding or assisting another entity in the commission of an internationally wrongful act does not appear to depend on the nature and character of the entities concerned.'[116] I propose to analyse Article 16 ASR and, where relevant, I will refer to the international organisations as the aiding or assisting entity.

Article 16 ASR has limited scope so that not every furnishing of aid or assistance from one State to another gives rise to derivative responsibility. Aid or assistance only triggers derivative responsibility of the aiding or assisting State if three conditions are met: (i) there must be the element of aid or assistance; (ii) there must be an international obligation by which both states are bound; and (iii) there must be the element of knowledge.

Regarding the first condition with its 'element of aid or assistance', the Commentaries to Article 16 ASR explain that the role of the aiding or assisting state is a supporting one.[117] The furnishing of aid or assistance is a contribution to an internationally wrongful act of the State receiving the aid or assistance. On this point, the Commentaries specify: 'There is no requirement that the aid or the assistance should have been essential to the performance of the internationally wrongful act; it is sufficient if it contributed significantly to that act.'[118] In furnishing examples of aid or assistance, the Commentaries refer to the financing of an activity which amounts to a violation of an internationally wrongful act, the assistance by providing an essential facility or facilitating the abduction of persons on foreign soil. This last example shows that aid or assistance includes non-material aid.

Frontex's role in joint operations includes providing technical equipment or coordinating operational cooperation. This falls within the concept of aid or assistance referred to in Article 16 ASR.[119] For Frontex's joint

---

[116] *Yearbook*, 2011, p. 36, para (1).   [117] *Yearbook*, 2001, p. 65, para (6).

[118] *Ibid.*, p. 66, para (5).

[119] The articles of the ARIO which establish the derivative responsibility of an international organisation for internationally wrongful acts committed by a State include the situation in which the aided or assisted State is a member of the international organisation. The EU may thus be derivatively responsible for a wrongful act committed by an organ of one of its Member States as a consequence of aid or assistance provided by the EU. This possibility is envisaged by the International Law Commission in the Commentaries to Chapter IV of the ARIO, which states that: 'the relations between an international organisation and its members ... may allow the former organisation to influence the conduct of members *also in cases* that are not envisaged in Articles 16 and 18 on the responsibility of States for internationally wrongful acts', see *Yearbook*, 2001, p. 35, para (3), emphasis added. See also A. Reinisch, 'Aid or Assistance and Direction and Control between States and International Organizations in the Commission of Internationally Wrongful Acts' (2010) 7 *International Organizations Law Review* 63,

operations, as explained in Section 4.2.2, the 'organic model' applies when responsibility of the EU and its Member States for internationally wrongful acts must be assessed. Specifically, the 'organic model' is reflected in the provisions of the ARIO on derivative responsibility. Accordingly, in Frontex's joint operations, the ARIO provisions on derivative responsibility apply when the EU's international responsibility must be ascertained.

Given the ways in which aid or assistance have been defined, they could include any act which contributes to a State's commission of an internationally wrongful act. States establish various forms of cooperation with each other. Frontex's joint operations are one example. When States engage in such cooperation, they do not necessarily assume the risk of the aided or assisted State committing an internationally wrongful act due to their contributions. In an attempt to further substantiate the meaning of the term 'aid or assistance', the International Law Commission in its Commentaries requires there to be a clear nexus between the giving of the aid or assistance and the commission of the internationally wrongful act. Article 16 ASR only applies to those cases 'where the aid or assistance given is *clearly linked* to the subsequent wrongful conduct'.[120] However, the International Law Commission does not substantiate further the meaning of such 'clear link'. Thus, the interpretation of the term 'aid or assistance' remains quite broad. The element of 'knowledge', which I will analyse in Section 4.4.3.1, is therefore essential in limiting the scope of application of Article 16 ASR.[121]

Regarding the second condition, stipulating the existence of 'an international obligation by which both states are bound', Article 16 ASR only applies if the aiding or assisting State is bound by the same obligation whose breach would constitute an internationally wrongful act of the aided or assisted State.[122] In the Commentary to Article 16 ASR, the International Law Commission explains that this is the corollary of the principle according to which a State 'cannot do by another what it cannot do by itself'.[123] This means that Article 16 ASR does not require both States (or the aided State and the aiding international organisation)

68, on the responsibility of the International Monetary Fund for internationally wrongful acts committed by its members as a consequence of its financial assistance.

[120] *Yearbook*, 2001, p. 66, para (5). Emphasis added. See G. Nolte and H. P. Aust, 'Equivocal Helpers – Complicit States, Mixed Messages and International Law' (2009) 58 *International and Comparative Law Quarterly* 1, 10.

[121] *Yearbook*, 2001, p. 66, para (5), emphasis added. See also Nolte and Aust, 'Equivocal Helpers', 1, 10; B. Graefrath, 'Complicity in the Law of International Responsibility' (1996) 29 *Revue Belge de Droit International* 371, 374.

[122] *Yearbook*, 2001, p. 66, para (6).   [123] *Ibid.*

to be bound by exactly the same obligation, but that the conduct would also be wrongful if committed by the State which gives its aid or assistance.[124] This is particularly relevant to the case of the EU aiding or assisting its Member States in committing a breach of the principle of non-refoulement. Chapter 5 will scrutinise the extent to which the EU is bound by the principle of non-refoulement. Our immediate concern is a fuller discussion of condition three with its 'element of knowledge'.

4.4.4   The Element of 'Knowledge'

For one State to incur responsibility for its aid or assistance to another state, Article 16 ASR requires that it should furnish aid or assistance with 'knowledge of the circumstances of the internationally wrongful act'. According to a plain reading of this requirement, a State (or international organisation) is responsible if it is aware of the circumstances of the internationally wrongful act committed by another State. This interpretation is supported by the explanation of derivative responsibility in the Commentaries to Chapter IV of the ASR: 'the articles in this chapter require that the former State should be aware of the circumstances of the internationally wrongful act in question, and establish a specific causal link between that act and the conduct of the assisting ... State.'[125] However, in the Commentaries to Article 16 ASR, the International Law Commission poses a higher threshold for the responsibility of the aiding State (or international organisation). The Commentaries at first state that if the aiding or assisting State is 'unaware' of the circumstances in which its aid will be used by the receiving State, it cannot be held responsible.[126] Also, the Commentaries require the element of 'knowledge' along with the element of 'intent'. They explain: 'A State is not responsible for aid or assistance under Article 16 ASR *unless the relevant State organ intended*, by the aid or the assistance given, *to facilitate the occurrence of the wrongful conduct* and the internationally wrongful conduct is actually committed by the aided or assisted State.'[127] According to the Commentaries 'the aid or assistance must be given with a view to facilitating the commission of that act, and must actually do so.'[128] For our purposes, according to the Commentaries, this requirement also applies to human rights violations: 'Where the allegation is that

---

[124] *Ibid.* See den Heijer, *Europe and Extraterritorial Asylum*, 96.
[125] *Yearbook*, 2001, p. 65, para (8).   [126] *Ibid.*, p. 66, para (4).
[127] *Ibid.*, p. 66, para (5), emphasis added.   [128] *Ibid.*, p. 66, para (3).

the assistance of a State has facilitated human rights abuses by another State, the particular circumstances of each case must be carefully examined to determine whether the aiding State by its aid was aware of and intended to facilitate the commission of the internationally wrongful conduct.'[129]

The element of 'intent' is subjective and it expresses a willingness to cause harm. I must now examine whether the element of intent, together with the element of knowledge, is the appropriate threshold for making an aiding state (or international organisation) responsible under Article 16 ASR. In contrast to the element of knowledge, the element of intent is absent from the text of Article 16 ASR. Its absence reflects the *ratio* of the entire ASR which avoids requiring the element of wrongful intent and the intention to harm by stating that such an element pertains to the norms of primary law.[130] This notwithstanding, in the Commentaries the International Law Commission has specified that the element of knowledge is not sufficient and that Article 16 ASR applies only if the State (or the international organisation) has furnished aid or assistance to facilitate the occurrence of a specific wrongful conduct.[131]

Georg Nolte, a member of the International Law Commission, and Helmut Philipp Aust[132] have put forward three main arguments in favour of the inclusion of the element of intent in Article 16 ASR:

(i) the approach of the International Court of Justice in the *Genocide Convention Case*;[133]

(ii) the narrow scope of Article 16 ASR in order not to undermine international cooperation between States;

(iii) Article 16 ASR read in conjunction with Article 41(2) ASR.

In the *Genocide Convention Case*, the International Court of Justice was concerned with the genocide in Srebrenica allegedly perpetrated by Serbian soldiers in 1995. The International Court of Justice had to analyse the concept of complicity in genocide and the specific intent (*dolus specialis*) which characterises the crime of genocide and the motives of the accomplice.[134] As stated by Article III, paragraph (e) of the Genocide Convention, complicity in genocide is a criminal provision. The International Court of Justice stated first that complicity is not

---

[129] *Ibid.*, p. 67, para (9).

[130] *Ibid.*, p. 34, para (3); p. 36, para (10); p. 65, para (8). *Contra*, Nolte and Aust, 'Equivocal Helpers', 13.

[131] *Yearbook*, 2001, p. 66, para (3).   [132] Nolte and Aust, 'Equivocal Helpers'.

[133] *Genocide Convention Case*, para 43.   [134] *Ibid.*, para 421.

a concept that exists in the law of international responsibility. However, the Court stated that the concept of complicity is similar to a customary rule of the law of State responsibility, i.e. Article 16 ASR.[135] Thereupon, it stated that there is no reason to differentiate between 'complicity in genocide' and 'aid and assistance' under Article 16 ASR.[136] Therefore, to determine the meaning of 'complicity in genocide', by way of analogy the International Court of Justice examined whether organs of the respondent State furnished aid or assistance for the commission of the genocide according to the concepts of the general law of international responsibility.[137] When asked whether Article 16 ASR includes the element of intent, the Court replied as follows:

> But whatever the reply to this question, there is no doubt that the conduct of an organ or a person furnishing aid or assistance to a perpetrator of a crime of genocide cannot be treated as complicity in genocide unless *at the least* that organ or person acted knowingly, that is to say, in particular, was aware of the specific intent (*dolus specialis*) of the principal perpetrator.[138]

Nolte and Aust interpreted the above quotation from the judgment as follows:

> If the analogy to Article 16 is supposed to be meaningful, this entails that knowledge of the circumstances of the wrongful act is required *at the least* (as the Court has put it) also with respect to Article 16. The words 'at the least' suggest that, as a general rule, more than mere knowledge is required.[139]

Yet the interpretation rendered by these two authors is not necessarily correct. In the primary quotation from the judgment cited above, the International Court of Justice did not clearly answer the question of whether Article 16 ASR includes the element of intent, but limited itself to stating that the aiding or assisting organ is required to act *at least* knowingly (i.e. with awareness of the intent of the organ committing the crime).[140] In other words, aid or assistance provided with awareness that the aided state will commit a wrongful act appears to be sufficient for Article 16 ASR to apply. The absence of the element of intent does not prevent its application.

An additional issue is that Nolte and Aust favour a narrow application of Article 16 ASR, including the element of intent, in order not to

---

[135] *Ibid.*, para 419.   [136] *Ibid.*, para 420.   [137] *Ibid.*   [138] *Ibid.*, para 421.
[139] Nolte and Aust, 'Equivocal Helpers', 14.
[140] See den Heijer, *Europe and Extraterritorial Asylum*, 97.

undermine international cooperation between States. They maintain that a broader application of Article 16 ASR, requiring knowledge but not requiring intent, would discourage many forms of international cooperation.[141] The idea behind this argument appears to be that knowing that the aided State is using aid to commit a specific wrongful act is not sufficient. The State (or international organisation), Nolte and Aust affirm, should only incur responsibility when it intends to facilitate a wrongful act. In this argument the authors do not appear to consider that the inclusion of the element of intent would make Article 16 ASR applicable to only those very few cases in which a State (or international organisation) openly declared its intention to facilitate the commission of an internationally wrongful act. To avoid such responsibility, it would only be necessary to refrain from making an open declaration of such intent.[142] Moreover, the inclusion of the element of intent, when applying Article 16 ASR runs counter to the principle of objective responsibility, which is widely supported by legal doctrine and practice. Under the principle of objective responsibility, in order to establish the responsibility of a State, it is not necessary to show the intentional conduct of an organ acting on behalf of the State. The responsibility of the State will be established without regard to the good or bad faith of the acting organ.[143]

Further discussion is also warranted concerning the way Nolte and Aust justify the inclusion of the element of intent among the requirements of Article 16 ASR by reading Article 16 ASR in conjunction with Article 41(2) ASR. Article 41(2) ASR concerns 'serious breaches of obligations under peremptory norms of general international law'. It provides for a duty for States to abstain from giving aid or assistance in maintaining a situation created by a serious breach of obligations under peremptory norms of general international law.[144] According to the non-exhaustive examples in the Commentaries, these norms include prohibitions of slavery, genocide, racial discrimination, apartheid and torture.[145] Article 41(2) ASR concerns conduct after the fact and 'extends

---

[141] Nolte and Aust, 'Equivocal Helpers', 15.

[142] See K. Nahapetian, 'Confronting State Complicity in International Law' (2002) 7 *UCLA Journal of International Law and Foreign Affairs* 99, 110.

[143] See Shaw, *International Law*, 784.

[144] *Yearbook*, 2001, p. 114, para (4). Article 41(2) ASR refers to Article 40 ASR.

[145] *Yearbook*, 2001, pp. 112–113, paras (4) and (5). As discussed in Chapter 5, to the extent that the principle of non-refoulement is in connection with torture, it seems to be a peremptory norm of general international law. To this extent, the principle of non-refoulement may fall within this provision. However, Article 40 requires there to be a serious breach and 'a gross and systematic failure by the responsible State to fulfil the

beyond the commission of the serious breach itself to the maintenance of the situation created by the breach'.[146] Importantly, Article 41(2) ASR requires neither the element of knowledge nor the element of intent. As explained in the Commentaries, 'it is hardly conceivable that a State would not have notice of the commission of a serious breach by another State.'[147] Since the International Law Commission has lowered the standard so as to attribute responsibility only in the limited number of cases of serious breaches of obligations under peremptory norms, Nolte and Aust formulate an *a contrario* argument concerning Article 16 ASR. They assert that since the element of intent is not required when it is inconceivable that a state is unaware of serious breaches – as in Article 41(2) ASR – *a contrario*, where breaches are not serious, a higher standard is required for the attribution of responsibility (i.e. there must be intent).[148] Nolte and Aust's argument here does not appear to take into consideration one aspect concerning attribution of responsibility. An alternative to the absence of the subjective element can be the requirement of 'knowledge of the circumstances of the internationally wrongful act', without requiring that the aid or assistance be given with a view to facilitating the commission of an internationally wrongful act, as the element of intent would require.

Based on this analytical sequence, it is possible to conclude that intent is not a necessary requirement for assessing the derivative responsibility of the EU or its Member States pursuant to Article 16 ASR. Knowledge of the circumstances under which a breach will occur appears to be sufficient. This conclusion is confirmed by the ECtHR's ruling in the *M.M.S.* case.[149] The case concerned the return of an Afghan national from Belgium to Greece under the Dublin Regulation[150] and the alleged breach of Articles 2, 3 and 13 ECHR by both Belgium and Greece. In formulating its decision, the ECtHR relied on reports from the United Nations High Commissioner for Refugees, the Council of Europe Commissioner for Human Rights and international non-governmental organisations on the

---

obligation'. There is uncertainty about whether these two further requirements are met by a possible breach of the principle of non-refoulement in the context of operational cooperation through Frontex.

[146] *Yearbook*, 2001, p. 115, para (11).   [147] *Ibid.*

[148] Nolte and Aust, 'Equivocal Helpers', 16.

[149] *M.S.S.* v. *Belgium and Greece* App No. 30696/09 (ECtHR, 21 January 2011).

[150] Council Regulation (EC) 343/2003 of 18 February 2003 establishing the criteria and mechanisms for determining the Member State responsible for examining an asylum application lodged in one of the Member States by a third-country national OJ 2003 No. L50, p. 1.

treatment to which refugees were subjected once they were in Greece and, in particular, their risk of being refouled.[151] The ECtHR ruled that the Belgian authorities were responsible for the breaches since the general lack of refugee protection in Greece *was known* to them.[152] Thus, the ECtHR referred only to the element of knowledge and not the element of intent.

To conclude, a summation of this legal setting must affirm that aid or assistance is a contribution by an international organisation or a State to the commission of an internationally wrongful act. The aid can either be material or non-material. Additionally, there must be a clear link between the aid or assistance and the wrongful conduct. Finally, the subjective element required is knowledge: namely, awareness that the aid may be used for the commission of a wrongful act.

4.4.5   Aid or Assistance Given by a Home Member State and by Frontex

We return now to a consideration of the aid or assistance given by Member States or by Frontex in the context of joint operations. The secondment of personnel from a home Member State to EBGTs receiving instructions from the host Member State constitutes aid or assistance as described above. Chapter 3 examines the problems which beset the fact that Frontex must rely on the personnel contributions of the Member States. Equally, all the activities of Frontex addressed to the Member States can be considered aid or assistance: providing risk analysis; training of personnel; developing scientific research for use in controlling the external borders; deploying technical equipment to the Member States during operations; together with the coordination of the operations.

It is more problematic to prove the following: (1) the existence of a clear link between the aid or assistance and the subsequent wrongful conduct; and (2) the fact that the aiding Member State (or the EU) possesses sufficient knowledge that the wrongful act has been committed using its aid or assistance. This applies in particular to the activities of Frontex in support of joint operations which are not closely linked to some specific conduct: namely, risk analysis; the training of personnel; and developing scientific research. Conversely, concerning Frontex's

---

[151] *M.S.S.* v. *Belgium and Greece*, paras 348–349.
[152] *Ibid.*, para 352. See Goodwin-Gill, 'The Right to Seek Asylum', 454.

other activities – the deployment of technical equipment (for instance, vessels) and, most of all, the coordination of the operations – it may be possible to prove a clear link between the aid and the conduct, and the element of knowledge, by examining in more depth the conduct of these joint operations.[153] The same may apply to aid or assistance provided by the home Member State when it deploys its personnel to the EBGTs.

In regard to the EU's responsibility deriving from Frontex's coordination of joint operations, it is pertinent to recall Chapter 3, Section 3.3, which notes that Frontex's Executive Director draws up the operational plan for each operation and is also responsible for its implementation.[154] This means that if an internationally wrongful act occurs during an operation, Frontex's Executive Director, and indirectly the EU since Frontex is an EU body, may possess sufficient knowledge of the fact that the wrongful act would be committed with the contribution of Frontex's aid or assistance. The potential liability contained in this legal avenue is something that will be explored in a later chapter.[155]

There is an additional avenue for assessing the EU's derivative responsibility for coordinating the operations of border control carried out by Member States. This would directly involve the European Commission and not Frontex alone. Chapter 2 shows that the EU's use of Frontex to develop a common policy on external border control effectively means: (1) Frontex not only coordinates operations when technical and operational assistance is needed, but it also provides increased coordination; (2) the European Commission is involved in the planning of the operations. The operational plan of each operation is prepared in accordance with Frontex's annual programme of work, including its operational portfolio. Frontex's annual programme of work is adopted by Frontex's Management Board, in which the European Commission is represented, after receiving the European Commission's approval. Thus, the EU, in the form of the European Commission, may potentially possess knowledge that the aid or assistance provided in coordinating operations contributes to the commission of an internationally wrongful act. However, a mitigating factor here stems from the fact that Frontex's annual programme of work, while including detailed information on future operations, is still a general programme. Thus, it may prove

---

[153] See J. Rijpma, 'Building Borders: The Regulatory Framework for the Management of the External Borders of the European Union' (DPhil thesis, European University Institute, 2009), 230.

[154] Articles 3a(1) and 25(g) of the Frontex Regulation.

[155] I will analyse this aspect in Chapter 8.

difficult to establish the existence of a clear link between the aid or assistance and the subsequent wrongful conduct. Subsequently, it is unlikely that this legal avenue will trigger the 'derivative responsibility' of the EU via the involvement of the European Commission in the coordination of operations.

4.5 Conclusions

It is possible to assess the international responsibility of the EU since the EU has international legal personality, as stated in Article 47 TEU. In order to make any such assessment it is first necessary to focus on the element of attribution, which is one of the constitutive elements of an internationally wrongful act. My analysis has prioritised the 'organic model' of attribution. This model refers to the rules which determine the conditions under which the acts of organs of an international organisation can be attributed to it. The model also includes complementary rules of attribution, for instance, when attribution to the international organisation derives from the conduct of organs placed at the disposal of the international organisation.

I have established that the EU is not responsible for the conduct of the border guards of a Member State participating in a joint operation, since Frontex does not exercise 'effective control' over the conduct of the border guards. I have concluded that the conduct of a border guard of a host Member State is attributable to the host Member State under Article 4 ASR. Equally, I have emphasised that the conduct of border guards who are seconded by the home Member State to the EBGTs and who receive instructions from the host Member State is also attributable to the host Member State. Incorporating additional contingencies, I have noted that in joint operations it is possible for two or more Member States (or the EU and a Member State) to be responsible for the same breach. This occurs where the Member States (or the EU and a Member State) act independently. I have also devoted the latter sections of this chapter to analysing the extent to which the EU and its Member States may incur derivative responsibility for aid or assistance to another Member State which commits an internationally wrongful act. In this respect, I have concluded that for some of Frontex's aid and assistance activities (for instance, training of personnel) it appears difficult to establish: (1) a close link between the aid or assistance and the wrongful act; and (2) the knowledge possessed by Frontex that the aid would be used in the commission of a wrongful act. However, the same legal difficulty may not apply to the secondment of personnel by a home Member State to an EBGT and to Frontex's coordination of the joint operations. In the latter case, the EU's derivative responsibility is related to the involvement of Frontex's Executive Director in drawing up the operational plan of each joint operation and the resultant responsibility for implementing the operational plan. This requires further analysis which will be developed in Chapter 8.

The Principle of Non-Refoulement in the EU Legal Setting

5.1 The Interconnection of International Law and EU Law Sources

Analysing the complexities of the legal framework defining the principle of non-refoulement is a vital prerequisite to understanding any possible violations of the principle which may occur in the context of Frontex's joint operations, along with any potential triggering of EU and/or Member State responsibility. These complexities arise from the international instruments enshrining the principle of non-refoulement as well as from the provisions of EU primary and secondary law on the principle.

Under the principle of non-refoulement, it is prohibited to return individuals to territories where they may be at risk of persecution, torture or other ill-treatment. In terms of its formal standing, the principle has been embodied in the 1951 Convention relating to the Status of Refugees (1951 Refugee Convention) and the 1967 Protocol relating to the Status of Refugees (the 1967 Protocol),[1] the Convention against Torture (CAT),[2] the International Covenant on Civil and Political Rights (ICCPR)[3] and the European Convention on Human Rights (ECHR).[4] The principle of non-refoulement may also be considered a norm of customary international law. At the EU level, the principle is embodied in Article 19(2) of the Charter of Fundamental Rights (EU Charter or Charter).[5] Article 18 of the EU Charter enshrines the right to asylum, and Article 19(1) of the EU Charter prohibits collective expulsions. Article 78(1) of the Treaty on the

---

[1] 1951 Convention relating to the Status of Refugees (189 UNTS 137); 1967 Protocol relating to the Status of Refugees (606 UNTS 267).
[2] 1984 Convention against Torture and Other Cruel, Inhuman or Degrading Treatment or Punishment (1465 UNTS 85).
[3] 1966 International Covenant on Civil and Political Rights (999 UNTS 171).
[4] 1950 European Convention for the Protection of Human Rights and Fundamental Freedoms (213 UNTS 222).
[5] Charter of Fundamental Rights of the European Union OJ 2010 No. C83, p. 1.

Functioning of the European Union (TFEU) requires the EU to act in accordance with the 1951 Refugee Convention and other relevant treaties.[6] In addition, non-refoulement may be studied in the light of its potential reach as a general principle of EU law. Importantly, concerns that violations of the principle may occur in the context of border control and Frontex's activities have triggered the adoption of several provisions against refoulement in EU secondary legislation.

In this chapter, I will analyse the inter-connected sources of international law and EU primary and secondary law in order to understand the principle of non-refoulement in the EU. My analysis will draw a distinction between the obligations of non-refoulement which bind the EU and its Member States under international law (where a violation triggers the international responsibility of the EU and/or its Member States) and the EU legal domain's standard of protection from refoulement which affects EU institutions, agencies like Frontex and the EU Member States, when implementing EU law. Accordingly, Section 5.2 of this chapter will examine the obligations of non-refoulement incumbent on the EU and its Member States directly under international law. The section will then consider the extent to which the principle of non-refoulement is a norm of customary international law. Thereafter, the analytical focus will be on the sources of fundamental rights which prohibit refoulement according to the EU legal order (Section 5.3) as well as the provisions of EU secondary legislation on Frontex's joint operations at the EU's external borders which prohibit refoulement (Section 5.4). Finally, I will offer some conclusions about what the principle of non-refoulement means for the EU in this complex legal framework (Section 5.5).

At this point, we must keep in mind that complexity and multiplicity extend as far as our primary definitions. The definition of the principle of non-refoulement noted above (i.e. the prohibition of returning individuals to territories where they may be at risk of persecution, torture or other ill-treatment) summarises very concisely EU Member States' obligations in this respect. However, this formulation does not mean that there is an overarching principle of non-refoulement and that the various non-refoulement obligations can be conflated into a single concept. It is necessary to make a theoretical distinction and each non-refoulement obligation must be analysed independently. Conflating the different non-refoulement

---

[6] Consolidated versions of the Treaty on European Union and the Treaty on the Functioning of the European Union OJ 2010 No. C83, p. 1.

obligations risks undermining international protection by applying restrictions to one legal instrument which rightly pertains only to another one.[7] Making such a theoretical distinction has evident implications for the principle of non-refoulement in the EU legal domain where, as explained, both the 1951 Refugee Convention and the ECHR are legal sources.[8]

5.2 Obligations of Non-Refoulement Which Bind the EU and Its Member States Directly under International Law

5.2.1 Background to the EU's Non-Refoulement Obligations

Before examining the international sources of law which enshrine the principle of non-refoulement, my analysis will focus on how potential breaches of international obligations, including violations of the principle, have the capacity to engage the international responsibility of the EU and/or the Member States.

The EU is not party to any of the international treaties under discussion enshrining the principle of non-refoulement, though Article 6(2) of the Treaty on European Union (TEU) does require the EU to accede to the ECHR.[9] Conversely, all Member States are parties to the 1951 Refugee Convention and the 1967 Protocol, the ECHR, the CAT and the ICCPR.[10] Currently, then, the EU as an international organisation cannot be held responsible for violations of the principle of non-refoulement by the European Court of Human Rights (ECtHR), the

---

[7] See V. Chetail, 'Le Droit des Refugiés à l'Epreuve de la Jurisprudence de la Cour Europèenne des Droit de l'Homme sur l'Interdiction de Renvoi des Etrangers Menacés de Torture et de Traitements Inhumains ou Dégradants' (2004) 1 *Revue Belge de Droit International* 155, 193–195; F. Messineo, 'Non-refoulement Obligations in Public International Law: Towards a New Protection Status?' in S. Juss (ed.), *The Ashgate Companion to Migration Law, Theory and Policy* (Ashgate, 2013), 131–132.

[8] See Section 5.3 below.

[9] At the time of writing, the draft agreement on the accession of the European Union to the ECHR (CDDH-EU 47+1(2013)008rev2) has been rejected by the Court of Justice of the European Union (CJEU) with Opinion 2/13 of 18 December 2014 where the CJEU found the draft agreement incompatible with EU law. On the EU's accession to the ECHR, see e.g. Giorgio Gaja, 'Accession to the ECHR' in A. Biondi, P. Eeckhout and S. Ripley (eds.), *EU Law after Lisbon* (Oxford University Press, 2012); T. Lock, 'End of an Epic? The Draft Agreement on the EU's Accession to the ECHR' (2012) 31 *Yearbook of European Law* 162; C. Eckes, 'EU Accession to the ECHR: Between Autonomy and Adaptation' (2013) 76 *The Modern Law Review* 254; P. P. Craig, 'EU Accession to the ECHR: Competence, Procedure and Substance' (2013) 6 *Fordham International Law Journal* 1114.

[10] The status of treaties is accessible at United Nations Treaty Collection, www.treaties.un.org (accessed 13 November 2015).

Human Rights Committee established by the ICCPR[11] or the Committee Against Torture established by the CAT.[12] However, the European Commission on Human Rights and the ECtHR have ruled on applications against EU Member States, party to the ECHR, for alleged violations of the ECHR committed in relation to acts of the EU (or the European Community) or acts of EU Member States implementing legal obligations deriving from their membership of the EU (or the European Community).[13] In these ECtHR rulings, despite the transfer of competence from the EU Member States to the EU pursuant to EU law, the EU Member States remain the parties which may incur responsibility for human rights violations. This seeks to avoid a loophole in the protection of human rights.[14] As explained in Chapter 4, applying the 'competence model' in order to establish the respective responsibilities of the EU and its Member States for an internationally wrongful act – of which the case law above constitutes an example – is not the most suitable method for assessing any potential breaches of the principle of non-refoulement in Frontex's joint operations. Instead, the 'organic model' should be used.[15]

---

[11] Article 28 of the 1966 International Covenant on Civil and Political Rights.

[12] Article 17 of the 1984 Convention against Torture.

[13] E.g. *M and Co.* v. *Federal Republic of Germany*, App No. 13258/87 (Commission Decision, 9 February 1990); *Senator Lines GmbH* v. *The Fifteen Member States of the EU*, App No. 56672/00 (ECtHR, 10 March 2004); *Emesa Sugar NV* v. *Netherlands* App No. 62023/00 (ECtHR, 13 January 2005); *Bosphorus Hava Yollari Turizm Ve Ticaret Anonim Sirketi* v. *Ireland* App No. 45036/98 (ECtHR, 30 June 2005).

[14] See T. Ahmed and I. de Jesus Butler, 'The European Union and Human Rights: An International Law Perspective' (2006) 17 *European Journal of International Law* 771, 781–782. Specifically, in the *Bosphorus* case the ECtHR ruled on the extent to which an EU Member State action, interfering with the applicant's human rights, can be justified by its compliance with obligations deriving from its membership of the EU to which the EU Member State has transferred part of its sovereignty. Among the many contributions to the literature on the *Bosphorus* case, see e.g. C. Costello, 'The *Bosphorus* Ruling of the European Court of Human Rights: Fundamental Rights and Blurred Boundaries in Europe' (2006) 6 *Human Rights Law Review* 88; S. Peers, 'Bosphorus – European Court of Human Rights – Limited Responsibility of European Union Member State for Actions within the Scope of Community Law. Judgment of 30 June 2005, *Bosphorus Airways* v. *Ireland*, Application No. 45036/98' (2006) 2 *European Constitutional Law Review* 443; C. Eckes, 'Does the European Court of Human Rights Provide Protection from the European Community? – The Case of Bosphorus Airways' (2007) 13 *European Public Law* 47; T. Lock, 'Beyond Bosphorus: The European Court of Human Rights' Case Law on the Responsibility of Member States of International Organisations under the European Convention on Human Rights' (2010) 10 *Human Rights Law Review* 529.

[15] Chapter 4, Section 4.2.2.

Since, as noted, all EU Member States are party to the 1951 Refugee Convention and 1967 Protocol, the CAT, the ICCPR and the ECHR, a situation involving a conflict of norms between EU Member States' human rights obligations and EU law may arise. This would occur if EU Member States were required to breach obligations contracted under the above treaties in order to implement EU law. Solutions to any conflict of norms in the specific field of EU asylum and border control law are to be found by applying Article 351 TFEU (regulating potential conflicts between EU law and agreements concluded by the EU Member States) in combination with Article 78(1) TFEU (stating the international obligations of the EU when it develops a common policy on asylum). This will be discussed in Section 5.3.2 on the principle of non-refoulement and the relevance of international treaties in the EU legal order.

Article 2 of the Articles on Responsibility of States for Internationally Wrongful Acts (ASR)[16] and Article 4 of the Articles on Responsibility of International Organizations for Internationally Wrongful Acts (ARIO)[17] help to clarify some issues concerning the origin of international obligations which may trigger the international responsibility of the EU and/or its Member States. One of the conditions for the existence of an internationally wrongful act committed by a State or an international organisation is that conduct attributable to the relevant signatory should constitute a breach of an international obligation to which it is a party. Articles 12 ASR and 10 ARIO state that a State or international organisation must honour an international obligation 'regardless of its origin'. The Commentaries to both provisions explain that 'international obligations may be established by a customary rule of international law, by a treaty or by a general principle applicable within the international legal order'.[18] This indicates that if the other conditions for the existence of an internationally wrongful act are present, the EU and/or the Member States can be deemed internationally responsible for breaches of the principle of non-refoulement in so far as they are party to an international instrument in which the principle is enshrined. The same applies to the extent to which the EU is bound by the principle of non-refoulement as a rule of customary international law. Specifically, the CJEU has affirmed the obligation of the EU to comply with

---

[16] UN Doc. A/Res/ 56/83 (12 December 2001). For an examination of the legal authority of the ASR and the ARIO see Chapter 4.

[17] UN Doc. A/64/10 (2009); UN Doc. A/CN.4/L.778 (12 August 2011).

[18] *Yearbook of the International Law Commission*, 2001, Vol. II, Part Two, p. 55, para (3); and *Yearbook of the International Law Commission*, 2011, Vol. II, Part Two, p. 31, para (2). On the work of the International Law Commission, see Chapter 4, Section 4.2.4.

customary international law[19] and such an obligation is recognised as a consequence of its international legal personality.[20] With regard to the human rights obligations of international organisations, Armin von Bogdandy and Mateja Steinbruck Platise observe that ARIO seems to solve the problem of making international organisations responsible for human rights violations, not only when these human rights obligations are derived from treaties, but also when they are based on customary international law and *jus cogens*. These scholars refer to the existence of 'a rather general consensus' according to which 'international organisations must respect at least the most fundamental human rights'.[21]

Since the aim of this chapter is to look at the interconnection of various instruments of law concerned with the principle of non-refoulement in order to determine the standard of protection at EU level, the next section focuses on those features of the principle which illuminate the kind of protection afforded by each instrument. Although the importance of the ECHR for the protection of fundamental rights has been stated in primary EU law[22] (and therefore the ECHR should be placed among the sources of fundamental rights in the EU legal order together with the general principles of EU law and the EU Charter), the analysis of Article 3 ECHR which enshrines the prohibition against refoulement must be included in this section. This examination will allow us to compare the content of Article 3 ECHR with the other provisions prohibiting refoulement included in the other relevant international instruments.

---

[19] Case C-286/90 *Anklagemyndighenden* v. *Peter Michael Poulse and Diva Navigation Corp.* [1992] ECR I-6019, para 9; Case T-115/94 *Opel Austria GmbH* v. *Council* [1997] ECR II-39, para. 90; Case C-162/96 *Racke* [1998] ECR I-3655; [1998] 3 CMLR 219, para 45–46; Case C-63/09 *A. Walz* v. *Clickair SA* [2010] ECR I-4239, para 16; Case C-366/10 *Air Transport Association of America and Others* v. *Secretary of State for Energy and Climate Change* [2011] ECR I–13755; [2012] 2 CMLR 4, para 101; C-410/11 *Espada Sanchez and Others* [2012] judgment of the Court of 22 November 2012; [2013] 1 CMLR 55, para 21; Case C-27/11 *Vinkov* [2012] judgment of the Court of 7 June 2012; [2012] 3 CMLR 22, para 33.

[20] A. Giannelli, 'Customary International Law in the European Union' in E. Cannizzaro, P. Palchetti and R. Wessel (eds.), *International Law as Law of the European Union* (Brill Nijhoff, 2011), 93.

[21] A. von Bogdandy and M. Steinbrück Platise, 'ARIO and Human Rights Protection: Leaving the Individual in the Cold' (2012) 9 *International Organizations Law Review* 67, 69.

[22] Article 6 TEU empowers the EU to accede to the ECHR and reiterates that fundamental rights guaranteed by the ECHR are general principles of EU law.

5.2.2 The 1951 Refugee Convention and 'the Other Relevant Treaties'[23]

The 1951 Refugee Convention is the most important international instrument providing protection against refoulement. It is the only instrument which gives refugees a status that is recognised in national law.[24] For our purposes, there are references to the 1951 Refugee Convention in the EU Treaties[25] and in the EU Charter,[26] as will be seen below.

Article 33 of the 1951 Refugee Convention prohibits signatory States from returning individuals who fall within the definition of 'refugee' to territories where they would be at risk of persecution. The recognition of refugee status is not constitutive but declaratory in nature:

> A person is a refugee within the meaning of the 1951 Refugee Convention as soon as he fulfils the criteria contained in the definition. . . . He does not become a refugee because of recognition, but is recognised because he is a refugee.[27]

It follows that protection under Article 33 applies to both recognised refugees and refugees seeking asylum.[28] The non-refoulement obligation incurred under the 1951 Refugee Convention does have exceptions. Article 33(2) of the 1951 Refugee Convention establishes the right of a State to return refugees who are dangerous to it. If the CAT, the ICCPR

---

[23] The term 'the other relevant treaties' is included in Article 78(1) TFEU which gives competence to the EU to develop a common policy on asylum, subsidiary protection and temporary protection in accordance with the 1951 Refugee Convention and the international treaties relevant for the establishment of the common policy, i.e. CAT, ICCPR and ECHR.

[24] See H. Lambert, 'Protection Against Refoulement from Europe: Human Rights Law Comes to the Rescue' (1999) 48 *International Comparative Law Quarterly* 519.

[25] Article 78 TFEU. [26] Article 18 of the EU Charter.

[27] UNHCR, 'Handbook on Procedures and Criteria for Determining Refugee Status under the 1951 Convention and the 1967 Protocol relating to the Status of Refugees', HCR/IP/4/Eng/REV.1, January 1992, www.unhcr.org (accessed 13 November 2015); UNHCR, 'Note on International Protection', UN Doc A/AC.96/815 (1993), para 11. See J. C. Hathaway, *The Rights of Refugees under International Law* (Cambridge University Press, 2005), 158–160, 303–304; and G. S. Goodwin-Gill and J. McAdam, *The Refugee in International Law* (Oxford University Press, 2007), 232–233; K. Wouters, *International Legal Standards for the Protection from Refoulement* (Intersentia, 2009), 46–47.

[28] See also UNHCR Executive Committee Conclusion No. 79 (XLVII) 1996, para (j); Hathaway, *The Rights of Refugees under International Law*, 278–279, 300–302; E. Lauterpacht and D. Bethlehem, 'The Scope and the Content of the Principle of Non-refoulement: Opinion' in E. Feller, V. Türk and F. Nicholson (eds.), *Refugee Protection in International Law: UNHCR's Global Consultation on International Protection* (Cambridge University Press, 2003), 113. See also Lambert, 'Protection Against Refoulement from Europe', 522.

and the ECHR, which complement the protection provided by the 1951 Refugee Convention, apply to a case in which a refugee is considered a danger to the security of the country of asylum under Article 33(2), the refugee cannot be returned.[29] Regarding the place (or places) to which refoulement is prohibited, Article 33 refers to 'territories'. This means that the prohibition includes returning a refugee to any territory where this individual would be at risk, and not only the refugee's country of origin.[30]

Unlike Article 33 of the 1951 Refugee Convention, Article 3 CAT protects every person against the risk of torture (not just refugees) so the personal scope covered by Article 3 CAT is broader.[31] Conversely, the scope of protection afforded by Article 3 CAT is narrower than that under Article 33(1) of the 1951 Refugee Convention. Article 3 CAT provides protection against the risk of torture,[32] whereas Article 33(1) of the 1951 Refugee Convention provides protection against any threat to life or freedom on account of a person's race, religion, nationality, membership of a particular social group, or political opinion.[33] Under both provisions, the way in which an act of return is qualified is irrelevant to the prohibition.[34] It is also noteworthy that unlike Article 33(1) of the 1951 Refugee Convention, Article 3 CAT does not admit any exception. This is specifically stated in Article 2(2) CAT, which expressly establishes

---

[29] See Goodwin-Gill and McAdam, *The Refugee in International Law*, 243–244; Hathaway, *The Rights of Refugees under International Law*, 342–355; and Lauterpacht and Bethlehem, 'The Scope and the Content of the Principle of Non-refoulement', 128–140, identifying a trend against exceptions to Article 33 of the 1951 Refugee Convention. Messineo, 'Non-refoulement Obligations in Public International Law', 135. On the implications of the application of complementary protection instruments and Article 33(2) of the 1951 Refugee Convention, see Wouters, *International Legal Standards for the Protection from Refoulement*, 114. More generally, on the relationship between the 1951 Refugee Convention and the protection provided by human rights law instruments, see J. McAdam, *Complementary Protection in International Refugee Law* (Oxford University Press, 2007), 19.

[30] Lauterpacht and Bethlehem, 'The Scope and the Content of the Principle of Non-refoulement', 121–122.

[31] See also Wouters, *International Legal Standards for the Protection from Refoulement*, 434–435.

[32] Article 3 CAT must be read together with Article 1 CAT which provides a definition of torture. On the interpretation of this definition, see, *inter alia*, J. H. Burgers and H. Danelius, *The United Nations Convention Against Torture: A Handbook on the Convention Against Torture and Other Cruel, Inhuman or Degrading Treatment or Punishment* (Martinus Nijhoff, 1988), 114–123; and M. Nowak and E. McArthur, *The United Nations Convention Against Torture* (Oxford University Press, 2008) 27–86.

[33] Nowak and McArthur, *The United Nations Convention Against Torture*, 195 and 197.

[34] *Ibid.*, 195, 196.

the absolute nature of the principle of non-refoulement under CAT by affirming that '*no exceptional circumstances whatsoever*, whether a state of war or a threat of war, internal political instability or any other public emergency, may be invoked as a justification of torture'.[35]

The Human Rights Committee has interpreted Article 7 ICCPR as a prohibition against any refoulement that would lead to torture or inhuman or degrading treatment or punishment.[36] The prohibition of such refoulement under Article 7 ICCPR is absolute, and precludes the return of an individual to any place where personal rights may be breached under the ICCPR.[37] Article 7 ICCPR has a broader scope of application than Article 3 CAT. In fact, Article 3 CAT only prohibits refoulement when there is a risk of torture upon return, whereas Article 7 ICCPR also covers inhuman or degrading treatment.[38]

As already observed, the ECHR has a special position in the EU legal order since the fundamental rights guaranteed by the ECHR constitute general principles of EU law[39] and since the EU Charter re-affirms the rights resulting from the ECHR.[40] Indeed, the EU's accession to the ECHR is an express obligation stated in the TEU.[41] The wording of Article 3 ECHR is very similar to the wording of Article 7 ICCPR.[42] The ECtHR has interpreted this provision as a prohibition against returning individuals if there is a risk of torture or inhuman or degrading treatment or punishment.[43] As in Article 3 CAT and the interpretation

---

[35] Emphasis added. See Messineo, 'Non-refoulement Obligations in Public International Law', 137.

[36] It is beyond the scope of this book to enter into further analysis of the wording of Article 7 ICCPR and its various interpretations by the Human Rights Committee. On the Human Rights Committee, see e.g. General Comment No. 20, HRI/GEN/1/Rev.6 at 30 (1992), para 9; General Comment No. 31, CCPR/C/21/Rev.1/Add.13 (2004), para 12. See also Goodwin-Gill and McAdam, *The Refugee in International Law*, 302.

[37] S. Joseph and M. Castan, *The International Covenant on Civil and Political Rights: Cases, Materials, and Commentary* (Oxford University Press, 2013), 216.

[38] The definition of torture in Article 7 ICCPR is not limited by the definition given in Article 3 CAT. See Wouters, *International Legal Standards for the Protection from Refoulement*, 525; also on the interpretation of torture under the ICCPR and the CAT, 388–389. For a comparative study of the enforcement mechanisms of the three international instruments in respect of protection against refoulement, see Lambert, 'Protection Against Refoulement from Europe', 515–544. I will refer in Section 5.3.4 to the case law of the Court of Justice of the European Union where the Court has indicated the ICCPR as a source of general principles of EU law.

[39] Article 6(3) TEU.   [40] EU Charter, preamble.   [41] Article 6(2) TEU.

[42] Article 3 ECHR does not include the word 'cruel'.

[43] Before the ECtHR, the European Commission of Human Rights had already maintained that Article 3 ECHR could be interpreted as implying a prohibition of return; see e.g. X.

given to Article 7 ICCPR by the Human Rights Committee, protection under Article 3 ECHR applies to every person and not merely refugees.[44] Unlike Article 33(2) of the 1951 Refugee Convention, the prohibition in Article 3 ECHR cannot be subject to any exception, derogation[45] or limitation. In fact, an individual must benefit from the principle of non-refoulement under Article 3 ECHR even if involved in criminal activities which threaten national security.[46] With no permissible exception, the content of the principle of non-refoulement under Article 3 ECHR is similar to the principle under Article 3 CAT, though the latter does not include inhuman or degrading treatment and is thus less comprehensive. In fact, the CAT contains a specific definition of torture, whereas there is no such definition limiting the interpretation of Article 3 ECHR.[47]

---

v. *Federal Republic of Germany* App No. 2457/65 (Commission Decision, 10 July 1967). See the case law of the ECtHR since *Soering* v. *United Kingdom* App No. 14038/88 (ECtHR, 7 July 1989) of which at the time of writing the most recent cases are: *Saadi* v. *Italy* App No. 37201/06 (ECtHR, 28 February 2008); and *M.S.S.* v. *Belgium and Greece* App No. 30696/09 (ECtHR, 21 January 2011).

[44] On this point, see N. Mole and C. Meredith, *Asylum and the European Convention on Human Rights* (Council of Europe Publishing, 2010), 25.

[45] Article 15(2) ECHR, which allows a derogation from the ECHR rights in the event of an emergency, expressly excludes Article 3 ECHR from a derogation.

[46] *Soering; Chahal* v. *United Kingdom* App No. 22414/93 (ECtHR, 15 November 1996); *Ahmed* v. *Austria* App No. 25964/94 (ECtHR, 17 December 1996); *Ramzy* v. *Netherland*, App No. 25424/05 (ECtHR, 20 July 2010); *Yankov* v. *Bulgaria* App No. 39084/97 (ECtHR, 11 December 2003); and *Saadi* v. *Italy*, para 138. For an analysis of the protection provided by Article 3 ECHR in the light of Article 33 of the 1951 Geneva Convention, see Mole and Meredith, *Asylum and the European Convention on Human Rights*, 30. On the absolute character of the prohibition of refoulement in the ECHR, see Wouters, *International Legal Standards for the Protection from Refoulement*, 307; Messineo, 'Non-refoulement Obligations in Public International Law', 140.

[47] It is not the purpose of this section to analyse in depth the wording of Article 3 ECHR, which has been referred to as a description of 'a hierarchy of ill-treatment, with torture the most extreme form' (Goodwin-Gill and McAdam, *The Refugee in International Law*, 313). The ECtHR has recognised that, in principle, other provisions of the ECHR can form the legal basis for preventing the removal of individuals. According to the ECtHR, claims for protection can be lodged under Articles 2, 5 and 6. Claims may also be lodged under Articles 8, 9 and 13 in combination with Article 3 ECHR. For instance, see *Ullah* v. *Secretary of State of the Home Department* [2004] UKHL 26; *Soering*, para 91; *Vilvarajah* v. *United Kingdom* App No. 13163/87 (ECtHR, 30 October 1991), para 103; and, *Cruz Varas* v. *Sweden* App No. 15576/89 (ECtHR, 11 July 1990), paras 69–70. See recent statements on the right to a fair trial (Article 6 ECHR) in *Othman (Abu Qatada)* v. *the United Kingdom* App No. 8139/09 (ECtHR, 17 January 2012), paras 281–285. On this point, see, *inter alia*, Mole and Meredith, *Asylum and the European Convention on Human Rights*, 87; H. Lambert, 'The European Convention on Human Rights and the Protection of Refugees: Limits and Opportunities' (2005) 24 *Refugee Survey Quarterly* 39; M. den Heijer, 'Whose Rights and Which Rights? The Continuing Story of Non-refoulement

Finally, the principle of non-refoulement enshrined in Article 33 of the 1951 Refugee Convention, Article 3 CAT and Article 3 ECHR entails the prohibition of indirect refoulement, i.e. sending an individual to a country where he would be at risk of being sent to another country where his life or freedom may be at risk.[48]

5.2.3 The Principle of Non-Refoulement as Customary International Law

In analysing whether the principle of non-refoulement is a customary norm of international law (i.e. 'is evidence of a general practice accepted as law'),[49] a distinction may be drawn between the principle of non-refoulement as incorporated in Article 33 of the 1951 Refugee Convention and the rendering of non-refoulement as expressed in the prohibition of torture and inhuman or degrading treatment or punishment. An international organisation or State is subject to the principle of non-refoulement as customary international law, even if the organisation or State is not a signatory to any international instrument which prohibits refoulement.[50]

We must first examine whether the principle of non-refoulement in Article 33 of the 1951 Refugee Convention is a customary norm of

under the European Convention on Human Rights' (2008) 10 *European Journal of Migration and Law* 277. On the extent to which poverty and a lack of medical care in the country of origin can prevent the removal, see *D* v. *UK* App No. 30240/96 (ECtHR, 2 May 1997); *SCC* v. *Sweden* App No. 46553/99 (Commission Decision, 15 February 2000); and *Sufi and Elmi* v. *United Kingdom* App No. 8319/08 and 11449/07 (ECtHR, 28 June 2011), paras 282–283.

[48] For Article 33 of the 1951 Refugee Convention, cf. Hathaway, *The Rights of Refugees under International Law*, 322–323; Lauterpacht and Bethlehem, 'The Scope and the Content of the Principle of Non-refoulement', 122–123; and Goodwin-Gill and McAdam, *The Refugee in International Law*, 252. For Article 3 CAT, see Report of the Committee against Torture, UN GAOR 53rd Session Supp. No. 44 Annex IX, 52–53, UN doc. A/53/44 (1998); *Korban* v. *Sweden*, Comm. No. 88/1997 (16 November 1998) UN doc. CAT/C/21/D/88/1997, para 7; Wouters, *International Legal Standards for the Protection from Refoulement*, 508. For Article 3 ECHR, *TI* v. *United Kingdom* App No 43844/98 (ECtHR, 7 March 2000), paras 14–15. The prohibition of indirect refoulement seems not to be found in relation to Article 7 ICCPR. However, the jurisprudence of the Human Rights Committee is likely to be consistent with that of the Committee against Torture since CAT expands on the scope of obligations not to commit torture and, to a lesser extent, other heinous forms of punishment and treatment. See Joseph and Castan, *The International Covenant on Civil and Political Rights*, 216.

[49] Article 38(1)(b) of the Statute of the International Court of Justice, San Francisco 24 October 1945.

[50] A. Cassese, *International Law* (Oxford University Press, 2005), 157. See also Section 5.2.1 of this chapter.

international law. In the *North Sea Continental Shelf Cases*, the International Court of Justice (ICJ) decided that a rule of customary international law can arise from the practices of States in accordance with a conventional rule. The case concerned the delimitation of the boundaries in the North Sea between the continental shelf areas of the States that are party to the 1958 Geneva Convention on the Continental Shelf. Pertinently to our question, the ICJ stated that for a conventional rule to be considered customary international law there should be 'a very widespread and representative participation in the convention . . . provided it included that of States whose interests were specially affected'.[51] In regard to the principle of non-refoulement, as of May 2015, 145 countries are parties to the 1951 Refugee Convention and 146 to the 1967 Protocol.[52] Walter Kälin, Martina Caroni and Lukas Heim have noted that some of the countries whose interests are particularly affected by the issue of non-refoulement are not parties to either the 1951 Refugee Convention or the 1967 Protocol 'but the fact that they have hosted large numbers of refugees for many years indicates that their behaviour is in line with the requirement of the principle of non-refoulement'.[53] Furthermore, whenever States which are not party to the 1951 Refugee Convention breach it, they always refer to the principle and claim that they have not breached it, thereby implicitly recognising that they are bound by the principle.[54] As for the *opinio juris et necessitatis*, the second requirement for the existence of customary international law, in the *North Sea Continental Shelf Cases* the ICJ required that States' practice be 'evidence of a belief that this practice is rendered obligatory by the existence of a rule of law requiring it'.[55] States that are parties to the 1951 Refugee Convention have affirmed the existence of the principle of non-refoulement on many occasions[56] as have resolutions of the United Nations General Assembly,[57] which includes all United Nations Members

---

[51] *North Sea Continental Shelf Cases* (Judgment), ICJ Reports 1969, para 73.

[52] Status of the 1951 Refugee Convention, www.treaties.un.org (accessed 13 November 2015).

[53] W. Kälin, M. Caroni and L. Heim, 'Article 33, para. 1' in A. Zimmermann (ed.), *The 1951 Convention Relating to the Status of Refugees and its 1967 Protocol: A Commentary* (Oxford University Press, 2011), 1343–1344. Pakistan, Syria, Jordan, Lebanon, Malaysia, Nepal and Thailand are examples of countries who hosted a significant refugee population in their own territories; but they are not party either to the 1951 Refugee Convention or the 1967 Protocol.

[54] Goodwin-Gill and McAdam, *The Refugee in International Law*, 352.

[55] *North Sea Continental Shelf Cases*, para 77.

[56] UN Doc. HCR/MMSP/2001/09 (2001), para 4.

[57] See A/RES/41/124 (1986), A/RES/42/109 (1987), A/RES/43/117 (1988): subsequently at least one resolution per year until the most recent A/RES/66/134 and A/RES/66/150 (2011).

(UN Members), including States that are not party to the 1951 Refugee Convention. In addition, given that a customary rule may arise from States' practices based on a convention, the ICJ required rigorous proof of *opinion juris*.[58] According to the ICJ, in order to form a rule of customary international law in compliance with a conventional rule, the conventional rule must have a 'norm-creating character' in the sense of:

> a norm-creating provision which has constituted the foundation of, or has generated a rule which, while only conventional or contractual in its origin, has since passed into the general *corpus* of international law, and is now accepted as such by the *opinio juris*, so as to have become binding even for countries which have never, and do not, become parties to the Convention.[59]

A 'norm-creating character' means that the provision of the conventional rule 'could be regarded as forming the basis of a general rule of law',[60] 'as opposed to the mere expression of contractual obligations'.[61] The extent to which Article 33 of the 1951 Refugee Convention fulfils this requirement has been laid down by the United Nations High Commissioner for Refugees (UNHCR) Executive Committee in its Conclusions. The UNHCR Executive Committee is a subsidiary organ of the United Nations General Assembly and is given the task of advising the High Commissioner on exercise of their functions which include supervising the application of the 1951 Refugee Convention.[62] The UNHCR Executive Committee's members are elected 'on the widest possible geographical basis from those states with a demonstrated interest in ... the solution of the refugee problem'.[63] Thus, the Conclusions of the UNHCR Executive Committee, while not legally binding, enjoy wide support from those UN Members that are 'specifically affected' by issues concerning the principle of non-refoulement. The Executive Committee's agreed view on refoulement issues must be regarded as being derived from 'the most important forum for identifying the value attributed to the norm of non-*refoulement*'.[64] The UNHCR Executive Committee Conclusions declared that: 'the fundamental humanitarian principle of non-refoulement has found expression in various international instruments adopted at the universal and regional levels and is generally

---

[58] *North Sea Continental Shelf Cases*, paras 70–74.   [59] *Ibid.*, para 71.   [60] *Ibid.*, para 72.
[61] Lauterpacht and Bethlehem, 'The Scope and the Content of the Principle of Non-refoulement', 143.
[62] Article 8(a), General Assembly Resolution 428(V) 14 December 1950.
[63] General Assembly Resolution 1166 (XII), 26 November 1957.
[64] J. Allain, 'The Jus Cogens Nature of Non-refoulement' (2002) 13 *International Journal of Refugee Law* 533, 539.

accepted by States'.[65] The UNHCR Executive Committee has also 'reaffirmed the fundamental character of the generally recognised principle of non-refoulement'.[66] Most legal writers agree that the principle of non-refoulement in Article 33 of the 1951 Refugee Convention has become customary international law.[67] It follows that my own finding here is to note the far-reaching extent to which the principle of non-refoulement in Article 33 of the 1951 Refugee Convention has become crystallised as a norm of customary international law.[68]

Conclusions are less readily apparent when we turn to the investigation of whether non-refoulement equates with customary law based on

---

[65] UNHCR Executive Committee Conclusion No. 6 (XXVIII) 1977, para (a).

[66] UNHCR Executive Committee Conclusion No. 17 (XXXI) 1980, para (b). Among other relevant UNHCR Executive Committee conclusions see: for instance Conclusion No. 79 (XLVII) 1996, para (j), Conclusion No. 81 (XLVIII) 1997, para (i). See also the most recent Conclusion No. 108 (LIX) 2008, para (a).

[67] Among those who agree: Goodwin-Gill and McAdam, *The Refugee in International Law*, 345–347; Lauterpacht and Bethlehem, 'The Scope and the Content of the Principle of Non-refoulement', 149–150. *Contra*, Hathaway, *The Rights of Refugees under International Law*, 363–370; K. Hailbronner, 'Non-refoulement and "Humanitarian" Refugees: Customary International Law or Wishful Legal Thinking?' (1986) 26 *Virginia Journal of International Law* 857; and Hathaway, *The Rights of Refugees under International Law*, 363–370. On the status of the principle of non-refoulement, based on Article 33 of the 1951 Refugee Convention, as regional international custom in Europe, see N. Coleman 'Non-refoulement Revisited: Renewed Review of the Status of the Principle of Non-refoulement as Customary International Law' (2003) 5 *European Journal of Migration and Law* 23.

[68] There is a debate about whether the principle of non-refoulement in Article 33 of the 1951 Refugee Convention has become a peremptory norm of general international law or *jus cogens*. In favour, see Allain, 'The Jus Cogens Nature of Non-refoulement', who refers to UNHCR Executive Committee Conclusion No. 25 (XXXIII) 1982, UNHCR Executive Committee Conclusion No. 79 (XLVII) 1996, *Declaration on Refugees, Colloquium on the International Protection of Refugees in Central America, Mexico and Panama*, 22 November 1984 and *Mexico Declaration and Plan of Action to Strengthen International Protection of Refugees in Latin America*, 16 November 2004; Kälin, Caroni and Heim, 'Article 33, para. 1', 1345–1346; A. Orakhelashvili, *Peremptory Norms in International Law* (Oxford University Press, 2006), 55. Not taking a clear stance but referring to Executive Committee Conclusion and the Cartagena Declaration, see Lauterpacht and Bethlehem, 'The Scope and the Content of the Principle of Non-refoulement', 141. *Contra*, Goodwin-Gill and McAdam, *The Refugee in International Law*, 345 n. 421. Yet, more recently, see G. S. Goodwin-Gill stating that 'the principle of non-refoulement is an inherent aspect of the absolute prohibition of torture, even sharing perhaps in some of the latter's *jus cogens* character', see G. S. Goodwin-Gill, 'The Right to Seek Asylum: Interception at Sea and the Principle of Non-refoulement' (2011) 23 *International Journal of Refugee Law* 443, 444. On the implications of the recognition and acceptance of the principle of non-refoulement as a norm of *jus cogens*, see Wouters, *International Legal Standards for the Protection from Refoulement*, 30; and R. Bruin and K. Wouters, 'Terrorism and the Non derogability of Non-refoulement' (2003) 15 *International Journal of Refugee Law* 5, 26.

international instruments other than the 1951 Refugee Convention (i.e. non-refoulement obligations on the basis of torture, inhuman or degrading treatment or punishment). At least two approaches are possible. One approach separates non-refoulement on the basis of the prohibition of torture in Article 3 CAT from the prohibition of cruel, inhuman or degrading treatment or punishment. The prohibition enshrined in Article 3 CAT has become crystallised as a norm of customary international law and it has been recognised in some judgments as a norm of *jus cogens*.[69] Conversely, proving that there is sufficient evidence of State practice in relation to the prohibition of inhuman or degrading treatment or punishment, as distinct from the prohibition of torture, may limit this first approach.[70] The second approach considers torture *and* inhuman or degrading treatment or punishment as components of a single prohibition as in Article 7 ICCPR and Article 3 ECHR. Such a broad formulation of the provision is considered more promising for the purposes of our current investigation.[71]

5.3 Obligations of Non-Refoulement Which Bind the EU and Its Member States within the EU Legal Order

5.3.1 Introduction

In order to understand the nature of the protection from refoulement afforded under EU law it is necessary to identify a legal standard with

[69] See e.g. Human Rights Committee, General Comment No 24 (52) (1994), CCPR/C/21/ Rev. 1/Add.6, 2 November 1994, para 10; *Prosecutor* v. *Anto Funrundzija* Case no. IT-95–17/1-T10, Trial Chamber, Judgment 10 December 1998, paras 155–157; *Regina* v. *Bartle and the Commissioner of Police for the Metropolis and Others Ex Parte Pinochet; Regina* v. *Evans and Another and the Commissioner of Police for the Metropolis and Others Ex Parte Pinochet* (On Appeal from a Divisional Court of the Queen's Bench Division), 24 March 1999. See E. de Wet, 'The Prohibition of Torture as an International Norm of Jus Cogens and Its Implications for National and Customary Law' (2004) 15 *European Journal of International Law* 97–121; Nowak and McArthur, *The United Nations Convention Against Torture*, 118.

[70] For this approach, see Goodwin-Gill and McAdam, *The Refugee in International Law*, 348–350; Wouters, *International Legal Standards for the Protection from Refoulement*, 30 and note 130.

[71] For this approach, see Lauterpacht and Bethlehem, 'The Scope and the Content of the Principle of Non-refoulement', 153 who refer to Human Rights Committee, General Comment No. 24 (52) (1994), CCPR/C/21/Rev.1/Add.6, 2 Nov.1994, at para 8. Lauterpacht and Bethlehem's reasoning is followed by Messineo, 'Non-refoulement Obligations in Public International Law', 145–146 and A. Duffy, 'Expulsion to Face Torture? Non-refoulement in International Law' (2008) 20 *International Journal of Refugee Law* 373, 384–385; Nowak and McArthur, *The United Nations Convention Against Torture*, 118 and 575–576.

which EU institutions, bodies, offices and agencies (Frontex), and the Member States, when implementing EU law, must comply. The starting point here is to scrutinise the ways in which international law prohibiting refoulement permeates the EU legal order. The second step is to analyse the intricacies of the EU legal order itself where both EU primary law and secondary law regulate the issue.

5.3.2   The Principle of Non-Refoulement and the Relevance of International Treaties in the EU Legal Order: Article 78(1) TFEU

Notwithstanding the presence in the EU Treaties of several obligations which stipulate a respect for human rights,[72] the fact remains that the EU is not party to any of the main human rights treaties enshrining the principle of non-refoulement, or the 1951 Refugee Convention and its 1967 Protocol.[73] Thus, in the context of this lack of formal adherence such treaties have not become an integral part of the EU legal order since otherwise it would have been pursuant to Article 216(2) TFEU.[74] With regard to human rights treaties and the 1951 Refugee Convention and its 1967 Protocol, there has been no substitution of the EU to the EU Member States' obligations under these international instruments. Such a move would require an exclusive competence of the EU in the human rights field which has not been recognised by the CJEU.[75] The relevance

---

[72] See for instance Articles 3(5) TEU and Article 21(1) TEU.

[73] See Section 5.2.1 above on international law obligations of the EU and its Member States and their international responsibility. The only human right treaty of which the EU, as an international organisation, is party is the Convention on the Rights of Persons with Disabilities (2515 UNTS 3).

[74] Article 216(2) TFEU provides that 'agreements concluded by the Union are binding upon the institutions of the Union and on its Member States' and lays down the doctrine expressed in the *Haegeman* case by the CJEU that international agreements concluded by the EU (at that time EC) are acts of the EU institutions and are an integral part of EU law (Case 181/73 *Haegeman* v. *Belgian State* [1974] ECR 449; [1975] CMLR 515, para 3, 4 and 5). More specifically, on the issues of validity and direct effect in the EU legal order, see B. de Witte, 'Direct Effect, Primacy and the Nature of the Legal Order' in P. P. Craig and G. de Burca (eds.), *The Evolution of EU Law* (Oxford University Press, 2011), 336–337; F.G. Jacob, 'Direct Effect and Interpretation of International Agreements in the Recent Case Law of the European Court of Justice' in A. Dashwood and M. Maresceau (eds.), *Law and Practice of EU External Relations: Salient Features of a Changing Landscape* (Cambridge University Press, 2008), 16–23.

[75] See A. Rosas, 'The Charter and Universal Human Rights Instruments' in S. Peers, T. Hervey and Others (eds.), *The EU Charter of Fundamental Rights: A Commentary* (Hart/Beck, 2014), 1688; cfr. Ahmed and Butler, 'The European Union and Human Rights', 788–792, who maintain that under certain circumstances substitution of the EU to the human rights

of international human rights law in the EU legal order was the focus of the CJEU's decision in the *Kadi and the Al Baarakaat* case.[76] In this case, the CJEU ruled on the judicial review under human rights law of EU restrictive measures implementing United Nations Security Council Resolutions against individuals and entities, specifically Mr Kadi and the Al Baarakaat International Foundation, allegedly associated with Osama bin Laden and the Al-Queda network. In 2005, the Court of First Instance held that the EU is bound by the United Nations Charter – and the protection and promotion of fundamental rights therein – and that United Nations Security Council Resolutions are reviewable only under peremptory norms of international law.[77] It is a matter of ongoing discussion as to whether the Court of First Instance in this ruling indicates a case of substitution.[78] The Court of First

---

obligations of the EU Member States is possible. The CJEU has recognised substitution in only two cases (outside the human rights field). First, the 1947 General Agreement on Tariffs and Trade (GATT), see Joined Cases 21–24/72 *International Fruit Company* [1972] ECR 1219; second, the 1950 Convention on Nomenclature for the Classification of Goods in Customs Tariffs and 1950 Convention Establishing a Custom Cooperation Council, see Case 38/75 *Douaneagent* [1975] ECR 1439; [1976] 1 CMLR 167.

[76] Joined Cases C-402/05 P and C-415/05 P *Kadi and Al Barakaat International Foundation v. Council and Commission* [2008] ECR I-6351; judgments of the Court of First Instance, Case T-306/01 *Yusuf and Al Barakaat International Foundation v. Council and Commission* [2005] ECR II-3533, [2005] 3 CMLR 49; Case T-315/01 *Kadi v. Council and Commission* [2005] ECR I-3649. The literature analysing the *Kadi* case is very rich, see e.g. J. d'Aspremont and F. Dopagne, 'Kadi: The ECJ's Reminder of the Elementary Divide between Legal Orders' (2008) 5 *International Organizations Law Review* 371; M. Scheinin, 'Is the ECJ Ruling in *Kadi* Incompatible with International Law?' (2008) 28 *Yearbook of European Law* 637; L. van den Herik and N. Schrijver, 'Eroding the Primacy of the UN System of Collective Security: The Judgment of the European Court of Justice in the Cases of Kadi and Al Barakaat' (2008) 5 *International Organizations Law Review* 329; C. Tomuschat, 'The *Kadi* Case: What Relationship is there between the Universal Legal Order under the Auspices of the United Nations and the EU Legal Order?' (2009) 28 *Yearbook of European Law* 654; G. de Burca, 'The European Court of Justice and the International Legal Order after *Kadi*' (2010) 51 *Harvard International Law Journal* 1; J. Kokott and C. Sobotta, 'The Kadi Case – Constitutional Core Values and International law – Finding the Balance?' (2012) 23 *European Journal of International Law* 1016.

[77] Case T-306/01 *Yusuf and Al Barakaat International Foundation v. Council and Commission* [2005] ECR II-3533, paras 276–282.

[78] See d'Aspremont and Dopagne, 'Kadi: The ECJ's Reminder of the Elementary Divide between Legal Orders', 375–376; Kokott and Sobotta, 'The Kadi Case – Constitutional Core Values and International law – Finding the Balance?', 1017 and Rosas, 'The Charter and Universal Human Rights Instruments', 1688–1689 on how the legally binding character of the UN Charter on the EU does not amount to substitution of the EU to the EU Member States obligations; *contra*, Tomuschat 'The *Kadi* Case', 664 and L. M. Hinojosa Martínez, 'Bad Law for Good Reasons: The Contradictions of the *Kadi* Judgment' (2008) 5 *International Organizations Law Review* 339, 339–341.

Instance reached the conclusion that the EU restrictive measures were not unlawful. Conversely, in 2008, the CJEU overturned the Court of First Instance's judgment by ruling that the EU restrictive measures, implementing Security Council Resolutions, are subject to the principles of liberty, democracy and respect for human rights and fundamental freedoms enshrined in Article 6(1) EU (now Article 6 TEU) as a foundation of the European legal order.[79] This assertion of the autonomy of EU law by the CJEU has attracted criticisms.[80] The CJEU decided to annul the EU restrictive measures in so far as they placed Mr Kadi and the Al Barakaat International Foundation on the sanction list. I will return to the *Kadi* cases when I analyse the principle of non-refoulement as customary international law in the EU legal order.

In this wider setting (with its indications of the extent to which international human rights law is relevant in EU law) our abiding concern with EU asylum and border control law leads us to focus on Article 78(1) TFEU. This provision states: 'The Union shall develop a common policy on asylum ... with a view to ... ensuring compliance with the principle of *non-refoulement*'. It also states that the common policy on asylum must accord with the 1951 Refugee Convention and the other relevant treaties. The CJEU has ruled on Article 78 TFEU in several cases since the entry into force of the Treaty of Lisbon.

First, in the *B and D* judgment[81] on the interpretation of the clauses excluding recognition as a refugee in the EU Qualification Directive,[82] the CJEU affirmed that the EU Qualification Directive must be interpreted 'in a manner consistent with' the 1951 Refugee Convention and

---

[79] Joined Cases C-402/05 P and C-415/05 P *Kadi and Al Barakaat International Foundation* v. *Council and Commission* [2008] ECR I–6351, paras 285 and 303. Article 6 TEU differs in its wording from Article 6 EU by providing for the legal status of the EU Charter of Fundamental Rights as EU primary law and the obligation of the EU to accede to the European Convention of Human Rights.

[80] See, *inter alia*, de Burca, 'The European Court of Justice and the International Legal Order after *Kadi*', 2; Tomuschat 'The *Kadi* Case', 662–663; Hinojosa Martínez, 'Bad Law for Good Reasons: The Contradictions of the *Kadi* Judgment', 343.

[81] Joined Cases C-57/09 and C-101/09 *B and D* [2010] ECR I–10979.

[82] Council Directive 2004/83/EC of 29 April 2004 on minimum standards for the qualification and status of third-country nationals or stateless persons as refugees or as persons who otherwise need international protection and the content of the protection granted OJ 2004 No. L304, p. 12; and recast Directive 2011/95/EU of the European Parliament and of the Council of 13 December 2011 on standards for the qualification of third-country nationals or stateless persons as beneficiaries of international protection, for a uniform status for refugees or for persons eligible for subsidiary protection, and for the content of the protection granted OJ 2011 No. L337, p. 11.

the other relevant treaties referred to in Article 78(1) TFEU.[83] Second, in the *N.S. and M.E.* cases[84] on the interpretation of the EU Dublin Regulation,[85] the CJEU stated:

> All the Member States are contracting parties to the Geneva Convention and the 1967 Protocol ... The European Union is not a contracting party ... but Article 78 TFEU and Article 18 of the Charter provide that the right to asylum is to be guaranteed with due respect for the Geneva Convention and the 1967 Protocol.[86]

According to the CJEU, Article 78 TFEU is an internal obligation of primary law to act in accordance with the 1951 Refugee Convention and the other relevant treaties.[87] Thus, the principle of non-refoulement enshrined in the 1951 Refugee Convention and the other relevant treaties is part of the EU legal order by virtue of this primary law obligation.

Should EU asylum and border control law require a Member State to breach its obligations under international law, it would be invalid by virtue of Article 78 TFEU. As explained above, this provision obliges Member States to respect the 1951 Refugee Convention and the relevant human rights treaties and can be considered *lex specialis* pursuant to Article 351 TFEU. This latter provision establishes that the international agreements concluded by Member States before 1 January 1958 (the date of the entry into force of the Treaty establishing the European Community) or, for

---

[83] Joined Cases C-57/09 and C-101/09 *B and D* [2010] ECR I–10979, paras 76–78.

[84] Joined Cases C-411 and C-493/10 *N.S.* v. *Secretary of State of the Home Department* and *M.E. and Others* v. *Refugee Application Commissioner and another* (*N.S. and M.E.*), [2011] ECR I–13905; [2012] 2 CMLR 9. See also Case C-277/11 *M.M.* v. *Minister for Justice, Equality and Law Reform*, judgment of 22 November 2012, para 8; Joined Cases C-71 and C-99/11 *Y and Z*, judgment of 5 September 2012; [2013] 1 CMLR 5, para 48; and Case C-364/11 *El Karem El Kott*, judgment 19 December 2012, para 43.

[85] Council Regulation (EC) 343/2003 of 18 February 2003 establishing the criteria and mechanisms for determining the Member State responsible for examining an asylum application lodged in one of the Member States by a third-country national OJ 2003 No. L50, p. 1; Regulation (EU) 604/2013 of the European Parliament and of the Council of 26 June 2013 establishing the criteria and mechanisms for determining the Member State responsible for examining an application for international protection lodged in one of the Member States by a third-country national or a stateless person (recast) OJ 2013 No. L180, p. 31.

[86] *N.S. and M.E.*, para 4. See also Case C-4/11 *Bundesrepublik Deutschland* v. *Kaveh Puid*, judgment 14 November 2013, para 36, 38; Case C-394/12 *Shamso Abdullahi* v. *Bundesasylamt*, judgment of 10 December 2013, para 4; Case C-481/13 *Mohammad Ferooz Qurbani*, judgment 17 July 2014, para 25.

[87] Likewise see B. de Witte, 'The EU and the International Legal Order: The Case of Human Rights' in M. Evans and P. Koutrakos (eds.), *Beyond the Established Legal Orders: Policy Interconnections between the EU and the Rest of the World* (Hart Publishing, 2011), 130.

acceding States, before accession, are not affected by the provisions of the TEU and the TFEU. Accordingly, the application of Article 351 TFEU alone does not make the international treaties prevail over the EU Treaties in those cases in which a Member State has acceded to an international treaty after the 1 January 1958 or after accession, as in the case of France's ratification of the ECHR. By the application of Article 78 TFEU as *lex specialis*, the effect of international treaties is also maintained in this latter case.[88] The role of Article 78 TFEU as explicated above is of particular importance to the analysis of the provisions on the principle of non-refoulement in the EU Charter and in the EU secondary legislation which I will conduct, respectively, in Sections 5.3.5 and 5.3.6.

5.3.3   The Principle of Non-Refoulement as Customary International Law in the EU Legal Order

My analysis thus far has explored non-refoulement's standing as customary law and has emphasised the ways in which the EU and its Member States are bound under international law by this principle.[89] This section aims to identify whether customary international law (and specifically non-refoulement to the extent that it qualifies) is part of the EU legal order.[90]

Unless one considers the general duty of the EU to comply with international law in its external relations – expressed in Articles 3(5) TEU and 21(1) TEU – as an obligation to respect customary international law within the EU legal order,[91] the EU treaties do not provide for the reception of

---

[88] See S. Peers, 'Human Rights, Asylum and European Community Law' (2005) 24 *Refugee Survey Quarterly* 24, 28–29; M. Gil-Bazo, 'Refugee Status, Subsidiary Protection, and the Right to be Granted Asylum under Refugee Law' (2006) *New Issues in Refugee Research*, Research Paper No. 136, Refugee Studies Centre Oxford, 4–5.

[89] Sections 5.2.1 and 5.2.3.

[90] This section does not deal with the question of whether customary international law is invocable before the EU courts in a review of legality, deeming it a separate question from whether customary international law is part of the EU legal order. For a detailed analysis of this issue, see J. Wouters and D. Van Eeckhoutte, 'Giving Effect to Customary International Law Through European Community Law' in J. N. Prinssen and A. Schrauwen (eds.), *Direct Effect* (Europa Law Publishing, 2004).

[91] See A. Giannelli, 'Customary International Law', 101–107. *Contra*, F. Casolari, *L'Incorporazione del Diritto Internazionale nell'Ordinamento del Diritto dell'Unione Europea* (Giuffrè', 2008), 62–63. The CJEU has referred to Article 3(5) as providing for an obligation of the EU to comply with customary international law in *Air Transport Association*, para 101: 'Under Article 3(5) TEU, the European Union is to contribute to the strict observance and the development of international law. Consequently, when it

customary international law within EU law. The CJEU has ruled on the issue of reception of customary international law in the EU legal order in *Opel Austria*.[92] The case concerned an action for the annulment of Council Regulation (EC) No. 3697/93 of 20 December 1993 withdrawing tariff concessions originally granted under the Free Trade Agreement between the Community (now the Union) and Austria.[93] The Council Regulation was adopted one week after the conclusion of the European Economic Area Agreement (EEA), prohibiting charges of equivalent effect to custom duties, but two weeks prior its entry into force. The applicant, a company called Opel Austria GmbH which was engaged in exporting gearboxes to the EU and receiving Austrian government aid for its production, argued that the adoption of the above Council Regulation was contrary to the principle of customary international law not to defeat the object and purpose of a treaty prior to its entry into force as codified in the Vienna Convention of the Law of Treaties.[94] The CJEU ruled that 'the principle of good faith is a rule of customary international law whose existence is recognised by the International Court of Justice ... and it is therefore binding on the Community'.[95] The CJEU reached the same conclusion in *Racke*.[96] The *Racke* case concerned the applicability of the *pacta sunt servanda* rule of customary international law to challenge a Council decision suspending a trade concession established by agreement between the Community (now the Union) and the former Yugoslavia. In its judgment, the CJEU ruled that the Community must respect international law 'in the exercise of its powers'.[97] Accordingly, rules of customary international law 'are binding upon the Community institutions and form part of the Community legal order'.[98] Thus, the CJEU recognised that the rules of customary international law must be part of the EU legal order and that the legislation adopted by the EU institutions must comply with customary international law.[99] The case law outlined above does not clarify the

---

adopts an act, it is bound to observe international law in its entirety, including customary international law, which is binding upon the institutions of the European Union'.

[92] *Opel Austria*. In its judgment the CJEU referred also to *Diva Navigation Corp.*, para 9. Also on reception of customary international law in the EU legal order see Case 41/74 *Van Duyn* v. *Home Office* [1974] ECR 1337; [1975] 1 CMLR 1, para 23; and Case 244/80 *Pasquale Foglia* v. *Mariella Novello* [1981] ECR 3045; [1982] 1 CMLR 585, para 24.

[93] OJ 1993 No. L343, p. 1.

[94] Article 18 of the 1969 Vienna Convention on the Law of Treaties (1155 UNTS 331).

[95] *Opel Austria*, para 90.   [96] *Racke*, paras 45–46.

[97] *Ibid.*, para 45. See also *Diva Navigation Corp.*, para 9.   [98] *Racke*, para 46.

[99] See R. Holdgaard, *External Relations Law of the European Community* (Wolters Kluwer, 2007), 181; M. Cremona, 'External Relations of the EU and the Member States: Competence,

position of customary international law vis-a-vis EU primary law (i.e. whether customary international law, when received in the EU legal order, has a higher standing than EU primary law). However, per *Kadi*, as shown above, the adoption of EU legislation in compliance with customary international law cannot derogate from the principles and fundamental freedoms which constitute the foundations of the EU.[100]

There is no case law dealing specifically with the reception of the principle of non-refoulement as customary international law in the EU legal order. Yet since the case law of the CJEU shows that customary international law is part of the EU legal order, it seems reasonable to conclude that the principle of non-refoulement (as customary international law) constitutes part of it.

5.3.4   The Principle of Non-Refoulement as a General Principle of EU Law

In the *N.S. and M.E.* cases the CJEU was asked whether the protection conferred by the general principles of EU law (and in particular by the rights under the EU Charter) was wider than the protection conferred by Article 3 ECHR. In its assessment, the Court gave much more prominence to the rights under the EU Charter.[101] Nevertheless, in her opinion in the *Dominguez* case[102] Advocate General Trstenjak suggested a different approach. The case concerned the interpretation of Directive 2003/88/EC on certain aspects of the organisation of working time, and the CJEU was asked whether an employee is entitled to rely directly on the norms of EU law. In this connection, Advocate General Trstenjak looked at the relationship between rights under the EU Charter and rights under the general

Mixed Agreements, International Responsibility, and Effects of International Law' (2006) *EUI Working Papers Law* No. 2006/22, 26; Wouters and Van Eeckhoutte, 'Giving Effect to Customary International Law Through European Community Law', 197; H. Battjes, *European Asylum Law and International Law* (Martinus Nijhoff, 2006), 80–82, 120; P. Jan Kuijper, 'Customary International Law, Decisions of International Organisations and Other Techniques for Ensuring Respect for International Legal Rules in European Community Law' in J. Wouters (ed.), *International Law in the EU and Its Member States* (T.M.C. Asser Press, 2008), 87.

[100] See Giannelli on the ranking of customary international law among the EU law sources by virtue of Articles 3(5) and 21(1) TEU, Giannelli 'Customary International Law in the European Union', 105.

[101] Giannelli, 'Customary International Law in the European Union', paras 109–115.

[102] Opinion of Advocate General Trstenjak in Case C-282/10 *Maribel Dominguez* v. *Centre Informatique du Centre Ouest Atlantique and Préfet de la Region Centre*, judgment 24 January 2012; [2012] 2 CMLR 14.

principles of EU law. She suggested that they 'have equal status' but that 'nevertheless, one cannot rule out the possibility of fundamental rights deriving from general principles and developed further affording a greater degree of protection that those under the Charter'.[103] Thus, the Advocate General suggests that the general principles of EU law could have a broader scope than the EU Charter. On this point, Sionaidh Douglas-Scott observes that the Charter 'now seems to have become the first point of reference for fundamental rights in the EU' with its status of EU primary law. However, the reference to general principles of EU law still present in Article 6(3) TEU allows the EU courts to enforce rights not present in the Charter or the ECHR, or rights in the Charter which have a limited effect due to horizontal or limitation clauses.[104] Given this, despite the principle of non-refoulement's presence in the EU Charter it seems necessary to investigate the extent to which the principle is a general principle of EU law.

The CJEU stated that fundamental rights form an integral part of the general principles of EU law.[105] This has subsequently been affirmed by the Treaties.[106] Hence, Article 6(3) TEU states: 'fundamental rights, as guaranteed by the European Convention for the Protection of Human Rights and Fundamental Freedoms and as they result from the constitutional traditions common to the Member States, shall constitute general principles of the Union's law'.[107] The jurisprudence of the CJEU does not offer a clear interpretation of this provision on the status of the ECHR within the EU legal order through the general principles of EU law. The CJEU typically identifies 'international treaties for the protection of human rights on which the Member States have collaborated or to which they are signatories' as *guidelines* from which the CJEU draws inspiration. A 'special significance in this respect' is given to the

---

[103] Opinion of Advocate General Trstenjak in *Maribel Dominguez*, para 127.

[104] See S. Douglas-Scott, 'The European Union and Human Rights after the Treaty of Lisbon' (2011) 11 *Human Rights Law Review* 671 and the CJEU's case law referenced therein. See also Rosas, 'The Charter and Universal Human Rights Instruments', 1700.

[105] Case 5/88 *Wachauf* [1989] ECR 2609; [1991] 1 CMLR 328, para 17; Case C-274/99 P *Connolly* v. *Commission* [2001] ECR I-1611; [2001] 3 CMLR 58, para 17; and Case C-94/00 *Roquette Frères* [2002] ECR I-9011; [2003] 4 CMLR 1, para 23.

[106] Originally Article F(2) of the EU Treaty 1992. Today Article 6(2) of the Treaty of Amsterdam and today Article 6(3) TEU following the entry into force of the Treaty of Lisbon.

[107] For an account of the development of general principles of EU law as deriving from the constitutional traditions common to the Member States, see, *inter alia*, J.H.H. Weiler, 'Eurocracy and Distrust: Some Questions concerning the role of the European Court of Justice in the Protection of Fundamental Human Rights within the Legal Order of the European Communities' (1986) 61 *Washington Law Review* 1103, 1115 ff.

ECHR.[108] Notably, although a special role is afforded to the ECHR, the CJEU in this case law grants the same status to the Convention and the other international human rights treaties. Conversely, in another stream of cases – less robust than the stream we have just referenced – the CJEU seems to refer to the ECHR forming part of the EU legal order through the general principles of EU law.[109] The 'special significance' language of the aforementioned case law is avoided by the Court which clearly differentiates the role of the ECHR (part of EU law) from the role of the other international human rights treaties. The ambiguity in the interpretation of Article 6(3) TEU by the CJEU is also evident if one looks at how the provision is analysed by the doctrine. On the one hand, some legal scholars favour a reading of Article 6(3) TEU which maintains that the ECHR and the case law of the ECtHR are not part of EU law until the EU accedes to the Convention. Meanwhile, the ECHR and the jurisprudence interpreting it should be considered 'authoritative guidelines for determining the general principles of Community law which the Court applies'.[110] Such a reading of Article 6(3) TEU aligns with the most common interpretation given by the CJEU, as presented above. On the other hand, Bruno de Witte points to how the wording of Article 6(3) TEU spells out clearly that the rights of the ECHR are general principles of EU law and that the ECHR, 'through the formal intermediary of the general principles' is part of the EU legal order (i.e. binding on the EU institutions). Accordingly, de Witte states that there is no discretion to

---

[108] Case C-479/04 *Laserdisken ApS* v. *Kulturministeriet* [2006]ECR I-8089; [2007] 1 CMLR 6, para 61. See also Case 4/73 *Nold* [1974]ECR 491, [1974] 2 CMLR 338; Case 374/87 *Orkem* [1989] ECR 3283, para 18; Joined Cases C-297/88 and 197/89 *Dzodzi* [1990] ECR I-3763, para 68; *Opinion 2/94* [1996] ECR I-929; [1996] 2 CMLR 265, para 33; Case C-112/00 *Schmidberger* [2003] ECR I-5659; [2003] 2 CMLR 34, para 71; Case C-540/03 *Parliament* v. *Council* [2006] ECR I-5769; [2006] 3 CMLR 28, para 37; Case C-229/05 P, *PKK and KNK* v. *Council* [2007] I-439, para 76; Joined Cases C-402/05 P and C-415/05 P *Kadi and Al Barakaat* v. *Council* [2008] ECR I-6531, para 283; Case C-438/05 *International Transport Workers' Federation* [2007] ECR I-10779; [2008] 1 CMLR 51, para 43; C-341/05 *Laval un Partneri* [2007] ECR I-11767; [2008] 2 CMLR 9, para 89.

[109] T-351/03 *Schneider Electric* v. *Commission* [2007] ECR II-2237; [2008] 4 CMLR 22, para 181; Case C-450/06 *Varec* v. *Etat belge* [2008] ECR I-581; [2008] 2 CMLR 24, para 44–45; Case C-465/07 *Elgafaji* v. *Staatssecretaris van Justitie* [2009] ECR I-921; [2009] 2 CMLR 45, para 28.

[110] See, for instance, A. Rosas, 'Fundamental Rights in the Luxembourg and Strasbourg Courts' in C. Baudenbacher, P. Tresselt and T. Orlygsson (eds.), *The EFTA Court: Ten Years On* (Hart Publishing, 2005), 170–171; G. Harpaz, 'The European Court of Justice and its Relations with the European Court of Human Rights: The Quest for Enhanced Reliance, Coherence and Legitimacy' (2009) 46 *Common Market Law Review* 105–141, 112–113.

the CJEU on how to dispose of the rights of the ECHR since they have been incorporated within EU law.[111] The first reading of the doctrine of Article 6(3) TEU – viewing the ECHR as no more than 'authoritative guidelines' – is influenced by an understanding of the EU law/ECHR relationship which is, in the words of Harpaz, 'judicial made' (i.e. shaped by the case law of the CJEU without 'a systematic analysis ... for the precise legal force that the Luxemburg Regime should ascribe to the Strasbourg Regime').[112] De Witte's argument, conversely, supported by particular case law of the CJEU, appears to offer a fair representation of the status of the ECHR in the EU legal order and the enduringly important position of the general principles in this order. Thus, as asserted by the supporters of the first reading of Article 6(3) TEU, it is correct to state that the ECHR will be directly binding on the EU institutions and part of the EU legal order only after the accession to the ECHR pursuant to Article 216(2) TFEU. However, the fact that a provision of EU primary law, Article 6(3) TEU, states that the rights of the ECHR constitute a general principle of EU law should not be disregarded. On this point, as highlighted by de Witte, a parallel could be drawn between Article 6(3) TEU and Article 78(1) TFEU, analysed above, stating the obligation of EU primary law to act in accordance with the 1951 Refugee Convention and the other treaties relevant for refugee protection.[113] Both provisions – Article 6(3) TEU and Article 78(1) TFEU – identify an internal obligation to act in accordance with international instruments to which the EU, as an international organisation, is not yet party. All told, de Witte's view seems to be preferable although it has not been confirmed by consistent jurisprudence from the CJEU.

We must now apply these reflections to understand the extent to which the principle of non-refoulement is a general principle of EU law. Concerning the standard of protection from refoulement in EU law, we should turn to the *Elgafaji* case where the CJEU specifically ruled on the principle of non-refoulement, as laid down in Article 3 ECHR and the general principles of EU law.[114] The *Elgafaji* case, which was a reference for a preliminary ruling, concerned an application for a temporary residence permit in the Netherlands submitted by Mr and Mrs Elgafaji who

---

[111] De Witte, 'The EU and the International Legal Order', 129–131.
[112] Harpaz, 'The European Court of Justice and Its Relations with the European Court of Human Rights', 112.
[113] De Witte, 'The EU and the International Legal Order', 130. Cfr. Rosas, 'The Charter and Universal Human Rights Instruments', 1691.
[114] *Elgafaji*.

sought to prove the real risk to which they would be exposed if they were expelled to Iraq which was their country of origin. The CJEU was asked to rule on the interpretation of Article 15 of Council Directive 2004/83/EC (the Directive) in relation to Article 3 ECHR. The Directive establishes the minimum standards for the qualification and status of third-country nationals as refugees or as persons who otherwise need international protection, and it deals with the content of the protection granted. Specifically, Article 15 of the Directive, in conjunction with its Article 2(e), sets out the conditions under which an individual qualifies for subsidiary protection. In particular, the CJEU was asked whether Article 15(c) of the Directive is to be interpreted as offering protection only in those situations in which Article 3 ECHR applies (as interpreted by the ECtHR) or whether Article 15(c) offers supplementary protection. The CJEU was also asked to set out the criteria for determining whether a person who claims to be eligible for subsidiary protection status runs a real risk of serious and individual threat by reason of indiscriminate violence within the terms of Article 15(c).[115] The CJEU found that Article 15(c) must be interpreted as meaning that an applicant for subsidiary protection does not necessarily have to prove that: 'the existence of a serious and individual threat to the life or person of an applicant for subsidiary protection is not subject to the condition that that applicant adduce evidence that he is specifically targeted by reason of factors particular to his personal circumstances'.[116] The existence of a serious and individual threat can 'exceptionally be considered to be established' where the degree of indiscriminate violence in the country is of such a high level that simply by returning to that country the individual would face a real risk.[117] Through this ruling, the CJEU made the interpretation of Article 15(c) fully compatible with the case law of the ECtHR on Article 3 ECHR.[118] However, the Court denied that there is a direct correspondence between Article 15(c) of the Directive and Article 3 ECHR and stated that the interpretation of Article 15(c) requires an independent analysis. Such interpretation, the Court ruled, must have due regard for the fundamental rights guaranteed under the ECHR.[119] On this point, the Court stated: 'the fundamental right guaranteed under Article 3 of the ECHR forms part of the general principles of Community law, observance of which is ensured by the Court, and . . . the case-law of

---

[115] *Ibid.*, para 26.   [116] *Ibid.*, para 43.   [117] *Ibid.*

[118] *Ibid.*, para 44. For the interpretation of Article 3 ECHR by the ECtHR see *N.A. v. The United Kingdom* (Application No. 25904/07, 17 July 2008).

[119] *Elgafaji*, para 28.

the European Court of Human Rights is taken into consideration in interpreting the scope of that right in the Community legal order'.[120] It follows from this judgment that Article 3 ECHR and the case law of the ECtHR on this provision are sources of general principles of EU law. Pertaining to this, the CJEU states that the ECHR is part of the EU legal order and not only a source of guidance in determining the general principles of EU law. Another relevant judgment arose from the *N.S. and M.E.* cases[121] concerning applicants originating from Afghanistan, Iran and Algeria who travelled via Greece and claimed asylum in the United Kingdom and Ireland. The CJEU ruled incidentally that the right to asylum enshrined in Article 18 of the EU Charter is a general principle of EU law.[122] The *N.S. and M.E.* ruling confirmed the *Elgafaji* case by treating the principle of non-refoulement as a general principle of EU law. These rulings can be located in the particular stream of CJEU jurisprudence, identified above, according to which the ECHR through the general principles of EU law is deemed part of the EU legal order.

Article 6(3) TEU expressly refers to the ECHR, together with the constitutional traditions common to the Member States, as a source of general principles of EU law. Other international instruments, such as the 1951 Refugee Convention, the ICCPR and the CAT, are not explicitly mentioned. As noted above, the CJEU has made a distinction between the international treaties for the protection of human rights from which it is said to derive 'guidelines' for determining the general principles of EU law and the ECHR which holds *at least* a special significance in EU law. On several occasions, the CJEU has referred to international human rights instruments different from the ECHR. In the *Dynamic Medien* case, concerning the interpretation of Directive 2000/31/EC of the European Parliament and the Council on certain legal aspects of information society services in the internal market,[123] the CJEU focused on youth-protection via classification of mail-order sales of image storage media and ruled that the ICCPR is one of those international instruments concerning the protection of human rights 'of which it takes account in

---

[120] *Ibid.* [121] *N.S. and M.E.*, judgment 21 December 2011.
[122] *Ibid.*, para 109. In *Parliament v. Council*, para 38, before the EU Charter became legally binding, the Court of Justice affirmed that the EU Charter right to respect for private and family life corresponds to a general principle of EU law. On the relationship between the right to asylum and the principle of non-refoulement see Section 5.3.5.1 below.
[123] OJ 2000 No. L178, p. 1.

applying the general principles of Community law'.[124] Notably, in the *Nold* case by way of comparison, the CJEU was called on to rule on the infringement of the rights to property and to freedom to trade, as protected under the German Constitution, by new trading measures issued by the European Commission. In ensuring respect for human rights, the CJEU referred firstly to the constitutional traditions common to the Member States, and secondly to international human rights treaties. The CJEU referred not only to the ECHR but more broadly to 'international treaties for the protection of human rights on which the Member States have collaborated or of which they are signatories'.[125] The so-called *Nold* formula has been followed by the CJEU in subsequent judgments and has also been used by the Court after the entry into force of the EU Charter.[126] It follows that the CJEU takes international human rights instruments (other than the ECHR) into account, and that such instruments have been used by the CJEU as 'guidelines' for determining which fundamental rights are general principles of EU law. Arguably, the wording of Article 6(3) TEU confirms this interpretation.[127] Thus, it seems plausible to conclude that other international human rights instruments that are not mentioned expressly in the rulings of the CJEU, such as the 1951 Refugee Convention and the CAT, could also be included as sources of the general principles of EU law.

As far as the principle of non-refoulement is concerned, according to the CJEU Article 3 ECHR is a source of the general principles of EU law. The CJEU has not stated that the principle of non-refoulement, as enshrined in the other international instruments, different from the ECHR, is a source of the general principle of EU law. However, since the ICCPR has been used by the CJEU for identifying which fundamental rights are general principles of EU law, it seems possible to argue that the CJEU may in future include among the general

---

[124] Case C-244/06 *Dynamic Medien Vertriebs GmbH* v. *Avides Media AG* [2008] ECR I–505; [2008] 2 CMLR 23, para 39. Cfr. Case C-249/96 *Grant* v. *South West Trains Ltd* [1998] ECR I–621; [1998] 1 CMLR 993 where the CJEU held that a communication from the ICCPR Human Rights Committee concerning discrimination on grounds of sexual orientation could not be included as a source of the general principles of EU law. On the interpretation of the dismissal of the opinion of the ICCPR Human Rights Committee, see Peers, 'Human Rights, Asylum and European Community Law', 30.

[125] *Nold*, para 13.

[126] See Rosas, 'The Charter and Universal Human Rights Instruments', 1688 ff.

[127] See likewise A. Rosas, 'International Human Rights Instruments in the Case Law of the Court of Justice' in *Law in the Changing Europe: Liber Amicorum Pranas Kuris* (Mykolo Romerio Universiteto, 2008), 369.

principles of EU law the principle of non-refoulement as enshrined in these international instruments.

5.3.5 The EU Charter of Fundamental Rights

5.3.5.1 Overview

The Charter enshrines civil, political, social, economic and cultural rights in the EU legal order. Drafted in 2000, after a deliberation on its elaboration by the European Council in 1999,[128] the EU Charter was first enshrined in the Treaty of Nice[129] and was subsequently given full legal effect with the entry into force of the Treaty of Lisbon which grants the EU Charter the status of EU primary law.[130] As stated in its Preamble, the Charter is a reaffirmation of the rights resultant from the constitutional traditions and international obligations common to the EU Member States. In this connection, it largely refers to the ECHR and other international instruments such as the 1951 Refugee Convention and its 1967 Protocol.[131] Importantly, for our purposes, the Charter includes a prohibition of collective expulsion (Article 19(1)), a prohibition of refoulement (Article 19(2)) and the right to asylum (Article 18). The prohibition of collective expulsion stipulates an obligation to give individual consideration to one person's claim to stay in a State's territory before expulsion is performed. The most important international provision including such prohibition is Article 4 Protocol 4 ECHR which has been dealt with by the ECtHR mainly in cases of asylum applications.[132] This prohibition is strictly connected to the prohibition of refoulement (i.e. the prohibition that we have examined extensively concerning the return of individuals to territories where they may be at risk of torture or other inhuman or degrading treatment or punishment). In turn, the principle of non-refoulement is at the core of the right to asylum. This is shown in the text of the 1951 Refugee Convention which, although not including a right to asylum, lists a set of rights which are granted to the refugee by virtue of the process in which 'the bond strengthens between a particular refugee

---

[128] European Council, Tampere 15 and 16 October 1999, 16/10/1999, No. 200/1/99.
[129] OJ 2001 No. C80, p. 1.   [130] Article 6(1) TEU.   [131] Article 18(1) of the Charter.
[132] See E. Guild, 'Article 19' in S. Peers, T. Hervey and Others (eds.), *The EU Charter of Fundamental Rights: A Commentary* (Hart/Beck, 2014), 549 and the ECtHR's jurisprudence referred to. See also on the prohibition of collective expulsion I. Bryan and P. Langford, 'Impediments to the Expulsion of Non-nationals: Substance and Coherence in Procedural Protection under the European Convention on Human Rights' (2010) 79 *Nordic Journal of International Law* 457–479, 459.

and the state party in which he or she is present'.[133] Importantly, in this framework of entitlement under the 1951 Refugee Convention, the principle of non-refoulement constitutes a right benefiting all refugees as soon as they come under the jurisdiction of the asylum State.[134] Nevertheless, the right to asylum is not limited to the principle of non-refoulement. It is commonly understood as an individual right to be admitted to the relevant State's territory, to have access to an asylum procedure and, in the long term, to obtain a durable solution of integration.[135] Since States cannot agree in terms recognising this right, or on recognising a concurrent binding international obligation, the right to asylum has been identified as a procedural right. This is a right to have access to an asylum procedure in line with the wording of Article 14 of the Universal Declaration of Human Rights enshrining 'a right to seek and enjoy asylum'.[136] However, a different interpretation may be given of the right to asylum in Article 18 under the Charter which will be discussed and developed below.

Yet before scrutinising the specific provisions of the EU Charter on the principle of non-refoulement, collective expulsions and the right to asylum, I will briefly analyse Article 6 TEU, which states the legal value of the EU Charter. Under Article 6 TEU, the EU Charter 'shall have the same legal value as the Treaties', so that compliance with the Charter is necessary for the validity of EU legislation. According to Article 51(1) of the EU Charter, which is the first of the general provisions governing the interpretation and application of the Charter, its provisions (embodying the principle of non-refoulement, the prohibition of collective expulsions and the right to asylum) are addressed to the institutions and agencies of the EU, as well as to the Member States when they implement EU law.[137] Asylum and migration are part of the Area of Freedom, Security and Justice where competence is shared between the Member States and the

---

[133] Hathaway, *The Rights of Refugees under International Law*, 154.   [134] *Ibid.*, 160.
[135] *Ibid.*, 300–302; Goodwin-Gill and McAdam, *The Refugee in International Law*, 356.
[136] Goodwin-Gill and McAdam, *The Refugee in International Law*, 358; T. Gammeltoft-Hansen and H. Gammeltoft-Hansen, 'The Right to Seek – Revisited. On the UN Human Rights Declaration Article 14 and Access to Asylum Procedures in the EU' (2008) 10 *European Journal of Migration and Law* 439–459, 446. On the complex interface between the right to asylum and the principle of non-refoulement, see McAdam, *Complementary Protection in International Refugee Law*, 54 ff.; Mole and Meredith, *Asylum and the European Convention on Human Rights*, 19 ff.; Messineo, 'Non-refoulement Obligations in Public International Law', 147–149; M. den Heijer 'Article 18' in S. Peers, T. Hervey and Others (eds.), *The EU Charter of Fundamental Rights: A Commentary* (Hart/Beck, 2014), 522, 534.
[137] Article 51(1) of the EU Charter.

EU in so far as competences have been transferred to the EU. Compliance with the EU Charter is only required in those areas of Member States' activities which fall within the competences transferred to the EU. Member States' activities outside the EU's competence are subject to the international obligations of the Member States.[138] Article 6 TEU and Article 51(2) of the EU Charter also state that the EU Charter does not extend the competences of the EU. Finally, Article 6 TEU and Article 52(7) of the EU Charter refer to the Explanations relating to the Charter of Fundamental Rights (EU Charter Explanations),[139] which set out the sources of the Charter's provisions and must be used when interpreting its rights, freedoms and principles.

In terms of the relationship between the EU Charter and the ECHR, until the EU becomes party to the ECHR, as required by Article 6(2) TEU, the EU itself is not subject to the ECtHR's jurisdiction. However, the EU is bound by ECHR rights to the extent that such rights are guaranteed by the EU Charter. Article 52(3) of the EU Charter states: 'In so far as this Charter contains rights which correspond to rights guaranteed by the Convention for the Protection of Human Rights and Fundamental Freedoms [ECHR], the meaning and scope of those rights shall be the same as those laid down by the said Convention'. This means that since the EU Charter is legally binding 'the EU [does not] enjoy the autonomy to breach the rights in the ECHR . . . because it will thereby be violating a domestic obligation to ensure that the ECHR rights are guaranteed within the EU legal order'.[140]

5.3.5.2 Specific Non-Refoulement Provisions; Collective Expulsions; the Right to Asylum and Their Legal Interaction with the General Provisions of the EU Charter

Article 19(2) of the EU Charter establishes that: 'No one may be removed, expelled or extradited to a State where there is a serious risk that he or she

---

[138] A. Dashwood, 'The Relationship between the Member States and the European Union/ European Community' (2004) 41 *Common Market Law Review* 355, 371. Regarding the scope of application of Article 51(1) of the EU Charter, the CJEU in Case C-617/10 *Åklagaren v. Hans Åkerberg Fransson*, judgment 26 February 2013; [2013] 2 CMLR 46, para 29, excluded a narrow interpretation of this provision and gave a very broad interpretation of the scope of EU Law. See on the limitations to the scope of application of the EU Charter, K. Lenaerts, 'Exploring the Limits of the EU Charter of Fundamental Rights' (2012) 8 *European Constitutional Law Review* 375.

[139] Explanations relating to the Charter of Fundamental Rights OJ 2007 No. C302, p. 2.

[140] S. Peers, 'Taking Rights Away? Limitations and Derogations' in S. Peers and A. Ward (eds.), *The European Union Charter of Fundamental Rights* (Hart Publishing, 2004), 171.

would be subjected to the death penalty, torture or other inhuman or degrading treatment or punishment'. Article 19(1) of the EU Charter prohibits collective expulsion. Article 18 of the EU Charter establishes that: 'The right to asylum shall be guaranteed with due respect for the rules of the Geneva Convention of 28 July 1951 and the Protocol of 31 January 1967 relating to the status of refugees and in accordance with the Treaty on European Union and the Treaty on the Functioning of the European Union'.

Article 19(2) of the EU Charter does not reproduce the text of Article 3 ECHR verbatim, but it does express the case law of the ECtHR on Article 3 ECHR.[141] Conversely, the text of Article 3 ECHR is repeated verbatim in Article 4 of the EU Charter, which states: 'No one shall be subjected to torture or to inhuman or degrading treatment and punishment'. The reason for expressing the two prohibitions in two different provisions of the EU Charter is to be found in the Charter's preamble which states: 'it is necessary to strengthen the protection of fundamental rights in the light of changes in society . . . by making those rights more visible in a Charter'. The principle of non-refoulement, as developed by the case law of the ECtHR on Article 3 ECHR, has probably been expressly included in the EU Charter to give it greater visibility.[142] A first question, with regard to the interaction between Article 19(2) of the EU Charter and the general provisions of the EU Charter, is whether Article 19(2) of the Charter is subject to any restrictions. It is established in the case law of the CJEU that: 'restrictions may be imposed on the exercise of fundamental rights . . . provided that those restrictions in fact correspond to objectives of general interest pursued by the [Union]'.[143] This case law is reflected in Article 52(1) of the EU Charter, which provides: 'any limitation on the exercise of the rights and freedoms recognised by this Charter must be provided for by law and respect the essence of those rights and freedoms'. It is not the purpose of the present analysis to examine the scope of such limitations. However, it must be acknowledged that Article 52(1) of the EU Charter does not itself limit rights in the Charter but provides rules of interpretation for *when* such rights are limited.[144] Thus, Article 52(1) of

---

[141] Article 19(2) of the EU Charter also refers to the death penalty.

[142] See S. Peers, 'Immigration, Asylum and the European Union Charter of Fundamental Rights' in E. Guild and P.E. Minderhoud (eds.), *The First Decade of EU Migration and Asylum Law* (Martinus Nijhoff, 2012), 460; Guild, 'Article 19', 545.

[143] See e.g. Case C-292/97 *Karlsson and Others* [2000] ECR I-2737; and, *Wachauf*.

[144] See Peers, 'Immigration, Asylum and the European Union Charter of Fundamental Rights', 455.

the EU Charter functions as an additional rule of interpretation.[145] It is therefore necessary to examine whether Article 19(2) of the EU Charter is subject to any restrictions which trigger the application of Article 52(1) of the EU Charter. If the requirements of Article 52(1) are met, it may be possible, under the EU Charter, to remove a person to a country where the risk of torture or other inhuman or degrading treatment is present.[146] In Section 5.2.2, I showed that Article 3 ECHR, as developed by the ECtHR to prohibit refoulement, is absolute. This means that no limitations are permitted. The question is whether Article 19(2) of the EU Charter is also absolute by virtue of the fact that it expresses the case law of the ECtHR on Article 3 ECHR. It might be argued that Article 19(2) of the EU Charter is subject to the restrictions derived from the case law of the CJEU mentioned above. Article 52(3) of the EU Charter states that the rights contained in the Charter have the same meaning and scope as the rights guaranteed by the ECHR if they correspond to rights laid down by the ECHR. It might seem that Article 52(3) of the EU Charter requires correspondence with a right expressly stated in the ECHR. Article 19(2) of the EU Charter does not enshrine a right laid down in the ECHR, as in the case of Article 4 of the EU Charter. As noted above, Article 19(2) of the EU Charter incorporates the case law of the ECtHR on Article 3 ECHR. There are three arguments against this latter position on Article 19(2) of the EU Charter. First, the EU Charter Explanations expressly state that Article 19(2) of the EU Charter corresponds to Article 3 ECHR as interpreted by the ECtHR. The EU Charter Explanations also clarify that, once correspondence has been established, it concerns meaning and scope 'including authorised limitations'. Since Article 3 ECHR is absolute, it is possible to conclude that the absoluteness also concerns Article 19(2) of the EU Charter. In other words, the fact that the terms 'meaning' and 'scope' also include 'authorised limitations' seems to permit a further step to be taken so that the terms 'meaning' and 'scope' also cover the absence of limitations. Second, Article 53 of the EU Charter prohibits the interpretation of any provision of the Charter 'as restricting or adversely affecting human rights and fundamental freedoms' as recognised in the ECHR. Applying any limitations to Article 19(2) of the EU Charter would have precisely this effect.[147] Third, the Member States have

---

[145] *Ibid.*

[146] See the EU Charter Explanations regarding Article 52(1) of the Charter which envisages that a limit may be imposed by Article 4(1) TEU on the grounds of national security.

[147] See Peers, 'Immigration, Asylum and the European Union Charter of Fundamental Rights', 460.

obligations under the ECHR and these would not be respected if the Member States had to apply limitations restricting the minimum protection afforded by the ECHR.[148] For all of these reasons, Article 19(2) of the EU Charter is not subject to any limitations, and, thus, Article 52(1) of the EU Charter does not apply.[149]

Article 19(1) of the EU Charter prohibits collective expulsions. The EU Charter Explanations on Article 52 state that Article 19(1) of the EU Charter corresponds to Article 4 of Protocol No. 4 to the ECHR. As Peers has observed, Article 19(1) of the EU Charter brings together Articles 3(1) and 4 of Protocol No. 4 to the ECHR. The prohibition of collective expulsions in Article 19(1) of the EU Charter includes both aliens and nationals. Article 3(1) of the Protocol refers to nationals and Article 4 of the Protocol refers to aliens. However, since Article 19(1) of the EU Charter includes both aliens and nationals, the scope of the application of Articles 3(1) and 4 of Protocol No. 4 to the ECHR has not been modified. Thus, the correspondence between Article 19(1) of the EU Charter and Article 4 of Protocol No. 4 is unaltered.[150] According to Article 52(3) of the EU Charter, since Article 19(1) of the EU Charter corresponds to Article 4 of Protocol No. 4 to the ECHR, it has the same meaning and scope as Article 4 of Protocol No. 4.[151] This is also stated in the EU Charter Explanations on Article 19(1) of the EU Charter.

Our consideration of the scope and interaction of provisions also benefits from examining the Article 15 ECHR derogation in relation to Article 19(1) of the EU Charter. The EU Charter Explanations on Article 52 of the EU Charter state:

> The Charter *does not affect the possibilities of Member States to avail themselves of Article 15 ECHR*, allowing derogations from ECHR rights in the event of war or of other public dangers threatening the life of the nation, when they take action in the area of national defence in the event of war and of the maintenance of law and order.[152]

Member States can avail themselves of the Article 15 ECHR derogation in relation to Article 4 of Protocol No. 4 to the ECHR, since Article 6 of the Protocol makes Article 4 of the Protocol additional to the Convention, and all the provisions of the ECHR, including Article 15, must apply accordingly. As noted above, the EU Charter Explanations make it clear that the terms 'meaning' and 'scope' also cover limitations to a right. The text of Articles 19(1) and 52(3) of the EU Charter and the EU Charter Explanations

---

[148] *Ibid.*   [149] Likewise, see Guild, 'Article 19', 559.   [150] Guild, 'Article 19', 450, 464.
[151] See Guild, 'Article 19', 554.   [152] Emphasis added.

do not point towards any difference between limitations and derogations in this respect. Since 'meaning and scope' also cover derogations, Article 19(1) of the EU Charter is subject to derogation in time of war or other public emergency threatening the life of the nation.[153]

Finally, Article 18 of the EU Charter provides that the right to asylum must be guaranteed 'with due respect for the rules of the Geneva Convention of 28 July 1951 and the Protocol of 31 January 1967 relating to the status of refugees'. The EU Charter Explanations on Article 18 declare that the text of the Article is based on Article 78 TFEU which requires the EU to respect the 1951 Refugee Convention.[154] Article 18 of the EU Charter also states that the right to asylum must be guaranteed 'in accordance with the Treaty on European Union and the Treaty on the Functioning of the European Union'. In this way, Article 18 of the EU Charter asserts that the right to asylum can be restricted by limitations pursuant to EU law. Such limitations must respect the general provisions governing the interpretation and application of the Charter stated in its Article 52(1) to (4).[155] Importantly, it follows that Article 18 of the EU Charter must be interpreted according to the additional rule of interpretation of Charter rights established in Article 52(1) of the EU Charter concerning the rules of interpretation for *when* rights are subject to limitations. However, as we have noted above, the right to asylum is part of the principle of non-refoulement which is enshrined in Article 19(2) of the EU Charter and does not admit limitations.[156] It may therefore be assumed that Article 18 of the EU Charter also has no limitations.[157]

The content of Article 18 of the Charter evokes a sequence of inquiry: namely, whether it is an individual's right to obtain entry to the territory

---

[153] *Contra*, Guild, 'Article 19', 559.

[154] The EU Charter Explanations also contain a reference to the Protocols relating to the United Kingdom, Ireland, and Denmark to define the extent to which Article 18 of the Charter is applicable to them. The Explanations also refer to the Protocol on Asylum for Nationals of Member States of the European Union annexed to the Treaties. This is the Protocol which excludes that a national of an EU Member State can apply for asylum in another EU Member State. On these references to the Protocols see den Heijer 'Article 18', 520–521; on the Protocol on Asylum see, for instance, G. Noll, *Negotiating Asylum. The EU Acquis, Extraterritorial Protection and the Common Market of Deflection* (Martinus Nijhoff, 2000), 553.

[155] See Peers, 'Immigration, Asylum and the European Union Charter of Fundamental Rights', 456. Cfr, den Heijer 'Article 18', 537.

[156] See likewise Peers, 'Immigration, Asylum and the European Union Charter of Fundamental Rights', 463.

[157] In *N.S. and M.E.* case, paras 109–115, the CJEU has stated that Article 18 of the EU Charter provides the same protection as Article 3 ECHR.

of the asylum State, and whether it is a corresponding obligation for the asylum State to grant admission, or whether it only corresponds to protection against expulsion once the asylum State has decided to admit the individual to its territory. A look at Article 52(4) of the EU Charter may shed some light on this issue. The provision concerns rights of the Charter resulting from the constitutional traditions common to the Member States which must be interpreted 'in harmony' with those traditions. On this point, while the 1951 Refugee Convention, the ECHR, the TEU and the TFEU do not guarantee an individual the right to asylum, it is evident that several EU Member States have recognised asylum as an individual right in their constitutions.[158] Therefore, it can be argued that if Article 18 of the EU Charter results from the constitutional traditions common to the Member States, according to Article 52(4) of the EU Charter, it must be interpreted 'in harmony' with those traditions thus guaranteeing a right of entry which goes beyond protection against expulsion.[159] Against this latter argument, it can be asserted (recalling the Charter Preamble) that the Charter was not adopted with the intention of creating new rights but for the purposes of reaffirming rights resulting from national constitutional traditions and also, importantly, international obligations common to the EU Member States. In this connection, as noted, no international instruments include an obligation to grant asylum. Accordingly, Article 18 of the Charter should not be interpreted as an individual right of entry since such an interpretation does not reflect EU Member States' international obligations.[160] A way forward in this debate will finally be offered by the CJEU when it rules on the matter.[161] Meanwhile, it is evident that

---

[158] S. Peers, *EU Justice and Home Affairs Law* (Oxford University Press, 2011), 98; and M. Gil-Bazo, 'The Charter of Fundamental Rights of the European Union' (2008) 27 *Refugee Survey Quarterly* 33, 46–47; den Heijer 'Article 18', 528–529; H. Lambert, F. Messineo and P. Tiedemann, 'Comparative Perspectives of Constitutional Asylum in France, Italy and Germany: *Resquiescat in Pace*?' (2008) 27 *Refugee Survey Quarterly* 32.

[159] See Peers, *EU Justice and Home Affairs Law*, 98; and Gil-Bazo, 'The Charter of Fundamental Rights of the European Union', 46–48.

[160] This argument is introduced by den Heijer who finally argues for Article 18 of the Charter to be considered an individual right: den Heijer 'Article 18', 530. See also C. Harvey, 'The Right to Seek Asylum in the European Union' (2004) 1 *European Human Rights Law Review* 17, 12.

[161] The CJEU has been asked to interpret the content of Article 18 of the Charter in two cases: *N.S. and M.E.* and Case C-528/11 *Halaf*, judgment of 30 May 2013. However, the CJEU has given no ruling on the issue. See, on this point, den Heijer 'Article 18', 531–532.

despite the fact that a right to asylum is not enshrined in any international obligation common to the EU Member States, Article 18 of the Charter may be interpreted as an individual right of entry to the territory of the asylum State. This solution relies on an interpretation in harmony with the constitutional traditions common to the EU Member States pursuant to Article 52(4) of the Charter and, moreover, on the nature of the Charter as a fundamental rights instrument.[162]

5.3.5.3 Scope and Application of the EU Charter's Principle of Non-Refoulement

Concerning the scope and interpretation of the rights and principles of the EU Charter, the last sentence of Article 52(3) of the Charter states that the EU is not prevented from providing more extensive protection than that afforded by the ECHR. The EU Charter Explanations on Article 52 of the Charter state: (i) the last sentence of Article 52(3) of the EU Charter means that the EU is allowed to guarantee more extensive protection; and (ii) 'in any event, the level of protection afforded by the Charter may never be lower than that guaranteed by the ECHR'. Thus, the protection afforded by the ECHR appears to be a minimum standard for EU protection of fundamental rights. Specifically, the following factors are relevant to the content of this minimum standard. First, both the EU Charter Explanations and the preamble to the EU Charter provide that the meaning and scope of the EU Charter provisions are determined by the ECHR case law and not merely by the text of its provisions. This does not affect the autonomy of EU law or of the CJEU.[163] Second, as stated in the EU Charter Explanations on Article 52, Article 19(2) of the Charter corresponds to the case law of the ECtHR on Article 3 ECHR. On this point, in her Opinion in the *N.S. and M.E.* cases, Advocate General Trstenjak put forward the view that the judgments of the ECtHR cannot be regarded 'as a source of interpretation with full validity in connection with the application of the Charter' but that 'significance and high importance are to be attached to the case law of the [ECtHR] in connection with the interpretation of the Charter of fundamental rights, with the result that it must be taken into consideration in interpreting the Charter'.[164] As such, it appears that the minimum standard is constituted both by the ECHR provisions and the case law of the ECtHR in respect of those provisions.

[162] See den Heijer 'Article 18', 531.
[163] See the EU Charter Explanations regarding Article 52 of the Charter.
[164] Opinion of Advocate General Trstenjak in *N.S. and M.E.*, para 146.

It follows that the EU secondary legislation in the field of asylum and border control must comply with the provisions of the EU Charter on the principle of non-refoulement and the right to asylum. In particular, the Charter prohibition of refoulement corresponds to the same prohibition in Article 3 ECHR. The implication is that Member States are required to comply with the principle of non-refoulement as enshrined in Article 3 ECHR and as interpreted by the ECtHR – both when implementing EU law and outside the domain of EU law. The fact that the EU Charter operates exclusively in the domain of EU law is irrelevant in the case of non-refoulement since the content and scope of the prohibition of refoulement are the same as the obligation to which Member States are subject under international law. However, as cited earlier, the EU may provide more extensive protection. Accordingly, when interpreting EU law, Member States may apply a higher standard of protection against refoulement than that provided for by Article 3 ECHR. The CJEU ruled on this in the *N.S. and M.E.* cases which concerned asylum seekers originating from Afghanistan, Iran and Algeria who travelled via Greece to eventually claim asylum in the United Kingdom and Ireland. According to Regulation (EC) 343/2003 (Dublin Regulation), having entered Greece irregularly, the asylum seekers were supposed to lodge their asylum applications there instead of moving to the United Kingdom or Ireland and claiming asylum there. Under the Dublin Regulation, the United Kingdom and Ireland ordered the transfer of the applicants to Greece and maintained that Greece was responsible for examining the asylum application since the applicants first entered the latter's territory irregularly (i.e. without the necessary documents under immigration rules). The applicants argued that the United Kingdom and Ireland should be responsible for examining their asylum applications since their transfer to Greece would risk breaching their fundamental rights under EU law, the ECHR and the 1951 Refugee Convention. According to the applicants, the United Kingdom and Ireland should have accepted responsibility by virtue of Article 3(2) of the Dublin Regulation. In this case, the CJEU ruled on whether the protection conferred by the EU Charter, in particular by its Articles 1, 18 and 47, is wider than the protection conferred by Article 3 ECHR. The question asked by the referring court was important at the time since the ECtHR had recently delivered its judgment in the *K.R.S. v. the United Kingdom* case.[165] In this case, the ECtHR rejected the application of an Iranian asylum seeker who

---

[165] K.R.S. v. *The United Kingdom* App No. 32733/08 (ECtHR, 2 December 2008).

argued that his removal to Greece by the United Kingdom would infringe Articles 3 and 13 ECHR. Thus, the referring UK court was faced with the question of whether the EU Charter ensures greater protection than that afforded by the ECHR. After the order for reference of the *N.S. and M.E.* cases was made, the ECtHR delivered its judgment in the *M.S.S.* v. *Belgium and Greece* case.[166] Among other matters, the ECtHR ruled that Belgium had breached Article 3 ECHR by sending the asylum seeker back to Greece since this exposed him to the risks linked to the deficiencies of the asylum system in Greece. This ruling meant that the question asked in the *N.S. and M.E.* cases may have ceased to be relevant, which in turn meant that Advocate General Trstenjak preferred in the context of her Opinion to rely on the question of whether, after the *M.S.S.* judgment, the transfer of asylum seekers to Greece could still be compatible with the EU Charter.

The CJEU answered the original question: namely, whether the protection conferred by the EU Charter, in particular by Articles 1, 18 and 47 EUCFR, is wider than the protection conferred by Article 3 ECHR. It first acknowledged that in delivering its *M.S.S.* judgment 'the [ECtHR] reviewed its position in the light of new evidence'.[167] It then stated that a Member State would infringe Articles 1, 18 and 47 of the EU Charter if it transferred an asylum seeker to the Member State responsible within the meaning of the Dublin Regulation if the circumstances described in the *M.S.S.* judgment in relation to Article 3 ECHR applied. The Court said that a Member State transferring the asylum seeker 'cannot be unaware' that in the Member State to which the asylum seeker is to be transferred there are systemic deficiencies in the asylum procedure and in the reception conditions that amount to breaches of the rights concerned.[168] Thus, in the *N.S.* and *M.E.* cases the CJEU stated that the extent of the protection conferred by Articles 1, 18 and 47 of the EU Charter is the same as the protection conferred by Article 3 ECHR. This ruling applies only to the case in question and does not exclude more

---

[166] *M.S.S.* v. *Belgium and Greece* App No. 30696/09 (ECtHR, 21 January 2011).

[167] *N.S. and M.E.*, para 112.

[168] *Ibid.*, para 113. The CJEU has clarified its position in 2013, in the *Abdullahi* case (Case C-394/12, judgment of 10 December 2013, para 60): 'In such a situation in which the Member State agrees to take charge of the applicant for asylum . . . the only way in which the applicant for asylum can call into question the choice of that criterion is by pleading systemic deficiencies in the asylum procedure and in the conditions for the reception of applicants for asylum in that latter Member State . . .'.

extensive protection being provided by Articles 1, 18 and 47 of the EU Charter in other cases.[169]

Hence, according to Article 52(3) of the EU Charter, Article 19(2) of the EU Charter has the same meaning and scope as Article 3 ECHR. Article 52(3) of the EU Charter states that Article 3 ECHR and the case law of the ECtHR constitute the minimum standard of protection. When the CJEU needs to verify whether EU secondary legislation complies with or is interpreted according to EU primary law, Article 3 ECHR is the applicable standard. The CJEU ruled in the *N.S.* and *M.E.* case that the extent of the protection conferred by Articles 1, 18 and 47 of the EU Charter is the same as the protection conferred by Article 3 ECHR. However, Article 52(3) of the EU Charter states that the EU can provide more extensive protection, opening this possibility also in the case of protection against refoulement under the Charter. Importantly, as noted above,[170] Article 18 of the EU Charter explicitly refers to the 1951 Refugee Convention and therefore effects a *renvoi* to Article 33 of the Convention. As we have also established,[171] a distinction needs to be maintained between Article 33 of the 1951 Refugee Convention and Article 3 ECHR. This is particularly relevant for the present discussion. The protection provided by Article 18 of the EU Charter is the same as the protection provided by Article 3 ECHR. However, the prohibition of non-refoulement in the EU Charter should not be seen as being merely equivalent to Article 3 ECHR, since both Article 3 ECHR and Article 33 of the 1951 Refugee Convention are separate and binding in the EU legal order. This is confirmed by Article 78 TFEU, which is a primary obligation of EU law and which states that the principle of non-refoulement enshrined in the 1951 Refugee Convention is part of the EU legal order. Therefore, the legal reach and standing of the principle of non-refoulement in the EU legal order should also take account of Article 33 of the 1951 Convention.

---

[169] Likewise see C. Costello, 'Courting Access to Asylum in Europe: Recent Supranational Jurisprudence Explored' (2012) 12 *Human Rights Law Review* 287, 327–328. We may witness a change of the jurisprudence of the CJEU after the ECtHR's *Tarakhel* judgment (*Tarakhel* v. *Switzerland* 2014 App No. 29217/12 (ECtHR, 4 November 2014), paras 116–122) which held that there would be a violation of Article 3 ECHR if the applicants were to be returned to Italy by the Swiss authorities without adequate reception conditions in Italian accommodation facilities for asylum seekers being guaranteed by the Italian authorities. Importantly, the ECtHR did not also require deficiencies in the Italian asylum procedures for violations of Article 3 ECHR to exist.
[170] Section 5.3.5.2.   [171] Section 5.1 of this chapter.

5.3.6 Non-Refoulement in EU Secondary Law Concerning Frontex's Joint Operations at the EU's External Borders

5.3.6.1 Introduction

Between 2002 and 2013, limiting our scope to those who were among the documented, 2282 third-country nationals died trying to reach Europe.[172] As a consequence of such upsetting figures, there has been an intensification of Frontex's border control as well as an increase in search and rescue operations in the Mediterranean. This, in turn, makes protection against refoulement an escalating matter of concern. Such urgency is reflected in the adoption of several legal provisions in the field of border control, Frontex's operations and asylum which aim at regulating the issue.

The following is an analysis of the provisions prohibiting refoulement in EU secondary legislation on Frontex's joint operations at the EU's external borders: the Schengen Borders Code (SBC),[173] the Frontex Regulation[174] and the Regulation establishing rules for the surveillance of the external sea borders in the context of operational cooperation coordinated by Frontex (External Sea Borders Regulation).[175] The relevant guidelines in the Practical Handbook for Border Guards (the Schengen Handbook) will also be a focal point.[176] The connected issue of non-refoulement and

---

[172] For a documented analysis of these figures see: Human Costs of Border Control, 'Deaths at the Borders of Southern Europe', www.borderdeaths.org; cfr. Fortress Europe, 'Nel Canale di Sicilia 7.065 tra morti e dispersi dal 1994', www.fortresseurope.blogspot.dk (accessed 13 November 2015).

[173] Regulation (EC) 562/2006 establishing a Community Code on the rules governing the movement of persons across borders (Schengen Borders Code) OJ 2006 No. L105, p. 1.

[174] Council Regulation (EC) 2007/2004 of 26 October 2004 establishing a European agency for the management of operational cooperation at the external borders of the Member States of the European Union [2004] OJ L349, p. 1, as amended by Regulation (EC) 863/2007 of the European Parliament and the Council of 11 July 2007 establishing a mechanism for the creation of Rapid Border Intervention Teams and amending Council Regulation (EC) 2007/2004 as regards that mechanism and regulating the tasks and powers of guest officers [2007] OJ L199/30, and by Regulation (EU) 1168/2011 of the European Parliament and the Council of 25 October 2011 amending Council Regulation (EC) 2007/2004 establishing a European agency for the management of operational cooperation at the external borders of the Member States of the European Union OJ L No. 304, p. 1.

[175] Regulation (EU) 656/2014 of the European Parliament and of the Council of 15 May 2014 establishing rules for the surveillance of the external sea borders in the context of operational cooperation coordinated by the European agency for the management of operational cooperation at the external borders of the Member States of the European Union OJ 2014 No. L189, p. 93.

[176] Commission Recommendation establishing a common 'Practical Handbook for Border Guards (Schengen Handbook)' to be used by Member States' competent authorities when carrying out the border control of persons, COM (2006) 5186 final. The Schengen

disembarkation in the context of Frontex's operations including search and rescue will be dealt with in Chapter 7.

5.3.6.2   How the Legal Instruments Are Connected

The SBC brings together 'common measures on ... border control at external borders'.[177] The Frontex Regulation, establishing the Frontex agency, concerns the implementation of the SBC. Article 1(2) of this Regulation states that Frontex's task is to 'facilitate and render more effective' the application of the SBC 'by ensuring the coordination of the actions of the Member States' and 'contributing to an efficient, high and uniform level of control on persons and surveillance of the external borders of the Member States'. Article 3b(3) of the Frontex Regulation requires border guards – seconded by Member States and deployed by Frontex in joint operations – to be treated as guest officers and have tasks and powers to carry out border checks in accordance with the SBC.[178] Article 3(3) of the Frontex Regulation requires Frontex to evaluate the results of joint operations by means of an incident-reporting scheme which in accordance with Recital 16 of the Regulation must report allegations of breaches of the SBC.

Furthermore, the External Sea Border Regulation applies to border surveillance operations carried out by Member States at their external sea borders in the context of operational cooperation coordinated by Frontex. The Regulation does not limit border surveillance 'to the detection of attempts at unauthorised border crossings but equally extends to ... arrangements intended to address situations such as search and rescue that may arise during a border surveillance at sea and arrangements intended to bring such an operation to a successful conclusion'.[179] Any measure taken in the course of a surveillance operation pursuant to this Regulation must be in accordance with the SBC.[180] The Regulation replaces the External Sea Borders Decision.[181] The Decision was adopted

Handbook 'is not intended to create any legally binding obligations upon Member States, or to establish new rights and duties for border guards or any other person who might be concerned by it', Schengen Handbook foreword.

[177] Recital (3) of the SBC.
[178] Article 3(b)(3) of the Frontex Regulation refers to Article 10 of the Rapid Border Intervention Teams Regulation.
[179] External Sea Borders Regulation, Recital (1).
[180] External Sea Borders Regulation, Recital (10).
[181] Council Decision 2010/252/EU of 26 April 2010 supplementing the Schengen Borders Code regarding the surveillance of the sea external borders in the context of operational cooperation coordinated by the European agency for the management of operational

to implement Article 12(5) SBC and to add rules specifically governing the surveillance of maritime external borders in the context of operational cooperation under Frontex's auspices. The External Sea Borders Decision included rules for sea border operations coordinated by Frontex (Part I) and non-binding guidelines for search and rescue situations and for disembarkation (Part II). Notably, in July 2010 the European Parliament brought an action for annulment of the Sea External Borders Decision before the CJEU.[182] Parliament's argument was that the Sea External Borders Decision modified essential elements of the SBC. As such, the Parliament contended that it should have been decided in accordance with the legislative procedure, with Parliament acting as a co-legislator. Instead, it had been adopted using the regulatory procedure with scrutiny under the comitology procedure. In 2012, the CJEU annulled the Sea External Borders Decision, in line with the Opinion of Advocate General Mengozzi,[183] by ruling incidentally that Part II (and not only Part I) of the External Sea Borders Decision was legally binding. The Sea External Borders Decision was upheld *ad interim* until new rules entered into force. Adopted in May 2014, the External Sea Borders Regulation takes into consideration the 2011 amendments to the Frontex Regulation and the ECtHR's case law concerning the principle of non-refoulement and search and rescue at sea.[184]

Finally, the Schengen Handbook brings together guidelines, best practice, and recommendations concerning the performance of border guards' duties to ensure that the rules on border control in the SBC 'are implemented in a uniform way by all national authorities competent for carrying out border control tasks'.[185] The Schengen Handbook was adopted in 2006, after the adoption of the SBC but before the adoption of the Sea External Borders Regulation. Since the Sea External Borders

cooperation at the external borders of the Member States of the European Union OJ 2010 No. L111, p. 20. For an analysis of the External Sea Borders Decision see V. Moreno Lax, 'The EU Regime on Interdiction, Search and Rescue, and Disembarkation: The Frontex Guidelines for Intervention at Sea' (2010) 25 *The International Journal of Marine and Coastal Law* 621.

[182] Case C-355/10 *European Parliament* v. *Council of the European Union*, judgment of 5 September 2012; [2013] 1 CMLR 1.

[183] Opinion of Advocate General Mengozzi in *European Parliament* v. *Council*.

[184] *Hirsi Jamaa and Others* v. *Italy* App No. 27765/09 (ECtHR, 23 February 2012). See Chapter 3, Section 3.2.2.2.4. On the process of negotiation of the External Sea Borders Regulation see S. Carrera and L. den Hertog, 'Whose *Mare*? Rule of Law Challenges in the Field of European Border Surveillance in the Mediterranean' *CEPS Paper in Liberty and Security in Europe* No. 79/January 2015, 10–13.

[185] Recital (2) of the Schengen Handbook.

Regulation was adopted in connection with the SBC, it is arguable that the Schengen Handbook guidelines are equally relevant to the implementation of the Sea External Borders Regulation. All told, the authorities of the Member States carrying out border controls at the EU's external borders in Frontex-led operations must always comply with the provisions of the Schengen Borders Code and the Schengen Handbook. When national authorities carry out surveillance at the sea external borders, they must also comply with the Sea External Borders Regulation.

5.3.6.3   The Prohibition of Refoulement

Regarding the provisions prohibiting refoulement, Article 3(b) of the Schengen Borders Code states that the Code applies to any person crossing the EU's external borders 'without prejudice to ... the rights of refugees and persons requesting international protection, *in particular as regard non-refoulement*'.[186] Article 4(3) SBC provides that the Member States must introduce penalties for unauthorised crossings of their external borders in accordance with their national law, unless this prejudices their international obligations to provide protection, including the principle of non-refoulement. Article 5(4) SBC provides that the international obligations of the Member States and humanitarian reasons are possible grounds for derogating from the conditions of entry set out in Article 5(1) SBC. Article 13(1) SBC provides that refusal of entry to the territories of the Member States 'shall be without prejudice to the application of special provisions concerning the right of asylum and to international protection'. Arguably, the standard of protection against refoulement and the right to asylum in these provisions must comply with the EU primary legislation (i.e. with Article 78(1) TFEU, the general principles of EU law, and Articles 18 and 19(1) of the EU Charter).

The External Sea Borders Regulation contains new rules on search and rescue at sea, disembarkation and, importantly, an entirely new provision, Article 4, devoted to the protection of fundamental rights and the principle of non-refoulement. Pursuant to this provision, 'no person shall ... be disembarked in, forced to enter, conducted to or otherwise handed over to the authorities of a country', if these actions are performed in violation of the principle of non-refoulement. In a manner which differs from the External Sea Borders Decision, which contained only a general prohibition of refoulement in the context of sea

---

[186] Emphasis added.

operations, Article 4 of the Regulation provides a rather encompassing definition of the principle of non-refoulement. It includes two grounds for the granting of 'subsidiary protection', for those individuals who do not fall within the definition of refugee according to the 1951 Refugee Convention, under the EU Qualification Directive and Article 33(1) of the 1951 Refugee Convention.[187] Thus, by virtue of this addition, the provision is appreciably strengthened.[188] Application of Article 4, as of all other provisions of the External Sea Borders Regulations, must be in full compliance with the Charter of Fundamental Rights and with the interpretation of the principle of non-refoulement delivered by the CJEU and the ECtHR.[189]

Also, under the External Sea Borders Regulation, it is an obligation under EU law for personnel of EU Member States taking part in a sea operation 'to identify the intercepted or rescued persons, assess their personal circumstances, inform them of their destination in a way that those persons understand ... and give them an opportunity to express any reason for believing that disembarkation in the proposed place would be in violation of the principle of non-refoulement'.[190] Such wording is in accordance with the *Hirsi* judgment decided by the ECtHR in 2012 which concerned an operation on the high seas in the Mediterranean where Italy returned individuals to the Libyan authorities. These were persons who had sought to flee Libya and who had come originally from Eritrea and Somalia.[191] Significantly, these procedural rights of intercepted or rescued persons in sea operations partially overlap with the provisions of the Schengen Handbook stating how safeguards of the principle of non-refoulement and the right to asylum must be implemented in all forms of border control operations (i.e. land, air and sea). Sections 10.1 and 10.2 in Part II of the Handbook set out some guarantees that apply to asylum seekers: all third-country nationals who apply for asylum at the borders must have their applications assessed; an asylum application consists of

---

[187] Added to the latter definition is the ground of 'social orientation'. Notably, the CJEU has ruled that homosexuals can form part of a particular social group under the EU Qualification Directive: Case C-199/12 to 201/12 X, Y and Z, judgment 7 November 2013, paras 41–49.

[188] See S. Peers, 'New Rules on Maritime Surveillance: Will They Stop the Deaths and Push-backs in the Mediterranean?' – Statewatch Analysis, February 2014, www.statewatch.org (accessed 13 November 2015).

[189] External Sea Borders Regulation, Recitals (12) and (19).

[190] External Sea Borders Regulation, Article 4(3).

[191] I deal with this issue when I analyse the principle of non-refoulement as interpreted by the ECtHR in the *Hirsi* case (Chapter 6, Section 6.2.2.2.4).

any expression of fear as to what might happen if the applicant were to return; and 'the wish to apply for protection does not need to be expressed in any particular form'. Importantly, these guarantees are also stated in the Directive on common procedures for granting and withdrawing international protection (Asylum Procedures Directive).[192] Article 6 of the Asylum Procedures Directive states that access to the asylum procedure must be guaranteed; Article 2(b) of the Directive states that an application for asylum is an application 'which can be understood to seek refugee status or subsidiary protection status', and includes applications for asylum made in any form. Thus, these guarantees are not merely included in a soft law instrument, the Schengen Handbook (to the extent that they do not overlap with the External Sea Borders Regulation), but they are included in an EU secondary law instrument and are therefore binding under EU law.[193] Because of the connections between the three legal instruments and the Schengen Handbook explained above, the provisions on the prohibition of refoulement in the SBC, the External Sea Borders Regulation and the guidelines in the Schengen Handbook apply when the Member States' authorities carry out border controls at the EU's external borders in a Frontex-led operation.[194]

5.4   Conclusions

This chapter has attempted to clarify questions concerning the principle of non-refoulement and its legal standing in the EU. It has endeavoured to disentangle the intricate international and EU legal framework in which the principle is embedded. This process has required scrutiny of how the several different legal provisions on refoulement engage the international responsibility of the EU and its Member States; how such international obligations permeate the EU legal domain; and also an

---

[192] Directive 2013/32/EU of the European Parliament and the Council of 26 June 2013 on common procedures for granting and withdrawing international protection (recast) OJ 2013 No. L180, p. 60 which replaces Council Directive 2005/85/EC of 1 December 2005 on minimum standards on procedures in Member States for granting and withdrawing refugee status OJ 2005 No. L326, p. 13.

[193] There are differences in the application of the Asylum Procedures Directive according to the opt-outs of the Member States. For instance, Denmark has not implemented the Asylum Procedures Directive as it is not bound by and not subject to some of the measures in the Area of Freedom, Security and Justice.

[194] The Frontex Regulation itself has a provision on safeguards against refoulement, see: Article 1(2) of the Frontex Regulation. See also Recitals (9) and (29).

analysis of the ways EU secondary law on Frontex's operations is inter-connected with the other provisions examined in the chapter and the ways it regulates protection against refoulement. Four points must be emphasised as we conclude. First, there is currently no international treaty body or court which can hold the EU responsible for possible violations of the principle of non-refoulement in the context of Frontex's operations. The process of the EU's accession to the ECHR, which would give the ECtHR jurisdiction to decide on the responsibility of the EU in relation to violations of the principle under Article 3 ECHR, has been delayed following the Opinion of the CJEU in December 2014 rejecting the accession agreement. Conversely, all EU Member States can be held responsible for such violations before the ECtHR, the Committee against Torture and the Human Rights Committee. Second, the prohibition of refoulement included in the 1951 Refugee Convention and its 1967 Protocol constitutes the international cornerstone for the protection of refugees. Its pertinence in the EU legal order is stated in Article 78(1) TFEU providing for an internal obligation of primary law to act in accordance with the 1951 Refugee Convention and other treaties relevant in the protection of refugees. Third, analysis of the case law of the CJEU shows that the standard of protection against refoulement within the EU legal order currently corresponds to Article 3 ECHR. This correspon-dence is revealed by including non-refoulement among the general principles of EU law. We have also noted that under the EU Charter of Fundamental Rights, Article 19(2) of the Charter corresponds to Article 3 ECHR and the corresponding jurisprudence of the ECtHR on this provi-sion. This does not exclude that more extensive protection can be granted by the EU in the future. Fourth, the Sea External Border Regulation provides an encompassing definition of the principle of non-refoulement with evident correspondence to the wording of the Qualification Directive and of Article 33 of the 1951 Refugee Convention.

6

Exploring the Legal Standing of Protection

The Ratione Loci *Application of the Principle of Non-Refoulement*

6.1 Introduction

We must now address the issue of space as we explore the legal setting related to rights protection, working methods at the borders of the EU and attendant questions of international responsibility. The material space in which Frontex's joint operations are performed spans the territory of EU Member States, the surrounding seas and potentially the territory of third countries. States' borders are often invisible to asylum seekers once in transit and such borders constitute lines on a map which may seem immaterial to individuals escaping injustice. However, this picture changes considerably if we delve into the relevant law and into the legal regimes which affect the 'integrated management' conducted at the borders of the EU. In this setting, territory, borders and sea are not only elements of the material space in which Frontex's joint operations are performed but concepts to which a legal meaning is attached. In particular, territory (generally perceived as the *locus* where sovereign power is exercised) represents not only the extent of national power's last defence but, at the same time, the limit of such power. Control exerted by a State acting upon space or individuals outside its own territory may acquire a strong juridical meaning. It is thus an urgent matter to clarify the protection from return which Frontex and Member States are expected to provide under the law (while also clarifying any variations which may depend on the area in which such authorities operate and the extent to which they have control on space and individuals).

In order to develop our understanding of these issues, we will investigate the *ratione loci* application of the principle of non-refoulement which brings juridical space into dialogue with the realm of material space. This is also a process that will clarify the link between exercise of sovereignty and protection obligations. We will investigate the matter under international law and under EU law. This chapter will examine the *ratione loci* application of non-refoulement from an international-law perspective which relates to this book's broader questions concerning any potential responsibility of the EU and its Member States for breaches of non-refoulement which might amount to an internationally wrongful act. The discussion in this section pertains to the juridical space in which a State is responsible for ensuring that an individual is protected against being returned to face persecution, torture or other ill treatment (Section 6.2). Thereupon, the chapter will examine the *ratione loci* application of non-refoulement from an EU law perspective. This is necessary in order to analyse the protection that EU legislation on Frontex's joint operations affords in the making of the operations (Section 6.3). In conclusion, I will present my findings on the legal standing of protection (Section 6.4).

This chapter will consider the exercise of jurisdiction by Member States involved in Frontex-led operations. As explicated in Chapter 4, the international responsibility of the EU can be established only derivatively for aid and assistance to Member States deemed to have committed an internationally wrongful act in the context of any joint operation. Hence, an examination of the extent to which the concept of 'jurisdiction' under international law is applicable and relevant to the EU – a non-State entity – falls outside the matters proposed for discussion here.[1]

6.2   A Matter of International Law

6.2.1   Crossing the Borders

During Joint Operation RABIT 2010, border control specialists from the then 27 Member States and Schengen Associated Countries were deployed

---

[1] In general, on the obligation of the EU to comply with international law in its external action, see Articles 3(5) and 21 Treaty on European Union (TEU) together with the analysis provided in Chapter 5 of this book regarding the international sources of law binding on the EU and its Member States. See, also, the relevant case law with a focus on the prohibition of *refoulement*. On the use of jurisdiction of the Member States to establish the competence of the EU to act pursuant to the EU Treaties (Article 5(1) and (2) TEU) see, *inter alia*, the following case law: Joined Cases 3/76, 4/76 and 6/76 *Cornelis Kramer and Others* [1976] ECR 1279; [1976] 2 CMLR 440, para 30–33 and Joined Cases 89/85, 104/85, 114/85, 116/85, 117/85 and 125/85 to 129/85 *A Ahlström Osakeyhtiö and Others v. Commission* [1994] ECR I–99; [1993] 4 CMLR 407, para 16–18. Specifically on jurisdiction in international human rights law, the draft agreement on the accession of the European Union to the European Convention on Human Rights (ECHR) (CDDH-EU 47+1(2013)008rev2), rejected by the Court of Justice of the European Union (CJEU) in December 2014, envisaged that the jurisdiction of the EU corresponds to the jurisdiction of the EU Member States.

by Frontex at the land border between Greece and Turkey in the Greek region of Orestiada. The aims of the operation were to patrol the border, to intercept irregular migrants crossing the border, to help Greek border guards with screening and interviewing designed to identify undocumented migrants and to gather information about smuggling networks. The deployment was requested by Greece to increase control and surveillance of Greece's external borders with Turkey because of the 'exceptionally high numbers' of migrants crossing the Greek-Turkish land border illegally'.[2] Two questions arise from this situation which pertains to the *ratione loci* application of the principle of non-refoulement. First, does the principle only benefit individuals who have crossed the Greek border and find themselves within Greek territory? Or, rather, are border guards, working on site in this situation, prevented from returning individuals who are in need of international protection even though these individuals are yet to enter Greek national territory?

Under general international law, the exercise of sovereignty is strictly related to territory: since it is territory that identifies the State as a legal entity and justifies rules to protect its inviolability.[3] One instance of EU rules designed to protect the inviolability of Member States' territory is the Schengen Borders Code (SBC).[4] The 'territory' of a State comprises its land, its territorial sea and its contiguous zone. A State exercises full jurisdiction over its land territory. The territorial sea consists of the waters surrounding the land of a coastal State, including bays, gulfs and straits.[5] It extends to 12 nautical miles from the baselines.[6] A coastal State also has full sovereignty over its territorial sea.[7] However, the sovereignty

---

[2] Frontex Press Release, 'Frontex Deploys Rapid Border Teams to Greece', 25 October 2010, www.frontex.europa.eu (accessed 13 November 2015).

[3] M. N. Shaw, *International Law* (Cambridge University Press, 2008), 488; G. Boas, *Public International Law: Contemporary Principles and Perspectives* (Edward Elgar Publishing, 2012), 163; A. Cassese, *International Law* (Oxford University Press, 2005), 82; I. Brownlie, *Principles of Public International Law* (Oxford University Press, 2008), 105–106.

[4] Regulation (EC) 562/2006 establishing a Community Code on the rules governing the movement of persons across borders (Schengen Borders Code) OJ 2006 L No. 105, p. 1.

[5] Cassese, *International Law*, 84; Shaw, *International Law*, 556–558; Brownlie, *Principles of Public International Law*, 176.

[6] Article 3 of the 1982 United Nations Convention on the Law of the Sea (1833 UNTS 3).

[7] Cassese, *International Law*, 85; Shaw, *International Law*, 556; D. D. Rothwell and T. Stephens, *The International Law of the Sea* (Hart Publishing, 2010), 58–59; Brownlie, *Principles of Public International Law*, 174. On the limitations to State sovereignty based on rules of international law, see M. Pallis, 'Obligations of States Towards Asylum Seekers at Sea: Interactions and Conflicts between Legal Regimes' (2002) 14 *International Journal of Refugee Law* 329, 343; A. Klug and T. Howe, 'The Concept of State Jurisdiction and the Applicability of the *Non-refoulement* Principle to Extraterritorial Interception Measures'

of a State is limited by the right of innocent passage, allowing foreign ships to navigate through the territorial sea as long as the passage does not prejudice the peace, good order or security of the coastal State.[8] The contiguous zone is different because it is a part of the 'territory' in which a coastal State can only exercise control deemed necessary to prevent or punish infringements of its immigration laws within its territory or territorial sea.[9] Specifically, the control necessary to *prevent* infringements of immigration law concerns ships which head from the high seas towards the land territories.[10] Finally, according to the theory of territoriality of ships,[11] registered ships are considered State territory and are subject to the jurisdiction of the flag State which can legislate and enforce its law on them.[12]

Under general international law, the borders of a State are part of its 'territory' in the sense that defining the borders of a State automatically defines the territory over which it exercises sovereignty.[13] As noted above, the EU's borders coincide with the Schengen States' external borders.[14] Under general international law, a State's treaty obligations also apply to its borders, deemed part of its territory. However, the applicability of the prohibition against refoulement at States' borders (whereby States' conduct in these specific spaces would be obliged to adhere to international refugee law and international human rights law) has remained a contentious issue. Since the relevant provisions of the

---

in B. Ryan and V. Mitsilegas (eds.), *Extraterritorial Immigration Control: Legal Challenges* (Martinus Nijhoff, 2010), 92.

[8] Article 14(4) of the Convention on the Territorial Sea and Contiguous Zone (516 UNTS 206).

[9] Article 33(1) of the 1982 United Nations Convention on Law of the Sea.

[10] On the contiguous zone, see Y. Tanaka, *The International Law of the Sea* (Cambridge University Press, 2012), 122.

[11] See *SS Lotus* (1928) PCIJ Series A No 10, p. 25. *Contra*, Tanaka, *The International Law of the Sea*, 152.

[12] Article 94 of the 1982 United Nations Convention on the Law of the Sea.

[13] See 'boundary treaties' as establishing or confirming title to territory in Shaw, *International Law*, 495–498, and the *uti possidetis* doctrine, according to which, after decolonisation, newly independent countries accepted the colonial boundaries existing at the time of independence, in Antonio Cassese, *International Law*, 83–84.

[14] Chapter 1, Section 1.3. On the concept of borders and how it is challenged by extra-territorial migration control mechanisms, see E. Guild, 'Moving the Borders of Europe', Inaugural Lecture at the University of Nijmegen, 30 May 2001, 52; E. Guild; D. Bigo; 'The Transformation of European Border Controls' in Ryan and Mitsilegas (eds.), *Extraterritorial Immigration Control*, 258; T. Kritzman-Amir and T. Spijkerboer, 'On the Morality and Legality of Borders: Border Policies and Asylum Seekers' (2013) 26 *Harvard Human Rights Journal* 1.

1951 Refugee Convention,[15] the International Covenant on Civil and Political Rights (ICCPR),[16] the Convention against Torture (CAT)[17] and the European Convention on Human Rights (ECHR)[18] do not specify whether the principle of non-refoulement applies at borders, some have interpreted these obligations as only prohibiting refoulement of persons who have crossed the borders of the State and are thus within its territory. On this point, Robinson wrote in 1953 that 'if a refugee has succeeded in eluding the frontier guards, he is safe; if he has not, it is his hard luck'.[19]

In this context of significant dispute, any broad application of the principle of non-refoulement at States' borders would create intricacies and potential problems of conduct which all affected States would need to monitor. Applying the principle may involve permission from a given State to cross its border and, in some cases, to remain in the territory until an asylum application has been processed. This may constitute a burden on the State which it might seek to avoid by not allowing individuals to enter its territory. Further analysis of such issues will follow in the subsequent sections.

6.2.1.1   Article 33 of the 1951 Refugee Convention

In Article 33 of the 1951 Refugee Convention, the principle of non-refoulement concerns the prohibition to 'expel' or 'return' (*refouler*) refugees (people who fall within the definition of Article 1A(2) of the Convention) 'in any manner whatsoever to the frontiers of territories' where their life is at risk. In order to analyse the scope of applying the principle *ratione loci*, I propose to look at the combination of Article 33 and Article 1A(2) of the 1951 Refugee Convention. Pursuant to Article 1A(2) of the 1951 Refugee Convention, for a person to be recognised as a refugee he or she must be outside the country of one's nationality or habitual residence. An individual cannot be considered a refugee if he or she has not crossed an international border.[20] Article 33 and Article 1A(2) of the Convention do not state what happens once a refugee leaves his or her country of

---

[15] 1951 Convention relating to the Status of Refugees (189 UNTS 137).

[16] 1966 International Covenant on Civil and Political Rights (999 UNTS 171).

[17] 1984 Convention against Torture and Other Cruel, Inhuman or Degrading Treatment or Punishment (1465 UNTS 85).

[18] 1950 European Convention for the Protection of Human Rights and Fundamental Freedoms (213 UNTS 222).

[19] N. Robinson, *Convention Relating to the Status of Refugees: Its History, Contents and Interpretation* (Institute of Jewish Affairs, 1953) reprinted by UNHCR 1997, 138.

[20] See J. C. Hathaway, *The Rights of Refugees under International Law* (Cambridge University Press, 2005), 307.

nationality and crosses an international border.[21] Is it enough to trigger the application of the principle of non-refoulement that a refugee reaches the border of the country of asylum? Or is it necessary for the refugee to be within the territory of the country of asylum, while those who do not manage to cross the borders are simply unlucky, as stated by Robinson?[22]

Although some writers have, in the past, supported the exclusionary reading according to which Article 33 of the 1951 Refugee Convention applies only within the territory of the asylum State and not at the borders,[23] today there is greater acceptance of giving the principle broad application so as to at least include the borders of States.[24] From this latter group of interpreters, different arguments have been posited to justify an inclusionary reading. Goodwin-Gill and McAdam maintain that no further understanding of the provisions derives from an interpretation of the text or an analysis of the motives which lead the High Contracting Parties to choose the specific wording of it. They look at the practices of States and conclude that Article 33 of the 1951 Refugee Convention applies within the territory and at the borders of the State.[25] Lauterpacht and Bethlehem argue in favour of an inclusionary reading by looking at key instruments in the field of refugee protection, the literal interpretation of the words 'return' and 'refouler', conclusions of the UNHCR's Executive Committee and resolutions of the General Assembly.[26] Similar arguments are used by Hathaway.[27] Other notable inclusionary views draw additional support and solidity from analysing

---

[21] See K. Wouters, *International Legal Standards for the Protection from Refoulement* (Intersentia, 2009), 49.

[22] Robinson, *Convention Relating to the Status of Refugees.*

[23] *Ibid.*, 163; A. Grahl-Madsen, *The Status of Refugees in International Law*, Vol. 2 (A. W. Sijthoff – Leiden, 1972), para 179(i).

[24] E.g. P. Weis, *The Refugee Convention, 1951: The Travaux Préparatoires Analyzed with a Commentary by Paul Weis* (Cambridge University Press, 1995), 341–342; E. Lauterpacht and D. Bethlehem, 'The Scope and Content of the Principle of Non-refoulement: Opinion' in E. Feller, V. Türk and F. Nicholson (eds.), *Refugee Protection in International Law: UNHCR's Global Consultation on International Protection* (Cambridge University Press, 2003), paras 76–86; Hathaway, *The Rights of Refugees under International Law*, 315; Wouters, *International Legal Standards for the Protection from Refoulement*, 48–56; G. Noll, 'Seeking Asylum at Embassies: A Right to Entry under International Law?' (2005) 17 *International Journal of Refugee Law* 542, 549; G. S. Goodwin-Gill and J. McAdam, *The Refugee in International Law* (Oxford University Press, 2007), 206–208.

[25] Goodwin-Gill and McAdam, *The Refugee in International Law*, 206–208.

[26] Lauterpacht and Bethlehem, 'The Scope and Content of the Principle of Non-refoulement: Opinion', paras 76–86.

[27] Hathaway, *The Rights of Refugees under International Law*, 315.

the Vienna Convention on the Law of Treaties (VCLT).[28] Among such scholars, both Noll and Wouters use the interpretative criteria of the VCLT by looking at the ordinary meaning of the words, the context, together with the object and purpose of the 1951 Refugee Convention to determine the scope of the *ratione loci* application of Article 33.[29] Importantly, both authors seem to propend for a broad application of the provision since, in Noll's words, 'it appears to be immaterial for the enjoyment of benefits under article 33 (1) CSR51 [1951 Refugee Convention] whether or not a person is located on state territory, as the emphasis is on the final destination of displacement, not its starting point'.[30] Wouters reaches this conclusion after examining the ordinary meaning of the words 'return' and 'refoulement', the remaining text of Article 33 of the 1951 Refugee Convention as well as other provisions of the Convention.[31] As such, both authors seem to argue for an application of Article 33 within the territory, at the border and also beyond the borders. What follows is an attempt to develop Noll and Wouters' lines of interpretation regarding Article 33. In doing so, I will also endeavour to explain why a more exhaustive interpretation of the provision should be preferred to a narrow one.

Exploring these concerns requires an understanding of the meaning of the terms 'expel', 'return' and 'refoulement' in Article 33 of the 1951 Refugee Convention pursuant to the general rule of interpretation of treaties as stated in Article 31(1) VCLT which states: 'a treaty shall be interpreted in good faith in accordance with the ordinary meaning to be given to the terms of the treaty in their context and in the light of its object and purpose'.[32] Article 31 VCLT, together with Article 32 VCLT establishing the supplementary means of interpretation, reflects pre-existing customary international law and, accordingly, can be applied to treaties concluded before the entry into force of the VCLT, including the 1951 Refugee Convention.[33] Importantly, Article 31 VCLT consists of

---

[28] 1969 Vienna Convention on the Law of Treaties (1155 UNTS 331).

[29] G. Noll, *Negotiating Asylum – The EU Acquis, Extraterritorial Protection and the Common Market of Deflection* (Martinus Nijhoff, 2000), 423–431; Noll, 'Seeking Asylum at Embassies', 549; Wouters, *International Legal Standards for the Protection from Refoulement*, 48–56.

[30] Noll, 'Seeking Asylum at Embassies', 553.

[31] Wouters, *International Legal Standards for the Protection from Refoulement*, 50–51.

[32] Article 31 VCLT.

[33] See O. Dörr and K. Schmalenbach, *Vienna Convention on the Law of Treaties: A Commentary* (Springer, 2012), 523–525. The pre-existing customary international law nature of Article 31 and 32 VCLT was recognised by the International Court of

one rule in which the elements of wording, context, object, purpose and the observance of the principle of good faith should be considered part of a single interpretative operation.[34] We must proceed here by looking at the ordinary meaning of the term which is a search for a meaning 'regular, normal and customary'.[35] If the term 'expel' – in the sense of 'to compel to quit a country'[36] – requires the presence of an individual within the territory of the country of asylum and the intervention by the authority of the State to force this person to leave, the same cannot be said of 'return', which means 'to go back to a place'.[37] As noted by Wouters (and also by Noll, though not necessarily in relation to the meaning of the single term), 'return' must be interpreted as having a broader meaning than 'expel', since it does not seem to require the presence of the individual within the territory of the country of asylum.[38] As for 'refoulement', the *travaux préparatoires* of the 1951 Refugee Convention show that, together with 'return', the Conference of Plenipotentiaries on the Status of Refugees and Stateless Persons required the insertion of '*refouler*'.[39] This insertion clarifies that the meaning of 'return' includes rejection at the frontiers.[40] Having investigated the ordinary meaning of the term, we can proceed in our interpretative operation pursuant to Article 31 VCLT by considering the context, object and purpose of the 1951 Refugee Convention since 'Article 31 para 1 does not allow establishing an abstract ordinary meaning of a phrase, divorced from the place

Justice in *Arbitral Award of 31 July 1989* (Judgment), ICJ Reports 1989, para 48 and subsequently reiterated by the same ICJ and other international courts and settlement bodies: e.g. International Tribunal for the Law of the Sea (Seabed Disputes Chamber) *Responsibilities and Obligations of States Sponsoring Persons and Entities with Respect to Activities in the Area* (Advisory Opinion), 1 February 2011, para 57; *Golder v. United Kingdom* App No. 4451/70 (ECtHR, 21 February 1975), para 29. The customary international law nature of these provisions overcomes the limitation posed by Article 4 VCLT stating that 'the Convention applies only to treaties which are concluded by States after the entry into force of the present Convention'.

[34] See Dörr and Schmalenbach, *Vienna Convention on the Law of Treaties: A Commentary*, 523.
[35] R. K. Gardiner, *Treaty Interpretation* (Oxford University Press, 2008), 164.
[36] See Oxford English Dictionary, www.oed.com (accessed 13 November 2015). [37] *Ibid.*
[38] Noll, 'Seeking Asylum at the Embassies', 553; Wouters, *International Legal Standards for the Protection from Refoulement*, 50–51.
[39] See Weis, *The Refugee Convention, 1951*, 335.
[40] For the definition of 'refoulement' see Larousse, www.larousse.com/en/dictionaries (accessed 13 November 2015). See Hathaway *The Rights of Refugees under International Law*, 153; Lauterpacht and Bethlehem, 'The Scope and Content of the Principle of Non-refoulement: Opinion', 113; Wouters, *International Legal Standards for the Protection from Refoulement*, 50.

which that phrase occupies in the text to be interpreted'.[41] Hence, an interpretation of the term in context, as stated by Article 31(2) VCLT, requires that we take into account the systematic structure of the treaty including its text, preamble and annexes.[42] In this connection, it must be observed that Article 33 of the 1951 Refugee Convention requires the application of the principle 'in any manner whatsoever', without specifying where the removal from the territory of the country of asylum takes place.[43] Second, other provisions in the 1951 Refugee Convention expressly include territorial limits to the enjoyment of rights, in a manner different from Article 33.[44] This means that the principle of non-refoulement in Article 33 of the 1951 Refugee Convention has no territorial limit and that it applies not only within the territories of the State of asylum but also at the borders.[45] A reading of this nature, which holds that the principle of non-refoulement in Article 33 has no territorial limit and that 'return' means to go back to a place, seems to open a path for an interpretation of Article 33 as applying not only at the borders but beyond the borders of the asylum State. In order to pursue this, our present interpretative assertion that Article 33 of the 1951 Refugee Convention has no territorial limitations can be considered in the light of what was expressed by the High Contracting Parties in the preamble to the Convention. This will promote our understanding of the context, object and purpose of the Convention. Notably, the preamble declares the social and humanitarian nature of the Convention, and it considers the United Nations' endeavour 'to assure refugees the widest possible exercise' of the fundamental rights and freedoms affirmed in the Charter of the United Nations and the Universal Declaration of Human Rights.[46] In the light of such considerations by the High Contracting

---

[41] Dörr and Schmalenbach, *Vienna Convention on the Law of Treaties: A Commentary*, 543.

[42] Article 31(2) VCLT also considers 'context' any agreement relating to the treaty which was made between the parties (or by one or more parties and accepted by the others) in connection with the conclusion of the treaty. Such elements are not relevant in the present interpretative operation.

[43] See Goodwin-Gill and McAdam, *The Refugee in International Law*, 246.

[44] On this point, see for instance Article 26 of the 1951 Refugee Convention, which imposes an obligation on States to allow refugees to choose their place of residence and to move freely within their territory only if the refugees are 'lawfully resident' in their territory. See Goodwin-Gill and McAdam, *The Refugee in International Law*, 246. On the structure of the 1951 Refugee Convention, granting rights to refugees on an incremental basis, see Hathaway, *The Rights of Refugees under International Law*, 154 ff.

[45] *Contra*, Grahl-Madsen, *The Status of Refugees in International Law*, para 179(i).

[46] Regarding the preamble of the 1951 Refugee and Article 3(3) of the 1933 Convention relating to the International Status of Refugees (159 LNTS 199), see the contextual argument furnished by Noll, *Negotiating Asylum*, 431.

Parties, a restrictive interpretation of Article 33 of the 1951 Refugee Convention, maintaining that the provision applies only within the territory of the asylum State, seems untenable.

Our interpretative operation must move further by considering 'subsequent practice in the application of the treaty which establishes the agreement of the parties regarding its interpretation' pursuant to Article 31(3)(b) VCLT.[47] For this purpose, acts of legislation and judicial decisions must be taken into consideration. Regulation (EU) No 604/2013 of the European Parliament and of the Council, which establishes the criteria and mechanisms for determining the Member States responsible for examining an application for international protection, provides: 'Member States shall examine any application for international protection by a third-country national or a stateless person who applies *on the territory of any one of them, including at the border* or in the transit zone'.[48] The same is stated in the SBC, which affirms in Article 1(9) that ' "border control" means the activity carried out at a border', and in Article 3 that the Schengen Borders Code applies to any person *crossing the external borders* of the Member States 'without prejudice to ... (b) the rights of refugees and persons requesting international protection, *in particular as regards non-refoulement*'.[49] Further, Directive 2013/32/EU of the European Parliament and of the Council, which contains common procedures for granting and withdrawing international protection, applies within the territory of the Member States, including at the border, in the territorial waters or in the transit zones of the Member States.[50]

As to the practice of States in judicial decisions, the jurisprudence on the application of Article 33 of the 1951 Refugee Convention at the borders is less clear-cut. In the *European Roma Rights Centre* case in the United Kingdom, the Court of Appeal and the House of Lords ruled on the pre-clearance procedures of the British authorities at Prague

---

[47] Article 31(3) VCLT states the elements that should be taken into consideration, together with the context, when a treaty is interpreted. Together with litera (b), Article 31(3) includes 'any subsequent agreement between the parties regarding the interpretation of the treaty or the application of its provisions' (litera a) and 'any relevant rules of international law applicable in the relation between the parties' (litera c). Only litera b is relevant to the present interpretation of the 1951 Refugee Convention.

[48] Article 3(1) of Regulation (EU) No 604/2013 of the European Parliament and of the Council of 26 June 2013 establishing the criteria and mechanisms for determining the Member State responsible for examining an application for international protection lodged in one of the Member States by a third-country national or a stateless person (recast) OJ 2013 No. L180, p. 31, emphasis added.

[49] Article 3(b) SBC, emphasis added.　　[50] OJ 2013 No. L180, p. 60, Article 3(1).

Airport under an agreement between the United Kingdom and the Czech Republic.[51] According to this agreement, British officers were allowed to screen passengers and grant or refuse permission to enter the United Kingdom before passengers boarded their scheduled plane. In the *European Roma Rights Centre* ruling, these pre-clearance procedures were subjected to legal scrutiny because six Czech nationals of Romani ethnic origins (the applicants) had been refused permission to enter the United Kingdom, even though three of them had expressly stated that they wanted to apply for asylum on arrival. The other applicants intended to seek asylum but did not expressly state it at the time. The applicants challenged the procedures as incompatible with the obligations of the United Kingdom under the 1951 Refugee Convention and under customary international law.[52] The UK Court of Appeal referred to the combination of Article 33 and Article 1A(2) of the 1951 Refugee Convention mentioned above, and excluded the application of the principle of non-refoulement to the operations at Prague Airport since the applicants were refused permission to enter the United Kingdom before leaving the Czech Republic (i.e. without leaving their country of nationality). They had not crossed an international border.[53] In the same case, the House of Lords upheld the Court of Appeal's argument and took a strict approach to the application of the principle as far as rejection at the borders was concerned. It stated:

> the prohibition of non-refoulement may only be invoked in respect of persons who are already present in the territory of the contracting state, and that *article 33 does not oblige it to admit any person who has not set foot there.*[54]

The House of Lords reached this conclusion by relying on an interpretation of the word 'return', which has a narrow meaning as it 'refers to

---

[51] *European Roma Rights Centre and Others v. the Immigration Officer at Prague Airport and the Secretary of State for the Home Department* [2003] EWCA Civ 666, Court of Appeal (Civil Division), 20 May 2003; and *Regina v. Immigration Officer at Prague Airport and Another, Ex parte European Roma Rights Centre and Others* [2004] UKHL 55, House of Lords, 9 December 2004.

[52] The applicants also asked the courts to determine whether the procedures involved unjustifiable discrimination on racial grounds. In the Court of Appeal the majority ruled against the appellants, but the House of Lords allowed the appeal on grounds of discrimination.

[53] *European Roma Rights Centre*, UK Court of Appeal, para 31.

[54] *European Roma Rights Centre*, UK House of Lords, judgment of Lord Hope of Craighead, para 70; see also the judgment of Lord Bingham of Cornhill, paras 11–17, emphasis added.

a refugee who is within the territory but is not resident there – to a person who has crossed the border and is on the threshold of initial entry'.[55] This represents a clear departure from the general rules of interpretation outlined above, whereby the term 'return' must be interpreted to mean not only forcible removal from within the territory but also rejection at the border. As an additional complication, in its judgment the House of Lords referred to the decision of the US Supreme Court in the *Sale* case.[56] The case concerned an executive order directing the US Coast Guard to intercept vessels on the high seas which were illegally transporting people from Haiti to the United States. The order was to return such people to Haiti without putting in place any measures to screen whether they qualified as refugees.[57] The US Supreme Court was asked whether the executive order infringed the Immigration and Nationality Act of 1952 (INA) and Article 33 of the 1951 Refugee Convention.[58] Interestingly, though, in the *Sale* case the US Supreme Court did not exclude the application of non-refoulement at the border as the House of Lords argued when referring to the decision. In fact, the executive order challenged in the *Sale* case concerned interceptions which were only made beyond the territorial sea of the United States. The *Sale* case did not concern rejection at the borders. Justice Stevens, who delivered the judgment of the Supreme Court, clarified:

> aliens *arriving at the border* ... are subject to an exclusion hearing ... In ... [an] exclusion proceeding the alien *may seek asylum as a political refugee* for whom removal to a particular country may threaten his life or freedom ... *The INA offers these statutory protections only to aliens who reside in or have arrived at the border of the United States.*[59]

According to Justice Stevens, then, the principle of non-refoulement applies at the borders. In specifying the meaning of 'return', the application of the principle of non-refoulement at the borders was not excluded: 'return means a defensive act of resistance or *exclusion at a border* rather

---

[55] *European Roma Rights Centre*, UK House of Lords, judgment of Lord Hope of Craighead, para 70.

[56] *European Roma Rights Centre*, UK House of Lords, judgment of Lord Bingham of Cornhill, para 17. *Sale* v. *Haitian Centers Council*, 509 US 155 (1993).

[57] For an analysis of the United States' interdiction programme and the related policy and legal problems, see S. H. Legomsky, 'The US and the Caribbean Interdiction Program' (2006) 18 *International Journal of Refugee Law* 677, 686.

[58] I will also analyse this case when I deal with the extraterritorial application of the principle of non-refoulement in Section 6.2.2.5.2.

[59] *Sale* v. *Haitian Centers Council*, paras 159–160, emphasis added.

than an act of transporting someone to a particular destination'.[60] The reason for this apparent contradiction in the judgment is that in the *Sale* case the US Supreme Court was not particularly concerned with excluding the application of the principle of non-refoulement at the borders. The focus of its analysis was the extraterritorial application of the principle, in particular on the high seas. Thus, the argument of the United Kingdom House of Lords in the *European Roma Rights Centre* case in favour of limiting the principle of non-refoulement so that it might only apply within the territory of the State is not supported by the interpretation of Article 33 of the 1951 Refugee Convention; and nor did the House of Lords strengthen its argument by referring to the *Sale* case.

Thus far, our interpretative operation clearly shows that the principle of non-refoulement in Article 33 of the 1951 Refugee Convention applies both to removal from within the territories of the asylum country and rejection at its borders. Hence, no further interpretation of the provision involving the supplementary means of interpretation under Article 32 VCLT in this respect is necessary. Conversely, it seems tenable to argue (but not absolutely clear) that because of the ordinary meaning of the terms ('return' and 'refouler') and the context, objective and purpose of the Convention (the arguments concerning the structure of the Convention and the Preamble of it), Article 33 might apply beyond the borders of the asylum State. In this respect, the meaning of the provision remains ambiguous at this juncture, and our analysis requires the use of Article 32 VCLT to determine it. I will do this in Section 6.2.2.5, in which I look at the extraterritorial application of the principle of non-refoulement in the 1951 Refugee Convention.

6.2.1.2   International Human Rights Instruments

Article 7 ICCPR does not expressly prohibit refoulement. However, in 1992 in one of its general comments the Human Rights Committee stated:

> States parties must not expose individuals to the danger of torture or cruel, inhuman or degrading treatment or punishment upon return to another country by way of their extradition, expulsion or *refoulement*.[61]

---

[60] *Ibid.*, para 182.

[61] The Human Rights Committee General Comment No. 20 replaces General Comment No. 7 concerning prohibition of torture and cruel treatment or punishment (Article 7): 10–03–1992, para 9, emphasis added. See also *GT* v. *Australia*, Communication No. 706/1996 (4 November 1997), UN doc. CCPR/C/61/0/706/1996, para 8.1. See Wouters, *International Legal Standards for the Protection from Refoulement*, 375–376.

As with Article 33 of the 1951 Refugee Convention, the use of the word 'refoulement' together with 'expulsion' clarifies that Article 7 ICCPR applies not only within the territories of States but also at their borders.

The wording of Article 3 CAT, which expressly prohibits expulsion, return (*refoulement*) or extradition to another State, resembles the wording of Article 33 of the 1951 Refugee Convention. My conclusion that the use of the term 'return' entails the prohibition of removal at the borders under Article 33 of the 1951 Refugee Convention also applies under Article 3 CAT.[62]

Article 3 ECHR does not expressly prohibit refoulement; but the European Court of Human Rights (ECtHR) has expanded the application of Article 3 ECHR to cases of extradition and expulsion where an applicant faces being sent to a territory where he or she may be at risk of harm.[63] Concerning the territorial application of the principle, there is no case law of the ECtHR dealing with the application of the principle at borders.[64] As noted above, though, the courts and legal doctrine have discussed the issue and emphasised its relevance to the principle of non-refoulement in the 1951 Refugee Convention, the ICCPR and the CAT. Since the ECtHR has not ruled in this respect, in the case of Article 3 ECHR it is necessary to examine the extraterritorial application of the principle. If it is found that the principle applies outside the territory of the State, then, *a fortiori*, it will also apply at the borders.[65]

---

[62] See Wouters, *International Legal Standards for the Protection from Refoulement*, 425 and 435; J. H. Burgers and H. Danelius, *The United Nations Convention against Torture: A Handbook on the Convention against Torture and other Cruel Inhuman or Degrading Treatment or Punishment* (Martinus Nijhoff, 1988), 35; M. Nowak and E. McArthur, *The United Nations Convention Against Torture* (Oxford University Press, 2008), 195. Cfr. Noll, *Negotiating Asylum*, 432–438.

[63] *Soering* v. *United Kingdom* App No. 14038/88 (ECtHR, 7 July 1989); *Chahal* v. *United Kingdom* App No. 22414/93 (ECtHR, 15 November 1996).

[64] But see *Al-Tayyar Abdelhakim* v. *Hungary* App No. 13058/11 (ECtHR, 23 January 2013), where the ECtHR seems not to question the applicability of the principle of non-refoulement to an application made at the borders. Further, the Council of Europe affirmed that States are responsible towards individuals present at the borders of the State: Committee of Ministers, Rec(94)5E, 21 June 1994 on guidelines to inspire practices of the Member States of the Council of Europe concerning the arrival of asylum seekers at European airports.

[65] See Noll, *Negotiating Asylum*, 441. I will examine the extraterritorial application of Article 3 ECHR in Section 6.2.2.2.2.

6.2.2   Beyond the Borders

The application of the principle of non-refoulement is extraterritorial when it refers to ensuring protection against return from 'outside the territory of the State'. Questions about the applicability of this principle are particularly relevant to Frontex and any participant Member States when joint operations are periodically performed outside the Member States' territories. The operational area of Frontex's activities is vast; and proffering some examples of Agency operations will provide the reader with the best understanding of this area's extent.

Joint Operation Hermes 2011 was launched in order to reinforce the surveillance of the southern borders of the Mediterranean and to deal with an 'extraordinary migratory situation in the Pelagic Islands'.[66] During the operation, which was requested and hosted by Italy, Frontex coordinated the deployment of personnel to patrol the central Mediterranean area – the high seas – 'with a view to detecting and preventing illegitimate border crossings to the Pelagic Islands, Sicily and the Italian mainland'.[67] According to Regulation (EU) No 656/2014 establishing rules for the surveillance of the external sea borders in the context of operational cooperation coordinated by Frontex (Sea External Borders Regulation), surveillance operations under Frontex's auspices at the sea external borders can, *inter alia*, lead to stopping, boarding and searching vessels; ordering vessels to change course outside the territorial waters of the coastal Member States; conducting vessels to a third country; or handing over vessels to the authorities of a third country.[68]

Activities on the high seas may extend to the territorial waters of third countries. Joint Operation Hera 2006 involved maritime surveillance of the area between West Africa and the Canary Islands. The operation led to the interception of migrants' boats close to the African coast, and diversion of these vessels to prevent them crossing the EU's external borders. It was conducted within the territorial waters of Senegal and Mauritania by virtue of an international agreement between Spain and

---

[66] Frontex Press Release, 'Request for Help over Migratory Pressure in Lampedusa', 15 February 2011, www.frontex.europa.eu (accessed 13 November 2015).

[67] Frontex Press Release, 'Hermes 2011 Running', 21 February 2011, www.frontex.europa.eu (accessed 13 November 2015).

[68] Regulation (EU) 656/2014 of the European Parliament and of the Council of 15 May 2014 establishing rules for the surveillance of the external sea borders in the context of operational cooperation coordinated by the European agency for the management of operational cooperation at the external borders of the Member States of the European Union OJ 2014 No. L189, p. 93, Article 7.

those countries. As to Frontex's mandate for coordinating operations in the territorial waters of third countries, it seems possible to identify a legal basis in Article 12 of the SBC regarding border surveillance and Article 14(1) and (7), which provides for the possibility of stipulating bilateral agreements with third countries where the Agency's role is to facilitate such cooperation.[69]

As an additional way of probing this specific legal setting, I wish to offer a hypothetical scenario designed to illustrate the extent to which clarity about rights protection and the legal contexts framing Agency operations will be an increasingly urgent matter in the future. In land border operations coordinated by Frontex, Member State personnel could conceivably be deployed to the territory of third country 'A' in order to apprehend irregular migrants coming from third country 'B' so as to prevent them trying to enter the EU. This deployment could take place by virtue of an agreement between a Member State and third country 'A'.[70] Notably, however, there is no provision in the Frontex Regulation which gives a mandate to the Agency to coordinate a joint operation in third-country territories.

In all the examples cited above, Member States' personnel taking part in Frontex-led joint operations act 'outside the territory' of the State as understood under general international law. Operations take place on the high seas, within the territorial waters of third countries and, possibly in future, in the territories of the third countries. Each of these operational areas has its own legal features which we will now address in turn. First, the high seas are the areas of the sea which lie beyond the contiguous zone and are not included in the exclusive economic zone, the territorial sea or the internal waters of a State.[71] Every State has freedom of navigation on the high seas[72] and has exclusive jurisdiction over its own ships.[73] Accordingly, as a general rule, a State cannot arrest a ship which flies the flag of another State on the high seas. However, there are many

---

[69] See J. Rijpma, 'The Patrolling of the European Union's External Maritime Border: Preventing the Rule of Law from Getting Lost at Sea' in A. Del Vecchio (ed.), *International Law of the Sea: Current Trends and Controversial Issues* (Eleven International Publishing, 2014), 95. Cfr. S. Carrera and L. den Hertog, 'Whose Mare? Rule of Law Challenges in the Field of European Border Surveillance in the Mediterranean' *CEPS Paper* No. 79/ January 2015, 11–12.

[70] On this point, see Chapter 1, Section 1.1, and Chapter 8, Section 8.3.2.

[71] Article 86 of the 1982 United Nations Convention on Law of the Sea. For a discussion of the law of the high seas, see Tanaka, *The International Law of the Sea*, 150.

[72] Article 87(1) of the 1982 United Nations Convention on Law of the Sea.

[73] Article 92(1) of the 1982 United Nations Convention on Law of the Sea.

exceptions to this rule.[74] The exception which is most relevant to our present analysis states that a warship, or a ship carrying out law-enforcement functions such as a coastguard ship, can board a foreign ship if 'there is reasonable ground for suspecting that ... the ship is without nationality'.[75] A flagless ship carrying migrants on the high seas commonly triggers interception and search operations coordinated by Frontex. On this point, the EU Sea External Borders Regulation provides that 'on the high seas, where there are reasonable grounds to suspect that a vessel is engaged in the smuggling of migrants by sea', the units participating in the operations must, among other measures, stop, board and search the vessel, in accordance with the Protocol against the Smuggling of Migrants.[76] Also, a ship flying the flag of another country may be boarded and searched with the consent of the flag State.[77] Second, operations in the territorial waters and territories of third countries are possible by agreement between a Member State and a third country. In regard to the circumstances in which a State can operate in the territory of a third country, general international law provides that if a State *legally* performs actions in foreign territory, the

---

[74] Exceptions to the exclusive jurisdiction of the flag State include the right to visit (Article 110(1) of the 1982 United Nations Convention on Law of the Sea) and the right to hot pursuit (Article 23 of the Geneva Convention on the High Seas and Article 111 of the 1982 United Nations Convention on the Law of the Sea). On the legal regime of interception of vessels on the high seas, see E. Papastavridis, *The Interception of Vessels on the High Seas: Contemporary Challenges to the Legal Order of the Oceans* (Hart Publishing, 2013), 259.

[75] Article 110(1) of the 1982 United Nations Convention on the Law of the Sea.

[76] Article 7 of the EU Sea External Borders Regulation. The regulation reiterates EU Member States' obligation to respect the United Nations Convention against Transnational Organised Crime and its Protocol against the Smuggling of Migrants by Land, Sea and Air during border surveillance operations: Recital (8), Articles 5, 6, 7. For an analysis of the Protocol see A. Gallagher, 'Human Rights and the New UN Protocols on Trafficking and Migrant Smuggling: A Preliminary Analysis' (2001) 23 *Human Rights Quarterly* 975 and T. Obokata, 'The Legal Framework Concerning the Smuggling of Migrants at Sea under the UN Protocol and the Smuggling of Migrants by Land, Sea and Air' in Ryan and Mitsilegas (eds.), *Extraterritorial Immigration Control*.

[77] For an analysis of the issues raised by irregular migration by sea and an overview of irregular migration practices, see M. Di Filippo, 'Irregular Migration and Safeguard of Life at Sea. International Rules and Recent Developments in the Mediterranean Sea' in Del Vecchio (ed.), *International Law of the Sea*, 9–10; F. Pastore, P. Monzini and G. Sciortino, 'Schengen's Soft Underbelly? Irregular Migration and Human Smuggling across Land and Sea Borders to Italy' (2006) 44 *International Migration* 95; P. Monzini, 'Sea-border Crossings: The Organisation of Irregular Migration to Italy' (2007) 12 *Mediterranean Politics* 163; S. Trevisanut, 'The Principle of Non-refoulement and the Deterritorialisation of Border Control at Sea' (2014) 27 *Leiden Journal of International Law* 661.

foreign State cannot interfere.[78] The legality of such actions depends on the consent of the foreign State.

Performance of joint operations on the high seas requires that all parties are fully cognizant of the consequences of a State engaging in activities outside its territory which may be contrary to the prohibition of refoulement. The essential legal questions framing such operations are multiple: (i) Is a State responsible for breaches of the principle of non-refoulement which it commits outside its borders? (ii) If, in the context of a joint operation on the high seas, coastguards deployed by Frontex intercept boats irregularly transporting people in need of international protection, are these coastguards prevented from returning them? (iii) Would the situation be different if the interception took place within the territorial waters or the territory of a third country?

6.2.2.1 The Concept of Jurisdiction in International Human Rights Law

The human rights treaties providing protection against refoulement do not necessarily link the application of each treaty to the territory over which a State has sovereignty. For instance, Article 1 ECHR states that 'the High Contracting Parties shall secure to everyone *within their jurisdiction* the rights and freedoms' included in the ECHR.[79] Conversely, Article 2(1) ICCPR states: 'each State party to the present Covenant undertakes to respect and to ensure to all individuals *within its territory* and subject to its jurisdiction the rights recognised in the present Covenant'. Article 2(1) CAT states: 'each State Party shall take effective legislative, administrative, judicial or other measures to prevent acts of torture *in any territory* under its jurisdiction'. Thus, the jurisdictional clauses in the ICCPR and the CAT have 'a stronger territorial focus than Article 1 ECHR', since their provisions refer to 'territory'.[80] Notwithstanding the different focal points concerning territory in the wording of the human rights treaties, in all cases the word 'jurisdiction' must be interpreted in the light of the object and purpose of the treaty concerned. The above provisions identify the area

---

[78] This principle of general international law (*par in parem non habet imperium*) applies to agreements permitting one State to intercept vessels in the territorial waters of another State, and also to the arrest of individuals in foreign territory by a State after the issue of an arrest warrant. See Cassese, *International Law*, 98.

[79] Emphasis added.

[80] D. McGoldrik, 'Extraterritorial Application of the International Covenant on Civil and Political Rights' in F. Coomans and M. T. Kamminga (eds.), *Extraterritorial Application of Human Rights Treaties* (Intersentia, 2004), 47.

within which the obligations of the human rights treaties apply.[81] As shown above,[82] this area generally corresponds to the geographical space over which the State has sovereignty but it must not necessarily be identified with it. In fact, the notion of 'jurisdiction' to which the above provisions refer is not related to sovereignty according to general international law. Sovereignty of a State establishes the right that a State has to exercise authority over a specific territory. This makes the exercise of State's authority over the territory legal.[83] 'Jurisdiction' in human rights treaties states the factual control which the State has over territory or persons, this control being legal or illegal under international law.[84]

While a State is likely to have a high degree of actual control in the territory over which it has sovereignty, control beyond the State's border requires different circumstances.[85] In other words, if a State is obliged to ensure the rights of individuals, the extent of its obligations depends on its capability to ensure these rights. This capability is measured by the actual control that the State can exercise.[86] Rick Lawson has referred to

[81] On the ECHR, see A. Orakhelashvili, 'Restrictive Interpretation of Human Rights Treaties in the Recent Jurisprudence of the European Court of Human Rights' (2003) 14 *European Journal of International Law* 529, 540.

[82] See Section 6.1.

[83] For the concept of jurisdiction under general international law, see Shaw, *International Law*, 645–686; Cassese, *International Law*, 49–50; Brownlie, *Principles of Public International Law*, 299–307.

[84] On the meaning of jurisdiction in human rights treaties, see T. Meron, 'Extraterritoriality of Human Rights Treaties' (1995) 89 *The American Journal of International Law* 78; A. Orakhelashvili, 'Restrictive Interpretation of Human Rights Treaties'; M. Gondek, 'Extraterritorial Application of the European Convention on Human Rights: Territorial Focus in the Age of Globalization?' (2005) 52 *Netherlands International Law Review* 349; M. J. Dennis, 'Application of Human Rights Treaties Extraterritorially in Times of Armed Conflict and Military Occupation' (2005) 99 *The American Journal of International Law* 119; M. Milanovic, 'From Compromise to Principle: Clarifying the Concept of State Jurisdiction in Human Rights Treaties' (2008) 8 *Human Rights Law Review* 411; S. Miller, 'Revisiting Extraterritorial Jurisdiction: A Territorial Justification for Extraterritorial Jurisdiction under the European Convention' (2009) 20 *European Journal of International Law* 1223; M. Milanovic, *Extraterritorial Application of Human Rights Treaties* (Oxford University Press, 2011); M. den Hijer and R. Lawson, 'Extraterritorial Human Rights and the Concept of "Jurisdiction"' in M. Langford, W. Vandenhole, M. Scheinin and W. Genugten (eds.), *Global Justice, State Duties: The Extraterritorial Scope of Economic, Social, and Cultural Rights in International Law* (Cambridge University Press, 2014), 163.

[85] But see Milanovic, who observes: 'A state may have title over territory, but not have jurisdiction, i.e. *de facto* control, over it' in *Extraterritorial Application of Human Rights Treaties*, 8.

[86] See R. Lawson, 'Life after Bankovic: On the Extraterritorial Application of the European Convention on Human Rights' in Coomans and Kamminga (eds.), *Extraterritorial Application of Human Rights Treaties*, 84.

this approach as a 'gradual and context-related approach'[87] and Martin Scheinin has called it 'facticity determining normativity'.[88] Such control can be spatial or personal. The spatial model consists of understanding 'jurisdiction' as the exercise of control by a State over a territory and its inhabitants, or perhaps over a narrow area within the territory such as a prison. The personal model consists of understanding 'jurisdiction' as the control exercised by a State over persons. Jurisdiction established by the occupation of a territory by a State and control over its inhabitants is not relevant for the analysis of the responsibilities of the EU and its Member States in Frontex's joint operations. Conversely, it is important to establish the extent to which the personal model applies. This is relevant when the actions of border guards involve checks at borders, interception and the apprehension of individuals.

How is 'jurisdiction' established in the Frontex joint-operational examples cited above? What protection does the principle of non-refoulement afford in these situations? We must now attempt to answer these questions by analysing relevant provisions and related judgments of the decision-making bodies with a focus on the application of the personal jurisdictional model. The list of judgments considered is far from exhaustive; but the rulings have been selected for their pertinence to the present investigation.

6.2.2.2 European Convention of Human Rights and Fundamental Freedoms

6.2.2.2.1 Actual Control over Persons The ECtHR and the European Commission on Human Rights (which ceased to function in 1998) interpreted the concept of 'jurisdiction' in Article 1 ECHR in the *Bankovic* case. Here, the ECtHR ruled in favour of 'jurisdiction' as being primarily a territorial concept and considered the extraterritorial exercise of jurisdiction to be strictly exceptional.[89] When deciding the admissibility of the *Bankovic* case, the Grand Chamber of the ECtHR took the opportunity to analyse the meaning of 'jurisdiction' in Article 1 ECHR and the extraterritorial application of the ECHR. The case concerned the bombing of a radio station in the Federal Republic of

---

[87] *Ibid.*, 107.

[88] M. Scheinin, 'Extraterritorial Effect of the International Covenant on Civil and Political Rights' in Coomans and Kamminga (eds.), *Extraterritorial Application of Human Rights Treaties*, 93.

[89] *Bankovic and Others* v. *Belgium and Others* App No. 52207/99 (ECtHR, 12 December 2001).

Yugoslavia in 1999 in the context of a military campaign organised by NATO. Sixteen people were killed and another sixteen injured in the bombing. The applicants claimed that the NATO states involved in the bombing had breached Articles 2, 10 and 13 ECHR. The ECtHR ruled that the case was inadmissible because the acts of the NATO states did not fall within jurisdiction of the NATO states.[90] In the present context, I will focus my analysis on the extraterritorial application of the ECHR and the meaning of 'jurisdiction'. In the *Bankovic* ruling, the ECtHR interpreted 'jurisdiction' according to general international law, according to which 'jurisdiction' is essentially territorial and a competence primarily of a State over its own territory. The ECtHR rejected that 'jurisdiction' corresponds to the exercise of effective control. However, it has recognised that a contracting State may 'exceptionally' exercise extraterritorial jurisdiction.[91] The ECtHR has declared that extraterritorial jurisdiction arises when a party exercises 'effective control of the relevant territory and its inhabitants abroad as a consequence of military occupation', or when a party 'through the consent, invitation or acquiescence of the Government of that territory, exercises all or some of the public powers normally to be exercised by that Government'.[92] Thus, the ECtHR has established that effective control is a form of extraterritorial application of the ECHR only in the form of exception. 'Jurisdiction' is understood according to the spatial model (i.e. control over territory by military occupation or the exercise of public powers by virtue of the consent of the government of the territory).[93] The personal model of jurisdiction was disregarded by the ECtHR, though it was utilised in its previous case law.[94] In *Bankovic*, the ECtHR identified two other exceptions to the territorial concept of 'jurisdiction': (i) when a State's acts take place on-board vessels registered in or flying the flag of the State, and (ii) when there is the consent of the government of the foreign territory.[95]

In other case law affirming the extraterritorial exercise of jurisdiction, the ECtHR has clearly applied the personal model of jurisdiction.[96]

---

[90] *Ibid.*, para 82.   [91] *Ibid.*, para 71.   [92] *Ibid.*
[93] See also *Ilascu and Others* v. *Moldova and Russia* App No. 48787/99 (ECtHR, 8 July 2004), para 387.
[94] See e.g. *Stocke* v. *Germany* App No. 11755/85 (Commission Decision, 19 March 1991); *Cyprus* v. *Turkey* App No. 25781/94 (Commission Decision, 15 May 2001).
[95] *Bankovic*, para 73.
[96] See Gondek, 'Extraterritorial Application of the European Convention on Human Rights', 363. On this point see also Milanovic on the ECtHR's lack of explanation for the change from *Bankovic* to subsequent cases in *Extraterritorial Application of Human Rights Treaties*, 166. See *Ocalan* v. *Turkey* App No. 46221/99 (ECtHR, 12 May 2005); *Pad*

In particular, we must examine the *Ocalan* v. *Turkey* case, which concerned the circumstances pertaining to the issuing of an arrest warrant for Abdullah Ocalan, leader of the Kurdistan Workers' Party in Turkey, who was accused of terrorist acts.[97] After seeking refuge in many countries, the applicant was arrested in an aircraft within the area of Nairobi airport by Turkish officials, to whom he was handed over by Kenyan officials. After the arrest, Ocalan was returned to Turkey, detained, put on trial and sentenced to death. Ocalan claimed that Turkey had acted in breach of several provisions of the ECHR, including Article 5(1), which prohibits the unlawful deprivation of liberty. The ECtHR had to decide whether the ECHR could apply extraterritorially in the circumstances of Ocalan's arrest in Nairobi. The ECtHR first referred to the *Bankovic* judgment on the territorial concept of 'jurisdiction' and the extraterritorial exception.[98] The ECtHR upheld the extraterritorial application of the ECHR by stating that the Turkish officials exercised authority over the applicant and he was brought within Turkish jurisdiction by this exercise of authority. Thus, the personal model was applied by the ECtHR.[99]

In more recent cases, the ECtHR has shown uncertainty about which model to apply. In Al-*Saadoon and Mufdhi* v. *United Kingdom*,[100] the ECtHR dealt with the case of two individuals who had been detained in Iraq by the United Kingdom in the context of the occupation of Iraq in 2003 by a coalition of armed forces. The individuals were detained in detention facilities run by British forces. The applicants were initially detained pursuant to Security Council Resolution 1546. The basis for their detention changed when they were detained on the orders of the Iraqi judiciary and charged with specific crimes. Upon the withdrawal of United Kingdom forces from Iraq, the Iraqi authorities required the transfer to them of the two detainees. The applicants claimed that their transfer would amount to an infringement of Articles 2 and 3 ECHR and Article 1 of Protocol No. 13 to the ECHR since it would expose them to a risk of being sentenced to death.[101] It is not clear whether in these cases the ECtHR

---

and Others v. *Turkey* App No. 60167/00 (ECtHR, 28 June 2007); *Isaak and Others* v. *Turkey* App No. 44587/98 (ECtHR, 24 June 2008).

[97] *Ocalan* v. *Turkey.*   [98] *Ibid.*, paras 91–92.   [99] *Ibid.*, para 93.

[100] Al-*Saadoon and Mufdhi* v. *United Kingdom* App No. 61498/08 (ECtHR, 2 March 2010). For commentary, see C. Janik and T. Kleinlein, 'When Soering Went to Iraq: Problems of Jurisdiction, Extraterritorial Effect and Norm Conflicts in the Light of the European Court of Human Rights' Al-*Saadoon* Case' (2009) 1 *Goettingen Journal of International Law* 459.

[101] The Al-*Saadoon* case was also concerned with a norm conflict between the United Kingdom's obligations under Iraqi law and its obligations under the ECHR. For an analysis of this point, see Milanovic, *Extraterritorial Application of Human Rights*

applied the personal or the spatial model of jurisdiction, since it referred to control and authority both over the individuals and over the premises.[102]

The most recent important case in regard to the application of the personal model of jurisdiction is *Al-Skeini and Others* v. *United Kingdom*,[103] since it has been deemed that this 'judgment has placed the doctrine of extraterritorial jurisdiction on a sounder footing than ever before'.[104] As in *Al-Saadoon*, the case concerned the occupation of Iraq by a coalition of armed forces. British troops shot five individuals while on patrol in Basra. A sixth individual was killed in British detention. Relatives of the deceased claimed that those killed were within the United Kingdom's jurisdiction under Article 1 ECHR when they died, and that the United Kingdom did not comply with its duty to investigate the case under Article 2 ECHR. The ECtHR found in favour of the applicants. The Grand Chamber of the ECtHR applies the personal model of jurisdiction in such a way that 'jurisdiction' is established in all situations in which it is possible to identify a 'jurisdictional link' between the victims of breaches of the ECHR and the acts of a State.[105] In other words, the State exercises jurisdiction whenever it acts through its agents. 'Jurisdiction' is not related to a territory or to a smaller space such as detention facilities, but refers to the control which can be exercised over a person.[106] This personal model of jurisdiction seems to have a limitation. 'Jurisdiction' is established only when State's agents have assumed the exercise of 'public powers', as in the case of UK soldiers engaged in security operations in Basra. Thus, to some extent, the personal model of jurisdiction identified by the ECtHR in *Al-Skeini* requires some spatial connection with the territory in which the breach occurs.[107] However, it is not yet clear from

---

Treaties, 132; M. E. Cross and S. Williams, 'Between the Devil and the Deep Blue Sea: Conflicted Thinking in the *Al-Saadoon* Affair' (2009) 58 *International and Comparative Law Quarterly* 689, 701. I will return to this judgment when I discuss the extraterritorial application of the principle of non-refoulement, Section 6.2.2.2.3.

[102] *Al-Saadoon and Mufdhi*, paras 87–89.
[103] *Al-Skeini and Others* v. *The United Kingdom* App No. 55721/07 (ECtHR, 7 July 2011).
[104] Judge Bonello, concurring opinion in *Al-Skeini*.   [105] *Al-Skeini*, para 149.
[106] *Ibid.*, para 136.
[107] See also M. Milanovic, who describes the ECtHR's solution in *Al-Skeini* as 'a rather bizarre mix of the personal model with the spatial one'; see M. Milanovic, 'Al-Skeini and Al-Jedda in Strasbourg' (2012) 23 *European Journal of International Law* 121, 131. For commentary of *Al-Skeini* before the ECtHR, see also C. Mallory, 'European Court of Human Rights Al-Skeini and Others v. United Kingdom (Application No. 55721/07) Judgment of 7 July 2011' (2012) 61 *International and Comparative Law Quarterly* 301; M. Zgonec-Rozej, 'Al-Skeini v. United Kingdom' (2012) 106 *American Journal of International Law* 131.

the judgment what constitutes 'public powers' and what their role is in establishing 'jurisdiction'.[108]

Two subsequent judgments, delivered by the ECtHR's Grand Chamber after *Al-Skeini*, have dealt with this matter. First, *Hassan* v. *United Kingdom* concerned the capture of the applicant's brother, Tarek Hassan, by British forces and his subsequent detention in the Camp Bucca facility in Iraq, where he was allegedly ill-treated.[109] The events occurred before 1 May 2003, which was the date when the United Kingdom assumed authority and responsibility for the maintenance of security in South-East Iraq. The applicant brought allegations concerning what he deemed the arbitrary arrest and detention of his brother; the discovery of the body in unknown circumstances; and a failure by the British authorities to investigate the circumstances around his brother's detention, ill treatment and death. The applicant complained of a violation of Articles 2, 3 and 5 ECHR. The ECtHR held the United Kingdom responsible only for the violation of Article 5 ECHR as regards the capture and detention of Tarek Hassan. In assessing whether Tarek Hassan was within the United Kingdom jurisdiction from the time of his capture to the time of drop-off at Camp Bucca, the ECtHR noted how the present case concerned an earlier period (a phase prior to the UK and the US occupation of South-East Iraq which was deemed be in effect and thus instrumental to the outcome of *Al-Skeini*).[110] Notwithstanding the absence of such assumption of public power by the United Kingdom in this phase, the ECtHR concluded that 'Tarek Hassan was within the physical power and control of the United Kingdom soldiers and therefore fell within United Kingdom jurisdiction' under the principles outlined in *Al-Skeini*.[111] Second, *Jaloud* v. *the Netherlands* concerned Dutch authorities' investigations into the circumstances surrounding the death of the applicant's son, Azhar Sabah Jaloud, who died of gunshot wounds on 21 April 2004 in a province of South-East Iraq.[112] Dutch personnel were involved in the circumstances of Jaloud's death. The ECtHR held that there had been a violation of Article 2 ECHR since the Netherlands had failed to carry out an effective investigation into the death of the applicant's son. The facts of this case occurred in an area of South-East Iraq

---

[108] See C. Costello, 'Courting Access to Asylum in Europe: Recent Supranational Jurisprudence Explored' (2012) 12 *Human Rights Law Review* 287, 299; and P. Ronchi, 'The Borders of Human Rights' (2012) 128 *Law Quarterly Review* 20, 22.

[109] *Hassan* v. *United Kingdom*, App No. 29750/09 (ECtHR, 16 September 2014).

[110] *Ibid.*, para 75.   [111] *Ibid.*, para 76.

[112] *Jaloud* v. *The Netherlands* App No. 47708/08 (ECtHR, 20 November 2014).

which was then under the operational control of a United Kingdom officer. The ECtHR established jurisdiction in respect of the Netherlands as follows: '[T]he Court points out that the status of "occupying power" ..., or the lack of it, is not *per se* determinative. ... The respondent Party is therefore not divested of its "jurisdiction", within the meaning of Article 1 of the Convention, solely by dint of having accepted the operational control of a United Kingdom officer.'[113] These two judgments, both reiterating the principles established in *Al-Skeini*, seem to exclude that the exercise of 'public powers' by the State allegedly responsible determines the jurisdiction of the said State within the meaning of Article 1 ECHR. In sum, with its ruling in *Bankovic*, the Grand Chamber of the ECtHR affirmed the essentially territorial nature of jurisdiction in Article 1 ECHR. Only as an exception has the ECtHR established 'jurisdiction' as actual control exercised by a State over territory. In subsequent cases, the ECtHR has exhibited a more open approach to the personal model of jurisdiction (e.g. *Ocalan*), though there have been other ECtHR rulings which reveal some uncertainty about which model to apply (e.g. *Al-Saadoon*). Finally, in the recent *Al-Skeini* ruling, the Grand Chamber defined 'jurisdiction' as actual control over individuals. The requirement in this latter judgment of a link to the territory through the exercise of public powers by the State's agents to establish jurisdiction seems to be excluded in later pronouncements of the Court.

In *Bankovic* the ECtHR established that there may also be extraterritorial application of jurisdiction pursuant to Article 1 ECHR with the consent of the government of the foreign territory.[114] In this connection, it is appropriate to recall Joint Operation Hera, described earlier, which was conducted within the territorial waters of Senegal and Mauritania under an international agreement between these nations and Spain. Did Spain exercise jurisdiction in the territorial waters of Senegal and Mauritania by virtue of their consent? Was obtaining this consent the source of Spain's potential responsibility for possible breaches of the principle of non-refoulement? As discussed above,[115] the interpretation of 'jurisdiction' in Article 1 ECHR as being primarily territorial according to general international law cannot be accepted, since it disregards the meaning of 'jurisdiction' in human rights law, which is based on actual control and not on the sovereignty of a State over its own territory. Accordingly, an exception to the territorial interpretation, based on the principle of general international law that a State cannot exercise

---

[113] *Ibid.*, paras 142–143.   [114] *Bankovic*, para 71.   [115] See Section 6.2.2.1.

jurisdiction in the territory of another State without the latter's consent, invitation or acquiescence, is untenable. The consent or acquiescence of the consenting State makes the actions of the acting State legal, but it does not determine the applicability of rights under the ECHR. Consent or acquiescence may constitute evidence that the acting State exercises control over individuals.[116] As we have noted, the obligation to ensure rights is linked to the degree of actual control exercised by the acting State, and this is a completely different issue from the exercise of 'jurisdiction' (competence) of States in their own territories or foreign territories. This argument is supported by several rulings of the ECHR and the ECtHR.[117] If we return to the specific example of Joint Operation Hera, in order to establish the responsibility of Spain for any potential breaches of the principle of non-refoulement in the territorial waters of Senegal or Mauritania, jurisdiction must be established on the basis of the control exercised by Spanish personnel over individuals and not because of the consent of third countries.

Further, in the *Bankovic* judgment, the ECtHR stated that, according to general international law, jurisdiction may be exercised extraterritorially when a State's acts take place on board crafts and vessels registered in, or flying the flag of, the State. In the example proffered above of joint operations launched to prevent irregular border crossing on the high seas, vessels with on-board Member State personnel can stop and board other vessels and hand over irregular migrants found on board the vessels to authorities of third countries in order to impede the irregular migrants entering the contiguous zone of a coastal State. If this conduct constitutes a breach of the principle of non-refoulement (for instance, if people are handed over to the authorities of a country where they may be at risk of persecution), we must establish an understanding of how 'jurisdiction' is established. Is 'jurisdiction' exercised by the State where the stopped and boarded vessel is registered? As our analysis has shown,[118] according to general international law, as a State exercises jurisdiction over its own territory, it has exclusive jurisdiction over vessels flying its flag. However, this is not the concept of 'jurisdiction' that applies to human rights treaties. In Section 6.2.2.1, I explained that 'human rights law jurisdiction' means control over territory or persons and it is not the same as the

---

[116] See likewise Klug and Howe, 'The Concept of State Jurisdiction', 93.

[117] *X and Y* v. *Switzerland; Freda* v. *Italy* App No. 8916/80 (Commission Decision, 7 October 1980); and *Altmann* v. *France* App No. 10689/83 (Commission Decision, 4 July 1984).

[118] Section 6.2.2.

definition of 'jurisdiction' under general international law. Thus, jurisdiction based on the flag of the State, as identified by the ECtHR, does not
seem to be legally correct. As in the case of the consent of the government
of a foreign territory, the flag-State jurisdiction may be evidence that the
acting State exercises control over individuals. My argument is supported
by the case law of the ECtHR on aircraft and vessels.[119] This issue was
dealt with expressly by the Grand Chamber of the ECtHR in the
Medvedyev and Others v. *France* case.[120] The case concerned the
boarding and search of a vessel, the *Winner*, flying the Cambodian flag.
This action was carried out by French authorities in an operation against
international drug trafficking. With the authorisation of the Cambodian
government, the French authorities boarded and searched the vessel,
where they found illegal drugs. The crew members, who made the
application, were detained on board the *Winner* for 13 days until they
were brought before a judge when the vessel reached the port of Brest in
France. They claimed that France's acts amounted to several breaches of
the ECHR, including Article 5(3), since their detention was unlawful and
they were not brought promptly before a judge. The ECtHR dealt with
the issue of jurisdiction as follows: the Court initially referred to the
essentially territorial concept of jurisdiction set out in the *Bankovic* case
and restated the exceptions to the territorial concept of jurisdiction,
including the general international law on jurisdiction over aircrafts
and vessels. However, there was no reason to restate these principles in
the judgment. The exception was not applicable to the case since the
Winner flew the Cambodian flag and it was not under French jurisdiction
according to general international law.[121] The ECtHR applied the control
doctrine to this case, and it was by virtue of this doctrine, not by the
application of general international law, that the applicants were subject
to French jurisdiction.[122] It was not clearly stated by the ECtHR whether

---

[119] See *Rigopoulos* v. *Spain* App No. 37388/97 (Commission Decision, 12 January 1999);
Xhavara c. Italie et Albanie App No. 39473/98 (Commission Decision, 11 January 2001);
and *Medvedyev* v. *France* App No. 3394/03 (ECtHR, 29 March 2010).

[120] *Medvedyev* v. *France*. For a complete analysis of the judgment, see E. Papastavridis,
'European Court of Human Rights *Medvedyev Et Al V France* (Grand Chamber,
Application No. 3394/03) Judgment of 29 March 2010' (2010) 59 *International and
Comparative Law Quarterly* 867.

[121] See Milanovic, *Extraterritorial Application of Human Rights Treaties*, 163.

[122] *Medevyev*, para 67. See likewise V. Moreno-Lax, '*Hirsi Jamaa and Others v Italy* or the
Strasbourg Court versus Extraterritorial Migration Control?' (2012) 12 *Human Rights
Law Review* 574, 581; K. Wouters and M. den Heijer, 'The Marine I Case: a Comment'
(2010) 22 *International Journal of Refugee Law* 1, 9.

the 'full and exclusive control ... in a continuous and uninterrupted manner' of the French authorities was exercised over the vessel or over the crew, in other words, whether it was personal or spatial control.[123] The reference to *Bankovic* in the quoted passage is difficult to reconcile with what was stated immediately prior to this by the ECtHR.[124] Thus, the exception identified in *Bankovic* was not used by the ECtHR to establish 'jurisdiction', and it seems the ECtHR, with this judgment, has overturned its previous case law in this respect. Thus, overall, the extra-territorial exercise of 'jurisdiction' based on general international law, when a State's acts take place on board vessels registered in, or flying the flag of, the State, seems to be considered as not legally correct given the meaning of 'jurisdiction' in human rights law as ruled by the ECtHR. In particular, in cases involving vessels and aircraft, the ECtHR has established 'Article 1 ECHR jurisdiction' by looking at the actual control exercised by a State over an applicant or, in the *Medvedyev* case, over a vessel. So if we return, once more, to our example of the joint-surveillance operations on the high seas coordinated by Frontex, 'juris-diction' is established by looking at the Member State which exercises 'continuous and uninterrupted control' over the vessel or over the indi-viduals when a vessel is stopped and handed over to the authorities of a third country.

6.2.2.2.2 Non-Refoulement under the ECHR

Having scrutinised the concept of jurisdiction under the ECHR, we are now ready to analyse how the ECtHR interpreted Article 3 ECHR and Article 4 of Protocol No. 4 ECHR prohibiting collective expulsion. An examina-tion of the issue of protection against refoulement and the law of the sea will also be part of the analysis. Two cases on the extraterritorial application of the principle of non-refoulement are particularly rele-vant for our purpose: *Al-Saadoon and Mufdhi v. United Kingdom* and *Hirsi v. Italy*.

6.2.2.2.3 The *Al-Saadoon* Case

We encountered the *Al-Saadoon* case in the previous discussion on the concept of jurisdiction under the ECHR. It must suffice to recall here that the case concerned the detention of two individuals by the United Kingdom in Iraq in the context of the occupation of Iraq in 2003. The Iraqi authorities requested the transfer to

---

[123] *Medevyev*, para 67.
[124] See Milanovic, *Extraterritorial Application of Human Rights Treaties*, 164.

them of the two detainees, and the detainees claimed that their transfer would expose them to a risk of being sentenced to death. The ECtHR found that jurisdiction was established by virtue of the control exercised by the United Kingdom, but (i) it is not clear from the judgment whether this control was personal or spatial; and (ii) it is not clear from the judgment whether the control was exercised *de facto* or *de jure*. *De jure* control would be control by virtue of the fact that the Iraqi authorities permitted the United Kingdom authorities to run the facilities. In its judgment, the ECtHR found that the transfer of the two applicants to the Iraqi authorities constituted a breach of the principle of non-refoulement under Article 3 ECHR.

Since the applicants were under the jurisdiction of the United Kingdom, the United Kingdom was considered responsible for their removal and for their exposure to the risk of death penalty.[125] Importantly, Article 3 ECHR was found to be infringed even though the applicants had not crossed an international border, since the detention facilities were within Iraqi territory.[126] In this respect, the protection against refoulement provided by Article 3 ECHR is broader than the protection provided by Article 33 of the 1951 Refugee Convention. In the latter provision, protection is only granted if individuals are not in their country of nationality or habitual residence (i.e. they are required to have crossed an international border).

In the *Al-Saadoon* case, the applicants encountered the United Kingdom because the United Kingdom arrested them.[127] Accordingly, the ECtHR found that the United Kingdom had a 'paramount obligation' not to *refoul* them. This is similar to what would happen if irregular migrants were to be apprehended in the territory of a third country by Member States' personnel (as in the hypothetical scenario of land border operations under Frontex's auspices outlined earlier). If, in a joint operation in the territory of a non-EU country, refugees are intercepted by the personnel of a Member State, it is the Member State which is responsible if a breach of the principle of non-refoulement occurs. The Member State is under a 'paramount obligation' not to send them to a territory where they can be at risk of persecution.

---

[125] *Al-Saadoon*, para 140.
[126] See likewise Janik and Kleinlein, 'When Soering Went to Iraq', 489; T. Gammeltoft-Hansen, *Access to Asylum: International Refugee Law and the Globalisation of Migration Control* (Oxford University Press, 2011), 138.
[127] *Al-Saadoon*, para 140.

6.2.2.2.4 The *Hirsi* Case The *Hirsi* v. *Italy* case was decided by the Grand Chamber of the ECtHR in 2012.[128] The case concerned the interception of 11 Somali nationals and 13 Eritrean nationals on the high seas by vessels of the Italian Revenue Police (*Guardia di Finanza*) and Coastguard (*Guardia Costiera*). After the interception, the applicants, who were fleeing from Libya, were transferred to Italian military vessels and returned to Tripoli, without being informed where they were being taken and without being identified. Notwithstanding their objection to being handed over to the Libyan authorities in Tripoli, the applicants were forced to leave the Italian vessel. The operation conducted by Italian authorities took place under a bilateral agreement between Italy and Libya to combat irregular migration.[129] The applicants argued that Italy infringed Articles 3, 13 and Article 4 of Protocol No. 4 to the ECHR.[130] The ECtHR ruled in favour of the applicants. It stated that in their interception activities, the Italian authorities acted in breach of the principle of non-refoulement and infringed the prohibition of carrying out collective removals.

In order to establish whether the principle of non-refoulement applied on the high seas, the ECtHR had to begin by ruling on the application of the ECHR on the high seas. The ECtHR started by referring to the case law on the extraterritorial application of the ECHR, analysed above,[131]

---

[128] *Hirsi Jamaa and Others* v. *Italy* App No. 27765/09 (ECtHR, 23 February 2012). Since the decision of the ECtHR has been examined by many scholars, my analysis will focus on the most relevant aspects for the purpose of this book. For a fuller account of the ECtHR's decision, see e.g. V. Moreno-Lax, '*Hirsi Jamaa and Others v Italy*', 574; M. Giuffré, 'Watered-Down Rights on the High Seas: *Hirsi Jamaa and Others v Italy*' (2012) 61 *International and Comparative Law Quarterly* 728; R. K. Holberg, 'Italy's Policy of Pushing Back African Migrants on the High Seas Rejected by the European Court of Human Rights in the Case of *Hirsi Jamaa & Others v. Italy*' (2012) 26 *Georgetown Immigration Law Journal* 467; M. den Heijer, 'Reflections on Refoulement and Collective Expulsion in the Hirsi Case' (2013) 25 *International Journal of Refugee Law* 265.

[129] 'Trattato di amicizia, partenariato e cooperazione tra la Repubblica italiana e la Grande Giamahiria araba libica popolare socialista', Benghazi, 30 August 2008, www.camera.it, followed by 'Processo verbale della riunione tra il ministro dell'interno della Repubblica italiana ed il ministro dell'interno della Libia', Tripoli, 3 April 2012, www.statewatch.org (both accessed 13 November 2015). For an analysis of the legal basis of Italy–Libya bilateral agreements as a component of Italy's practice of interdiction and return, see M. Giuffré, 'State Responsibility beyond Borders: What Legal Basis for Italy's Push-backs to Libya?' (2012) 24 *International Journal of Refugee Law* 692.

[130] For the purpose of the current investigation, my analysis of the Hirsi case is limited to what was decided by the ECtHR on Article 3 ECHR and Article 4 to Protocol No. 4 to the ECHR.

[131] See Section 6.2.2.2.1.

which affirms that 'jurisdiction' is primarily territorial, though some exceptions are admitted. The ECtHR referred to the exception to territoriality represented by the extraterritorial exercise of jurisdiction by a State in the case of vessels flying a State's flag.[132] The ECtHR started from this last exception and noted that in this case the vessel to which the individuals were transferred for transportation to Libya flew the Italian flag.[133] Accordingly, the ECtHR recognised the *de jure* control of the Italian State over the individuals (i.e. its jurisdiction).[134] To start with, 'jurisdiction' was established on this basis and the ECtHR referred to Italian legislation which refers to the same principle.[135] However, perhaps somewhat surprisingly, the ECtHR did not stop there but went on to refer to the *Medvedyev* case, in which the ECtHR found that France had jurisdiction by virtue of its exercise of full and exclusive control in a continuous and uninterrupted manner over a vessel flying a Cambodian flag. In this latter case, the ECtHR did not apply the State-flag principle but the effective-control principle. Finally, the ECtHR concluded:

> in the instant case the events took place entirely on board ships of the Italian armed forces, the crews of which were composed exclusively of Italian military personnel. In the Court's opinion, in the period between boarding the ships of the Italian armed forces and being handed over to the Libyan authorities, *the applicants were under the continuous and exclusive de jure and de facto control of the Italian authorities.*[136]

The ECtHR stated that there was *de jure* control since the vessel flew the Italian flag, but that there was also *de facto* control by the Italian authorities on board the ship. Thus, it is not clear from the judgment which criterion was used to establish jurisdiction on the high seas (i.e. whether it was the flag-State concept of jurisdiction or the control doctrine).[137] However, the ECtHR's statement that the Italian authorities exercised continuous and exclusive actual control over the individuals and its reference to the *Medvedyev* case show that, according to the ECtHR, the control doctrine may apply on the high seas. The implication of this observation is that the ECHR would apply, in future cases, when individuals remain on their own vessel (i.e. a vessel which does not fly the flag

---

[132] *Hirsi*, para 75.

[133] *Ibid.*, para 76. The interception started when the individuals were still on a vessel not flying the Italian flag and from that moment they were under the continuous and exclusive control of the Italian authorities. This element was apparently disregarded by the ECtHR.

[134] *Hirsi*, para 77.   [135] *Ibid.*, para 78.   [136] *Ibid.*, para 75, emphasis added.

[137] Cfr. Moreno-Lax, '*Hirsi Jamaa and Others v Italy*', 579–582.

of the intercepting State) but are under the continuous and exclusive control of the authorities of the intercepting State.[138]

Concerning the actual breach of the principle of non-refoulement under Article 3 ECHR, the ECtHR distinguished two aspects: (1) the exposure of the applicants to inhuman and degrading treatment in Libya; and (2) the risk of indirect refoulement (i.e. the transfer from Libya to countries where the applicants could be at risk of inhuman and degrading treatment, represented in this instance by the applicants' countries of origin).[139] On the first aspect, the ECtHR observed that the treatment of irregular migrants in Libya was clear from reports by several international bodies and non-governmental organisations, and that 'the Italian authorities knew or should have known that as irregular migrants, the applicants would be exposed in Libya to treatment in breach of the Convention and that they would not be given any kind of protection in that country'.[140] On the second aspect, after finding that the removal of individuals to Somalia and Eritrea would constitute a breach of the principle of non-refoulement under Article 3 ECHR and that there were not sufficient guarantees against indirect refoulement in Libya, the ECtHR stated that 'the Italian authorities knew or should have known that there were insufficient guarantees protecting the parties concerned from the risk of being arbitrarily returned to their countries of origin'.[141]

In analysing both aspects, the ECtHR defined the content of the principle of non-refoulement. In its submission the Italian government argued that Italy was not obliged to respect the principle of non-refoulement under Article 3 ECHR. According to the Italian government, the applicants had not sufficiently described the risk to which they could be exposed if returned to Libya since they had not applied to the Italian authorities for asylum.[142] The mere fact that the applicants opposed their disembarkation was not sufficient to trigger the prohibition.[143] The Italian authorities did not inform the applicants that they were being taken to Libya; nor did they screen them in order to identify them. Such a procedure would have

---

[138] See likewise den Heijer, 'Reflections on *Refoulement* and Collective Expulsion in the *Hirsi* Case', 9.

[139] Prohibition of indirect refoulement was established by the ECtHR in *T.I.* v. *the United Kingdom* App No 43844/ 98 (Commission Decision, 7 March 2000) and *M.S.S.* v. *Belgium and Greece*.

[140] *Hirsi*, para 131. On the relaxation of the burden of proof and the importance attached by the Court to country information to assess the level of risk to which the applicant is exposed, see Moreno-Lax, '*Hirsi Jamaa and Others v Italy*', 583.

[141] *Hirsi*, para 156.   [142] *Ibid.*, para 132.   [143] *Ibid.*

allowed the Italian authorities to understand the risk to which the applicants could be exposed in being returned to Libya.

According to the ECtHR, the threshold for triggering the prohibition
of refoulement is lower than that stated by the Italian government. It is
not necessary to make a formal asylum application, and it is the State's
duty to find out about the risk to which individuals are exposed by being
sent back.[144] In the words of Moreno-Lax, 'the State must undertake the
relevant investigation *proprio motu*'.[145] It is compulsory for the State to
declare where the individuals are being taken and to screen them in order
to identify their nationality and the risk to which they could be exposed.
Arguably, it can be inferred from the wording of the judgment that the
principle of non-refoulement entails the fulfilment of both these requirements by the State.[146] I have shown previously how similar safeguards are
ensured by the EU Asylum Procedures Directive and the Schengen
Handbook.[147] Regrettably, in the *Hirsi* judgment the ECtHR did not
clearly state the obligations of the Italian authorities after a vessel is
intercepted. It is clear from the ruling that the Italian authorities should
not have handed over the individuals to the Libyan authorities, but it is
not stated whether this means the Italian authorities should have given
the individuals access to an asylum procedure.[148]

In the *Hirsi* case, the ECtHR ruled for the first time on the extraterritorial application of Article 4 of Protocol No. 4 to the ECHR, which prohibits
the collective expulsion of aliens. The ECtHR had previously ruled on cases
in which alleged infringements of Article 4 of Protocol No. 4 to the ECHR
occurred in the territory of the State receiving the aliens.[149] In addition, the

---

[144] *Ibid.*, para 133.   [145] Moreno-Lax, '*Hirsi Jamaa and Others v Italy*', 583–584.

[146] Cfr. den Heijer, 'Reflections on *Refoulement* and Collective Expulsion in the *Hirsi* Case', 11.

[147] Chapter 5, Section 5.3.6.

[148] For a reading of the judgment according to which States have an obligation to ensure access to an asylum determination procedure, see M. Giuffré, 'Watered-Down Rights on the High Seas', 744–745.

[149] See, e.g. *Conka v. Belgium* App No. 51564/99 (ECtHR, 5 February 2002); *Dritsas v. Italy* App No. 2344/02 (ECtHR, 1 February 2011) and *Sharifi and Others v. Italy and France* App. No. 16643/09 (ECtHR, 21 October 2014). Also, see the Rule 39 *interim order* given to Malta by the ECtHR on 9 July 2013 to block the return of around 45 Somali migrants from Malta to Libya. The ECtHR gave Malta one month in which to individually assess the asylum applications of the migrants, www.maltatoday.com (accessed 13 November 2015). For a commentary on jurisprudence of the ECtHR on collective expulsions, see J. D. Howley, 'Unlocking the Fortress: Protocol No. 11 and the Birth of Collective Expulsion Jurisprudence in the Council of Europe System' (2006) 21 *Georgetown Immigration Law Journal* 117.

Xhavara and Others v. *Italy and Albania* case,[150] which was ruled on by the ECtHR, concerned the interception of Albanian nationals in Albanian waters by Italian authorities in order to prevent them reaching Italian territory. However, the ECtHR did not rule on the applicability of Article 4 of Protocol No. 4 to the ECHR on the ground of incompatibility *ratione personae*.

In the case of *Henning Becker* v. *Denmark*,[151] the collective expulsion of aliens was defined by the European Commission on Human Rights as follows: 'any measure of the competent authority compelling aliens as a group to leave the country, except where such a measure is taken after and on the basis of a reasonable and objective examination of the particular case of each individual alien of the group'.[152] Thus, according to the ECHR, the prohibition does not ban collective expulsion as such, but requires that any such measure must follow an examination of the particular circumstances of each individual in the group. The prohibition proscribes expulsions without procedural guarantees. In the *Conka* case, the ECtHR has clarified that where the above condition is satisfied, 'that does not mean that . . . the background to the execution of the expulsion orders plays no further role in determining whether there has been compliance with Article 4 of Protocol No. 4'.[153]

In the *Hirsi* case, it was not disputed that the Italian authorities did not provide any procedural guarantees to the intercepted individuals when embarking them on military vessels and disembarking them in Libyan territory.[154] However, it was disputed that Article 4 of Protocol No. 4 to the ECHR had extraterritorial application (i.e. that the provision was applicable on the high seas). The Italian government argued that Article 4 of Protocol No. 4 to the ECHR 'came into play only in the event of the expulsion of persons on the territory of a State or who has crossed the national border illegally'.[155] The Italian government maintained that the word 'expulsion' in Article 4 of Protocol No. 4 to the ECHR was an obstacle to the application of the provision outside the territory of the intercepting State.

The ECtHR decided as follows. First, it interpreted Article 4 of Protocol No. 4 to the ECHR according to the rules of interpretation of the VCLT. The ECtHR considered the ordinary meaning to be given to the terms in their context and in the light of the object and purpose of the

---

[150] *Xhavara.*
[151] *Henning Becker* v. *Denmark* App No. 7011/75 (ECtHR, 3 October 1975).
[152] *Ibid.*, para 235. [153] *Conka* v. *Belgium*, para 59. [154] *Hirsi*, para 185.
[155] *Ibid.*, para 160.

provision, and noted that Article 4 of Protocol No. 4 to the ECHR contains no reference to the word 'territory' so as to give the prohibition a territorial scope. The word 'territory' is present in Article 3 of the same Protocol and in Article 1 of Protocol 7.[156] However, in its analysis, the ECtHR did not mention the word 'expulsion'. Further, the ECtHR referred to the *travaux préparatoires* of the ECHR and noted that Article 4 of Protocol No. 4 to the ECHR does not only refer to individuals present within the territory of the receiving State.[157] Second, the ECtHR took an evolutive approach and sought a functional and teleological interpretation of Article 4 of Protocol No. 4 to the ECHR. It stated that the provision should be interpreted by looking at its purpose and meaning 'in the light of the present-day conditions' and 'in a manner which renders the guarantees practical and effective and not theoretical and illusory'.[158] In applying this approach the ECtHR stated:

> If, therefore, Article 4 of Protocol No. 4 were to apply only to collective expulsions from the national territory of the States Parties to the Convention, a significant component of contemporary migration patterns would not fall within the ambit of that provision, notwithstanding the fact that the conduct it is intended to prohibit can occur outside national territory and in particular, as in the instant case, on the high seas.[159]

Finally, the ECtHR ruled in favour of the extraterritorial application of Article 4 of Protocol No. 4 to the ECHR. Although the ECtHR interpreted Article 4 of Protocol No. 4 to the ECHR according to the rules of interpretation of the VCLT, it seems that it did not consider the word 'expulsion' in its interpretation. As pointed out above,[160] this word requires the presence of the individual within the territory of the country where asylum is sought and the intervention by the authority of the State forcing him or her to leave. 'Expulsion' refers to the territorial attachment prior to removal.[161] If it had considered the meaning of 'expulsion', the ECtHR would not have decided in favour of the extraterritorial application of Article 4 of Protocol No. 4 to the ECHR. Thus, it is not surprising that the evolutive approach together with the functional and teleological interpretation referred to above have greater prominence in the decision of the ECtHR. This approach, supported by the applicants in the case,[162]

---

[156] *Ibid.*, para 172.   [157] *Ibid.*, para 174.   [158] *Ibid.*, para 175.   [159] *Ibid.*, para 177.
[160] Section 6.2.1.1.
[161] Cfr. den Heijer, 'Reflections on *Refoulement* and Collective Expulsion in the *Hirsi* Case', 19.
[162] *Ibid.*, para 161.

makes it obligatory for States to provide procedural guarantees to examine the particular circumstances of the individuals in a group, both within and outside the national territory (i.e. where interception to combat irregular migration takes place). The ECtHR suggested that procedural guarantees should include trained personnel to conduct individual interviews, to assist with interpreting and to offer legal advice.[163]

In the *Hirsi* case, the Italian government argued that the interception of the individuals on the high seas took place in the context of a search-and-rescue-at-sea operation and not a maritime police operation. The Italian government maintained that, in this context, it was not obliged to respect ECHR rights and only had the obligation to assist vessels in distress, as required by the law of sea. The ECtHR dismissed the Italian government's argument and stated that human rights obligations under the ECHR cannot be circumvented by deeming an operation to be search and rescue at sea. This ruling is not surprising since the ECtHR had first stated in the *Medvedyev* case that 'the special nature of the maritime environment . . . cannot justify an area outside the law where ships' crews are covered by no legal system capable of affording them enjoyment of the rights and guarantees protected by the Convention'.[164] The main implication of this ruling concerns disembarkation in search-and-rescue-at-sea operations. Since the ECtHR found that ECHR obligations must be respected in search-and-rescue-at-sea operations, the rescuing State must ensure that disembarkation, which the law of sea requires to be in a place of safety, respects ECHR obligations. I will further analyse the legal regime governing search and rescue at sea in connection with the principle of non-refoulement in Chapter 7.

6.2.2.3   The International Covenant on Civil and Political Rights

Cognizant, now, of the extraterritorial scope affecting the application of non-refoulement, and mindful of the connected issue of personal jurisdiction under the ECHR, our investigation must explore the protection afforded by the principle of non-refoulement under the ICCPR. Article 2(1) ICCPR provides:

> Each State party to the present Covenant undertakes to respect and to ensure to all individuals *within its territory and subject to its jurisdiction* the rights recognized in the present Covenant.[165]

---

[163] *Ibid.*, para 185.   [164] *Medvedyev*, para 81.   [165] Emphasis added.

In order to investigate the extraterritorial application of the ICCPR, it is necessary to understand the meaning of 'within its territory and subject to its jurisdiction'. If we choose to pursue a literal interpretation of the provision, if the two elements are read conjunctively, individuals are protected under the ICCPR if they are *both* within the territory of a State *and* subject to its jurisdiction. Accordingly, individuals who are outside the territory of the State are not protected by the ICCPR. This is a literal interpretation of the provision which looks at the ordinary meaning of the terms.[166] However, the VCLT states that a treaty should be interpreted in good faith, not only in accordance with the ordinary meaning to be given to the terms of the treaty but also by looking at their context and in the light of the object and purpose of the treaty.[167] The 'context' comprises the text of the treaty, including its preamble and annexes, and any agreement or instrument made by the parties to the treaty in connection with the conclusion of the treaty,[168] including protocols.[169] The following derives, if this rule of interpretation is applied. First, it is stated in the preamble to the ICCPR that it is the object and purpose of the ICCPR to recognise inalienable rights of all members of the human family and to promote universal respect for those rights.[170] It would be contrary to the object and purpose of the ICCPR to maintain that these rights must be recognised and promoted only within the territory of a State, and not in situations whereby the State acts outside its territory. Second, Article 1 of the First Optional Protocol to the ICCPR requires individuals to be subject to a State's jurisdiction (but not also within the State's territory as in Article 2(1) ICCPR) in order to be protected under the ICCPR. 'Jurisdiction' must be interpreted in the light of the object and purpose of both the ICCPR and the Protocol.[171] Thus, the application of the rule of interpretation mentioned above leads to Article 2(1) ICCPR being read disjunctively. A State Party to the ICCPR must ensure the rights of all individuals who find themselves either within its territory or subject to its jurisdiction. Accordingly,

---

[166] For such interpretation of the provision, see Noll, 'Seeking Asylum at Embassies' 542, 557–564; Noll, *Negotiating Asylum*, 440.

[167] Article 31(1) VCLT.   [168] Article 31(2) VCLT.

[169] *Lithgow and Others v. the United Kingdom* (1981) Series A no 102, para 114.

[170] ICCPR preamble.

[171] See McGoldrik, 'Extraterritorial Application of the International Covenant on Civil and Political Rights', 48–49; V. Mantouvalou, 'Extending Judicial Control in International Law: Human Rights Treaties and Extraterritoriality' (2005) 9 *International Journal of Human Rights* 147, 155.

protection must also be given pursuant to the ICCPR when individuals find themselves outside the territory of the State.[172]

This was also the conclusion of the Human Rights Committee when it was called upon to decide on the issue. In *De Lopez* v. *Uruguay* the Human Rights Committee affirmed that the ICCPR also applies extraterritorially.[173] Notably, in terms which are relevant to our previous discussion, the Human Rights Committee did not link the accountability of a State for its acts abroad with a foreign State having given its consent. In addition, regarding Article 1 of the First Optional Protocol, the Human Rights Committee held that the reference to jurisdiction:

> is not the place where the violation has occurred, but rather *the relation-ship between the individual and the State* in relation to a violation of any of the rights set forth in the Covenant, wherever they occurred.[174]

The Human Rights Committee has given a very open interpretation of 'jurisdiction'. It applies the personal model of jurisdiction, since it refers to the control which a State exercises over individuals 'wherever they occur'. The 'relationship between the individual and the State' has subsequently been clarified by the ECtHR in the *Al-Skeini* case, analysed earlier in this chapter, which represented a step forward in respect to the case law on Article 1 ECHR.[175] Nevertheless, the interpretation of 'jurisdiction' in the *Al-Skeini* case is not as open as in *De Lopez*, since in *Al-Skeini* it is a requirement that the State should exercise some public powers normally exercised by the foreign government (although this requirement does seem to be mitigated by a later case law). In this respect, *De Lopez* lays down an easier threshold to meet for establishing jurisdiction. The content of the relationship between the individual and the State was clarified by the Human Rights Committee in a General Comment in 2004. In this General Comment, the Human Rights Committee reiterates its interpretation of 'jurisdiction' as amounting

---

[172] See likewise M. Nowak, *UN Covenant on Civil and Political Rights. CCPR Commentary* (Engel, 2005), para 29; S. Joseph and M. Castan, *The International Covenant on Civil and Political Rights: Cases, Material and Commentary* (Oxford University Press, 2013), 96–100.

[173] Human Rights Committee, *De Lopez* v. *Uruguay*, Communication No. 52/1979, UN doc. CCPR/C/13/D/52/1979, para 12.3. See also *Celiberti de Casariego* v. *Uruguay*, Communication No. 56/1979, UN doc. CCPR/C/13/D/56/1979, para 10.3. The same position was later adopted by the International Court of Justice in *Legal Consequences of the Construction of a Wall in the Occupied Palestinian Territory* (Advisory Opinion), ICJ Reports 2004, paras 108–111.

[174] *De Lopez* v. *Uruguay*, para 12.2, emphasis added.   [175] See Section 6.2.2.2.1.

to control over individuals.[176] However, the Human Rights Committee has also identified jurisdiction as control over territory or detention facilities.[177]

Thus, the interpretation of Article 2(1) ICCPR and an analysis of the decisions of the Human Rights Committee show that the ICCPR applies extraterritorially. This extraterritorial application is supported by an open interpretation of Article 2(1) ICCPR, based on a relationship between the individual and the State. The personal model of jurisdiction is endorsed. In terms of Frontex's coordinated activities, and our examples of Joint Operation Hermes, Joint Operation Hera and possible land border operations in third countries, the case law of the Human Rights Committee is not sufficiently detailed to allow an analysis of the different aspects which I have examined in relation to the ECHR. However, it is possible to say that, in all these examples, the jurisdiction of States is established on the basis of effective control over individuals.

6.2.2.3.1 Non-Refoulement under the ICCPR   There have been multiple instances in which the Human Rights Committee has dealt with the particular issue of the extraterritorial application of the principle of non-refoulement under the ICCPR. At first, in 2004, the Human Rights Committee affirmed that the ICCPR provides protection against refoulement pursuant to Articles 2, 6 and 7 ICCPR. However, it is not clear whether Article 7 ICCPR applies only within the territory of the State or also outside its territory.[178] The Human Rights Committee clarified the issue in a subsequent concluding observation and ruling. In its Concluding Observations on the United States of America's Report,[179] the Human Rights Committee clarified that detention outside US territory entails an obligation for the United States not to return an individual to a country where he or she can be at risk.[180]

---

[176] General Comment No. 31 [80], 'Nature of the General Legal Obligation Imposed on State Parties to the Covenant', 26 May 2004, CCPR/C/21/Rev.1/Add.13, para 10.

[177] Human Rights Committee, Concluding Observations on Israel, 18 August 1998, UN doc. CCPR/C/79/Add.93, para 10; Human Rights Committee, Concluding Observations on Israel, 21 August 2003, UN doc. CCPR/CO/78/ISR, para 11; Human Rights Committee, Concluding Observations on Croatia, 28 December 1992, UN doc. CCPR/C/79/Add.15, para 9.

[178] Human Rights Committee, General Comment No. 31 (2004), para 12.

[179] Human Rights Committee, Concluding Observations on the United States of America, 18 December 2006, UN doc. CCPR/C/USA/CO/3/Rev.1.

[180] *Ibid.*, para 16.

In another instance, the Human Rights Committee had the opportunity to make clear its view on the extraterritorial application of non-refoulement in the individual petition of *Arshdin Israil* v. *Pakistan*.[181] The petitioner was a Chinese national of Uighur origin who fled China fearing persecution by the Chinese authorities because he had cooperated with foreign media in shedding light on the killing of Uighur people. Once in Pakistan, he was detained and his asylum application was refused. He claimed there was a breach of Articles 2(3) and 9(1) ICCPR. The Human Rights Committee also found that the case raised issues under Articles 6 and 7 ICCPR. The issues arising from this latter setting are of most interest to this book. The case did not directly concern the extraterritorial application of non-refoulement, but the Human Rights Committee took a general view before analysing the specific issues in the case. The Committee seemed to place an emphasis on where the individual is taken.[182] Additionally, the Committee did not construe the application of the principle of non-refoulement as being exclusively territorial: it was held to refer to removal from jurisdiction, not from territory.[183]

The Human Rights Committee has also given its view on whether the principle of non-refoulement under Articles 6 and 7 ICCPR also applies when an individual seeking protection has not crossed an international border. The Committee expressed its view in the individual petition of *Mohammad Munaf* v. *Romania*.[184] The petition concerned a person with dual Iraqi and American nationality who had been handed over by the Romanian Embassy in Baghdad to the multinational force in Iraq. The petitioner was subsequently sentenced to death. He claimed that Romania infringed Articles 6 and 7 ICCPR, among others. Although the Human Rights Committee considered that Romania could not have known that by leaving its embassy the petitioner ran a risk of his rights under the ICCPR being breached,[185] it recognised that Romania had jurisdiction in the case. In other words, 'by allowing the author [of the petition] to leave the premises of the Romanian Embassy in Baghdad, [Romania] exercises jurisdiction over him in a way that exposed him to a real risk of becoming a victim of violations of his rights under Articles 6

---

[181] *Arshdin Israil* v. *Pakistan*, Communication No. 2024/2011, UN doc. CCPR/C/103/D/ 2024/2011.

[182] *Ibid.*, para 9.4.   [183] *Ibid.*, para 9.6.

[184] *Mohammad Munaf* v. *Romania*, Communication No. 1539/2006, UN doc. CCPR/C/96/ D/1539/2006.

[185] *Ibid.*, para 14.5.

and 7'.[186] Here, the Committee took the same view as the ECtHR with regard to Article 3 ECHR in the *Al-Saadoon* case,[187] differing from the interpretation generally given to Article 33 of the 1951 Refugee Convention,[188] that protection against refoulement requires asylum seekers to have left their country of nationality or habitual residence and to find themselves in a third country having crossed an international border.

The conclusion prompted by this legal sequence, then, is that the principle of non-refoulement under Articles 6 and 7 ICCPR applies extraterritorially.[189] There is no requirement for an individual to have crossed an international border for protection under this provision to apply.

6.2.2.4   Convention against Torture

Our analysis of the extraterritorial application of the principle of non-refoulement under international human rights law will conclude with an examination of the CAT. There is no single provision in the CAT which determines the *ratione loci* application of the Convention. Instead, there are distinct provisions in which a State is obliged to prevent acts of torture 'in any territory under its jurisdiction'.[190] In particular, Article 2(1) CAT states:

> Each State Party shall take effective legislative, administrative, judicial or other measures to prevent acts of torture *in any territory under its jurisdiction.*

Relative to the jurisdictional clauses studied prior to this – Article 1 ECHR and Article 2(1) ICCPR – Article 2(1) CAT has the clearest link between jurisdiction and territory.[191] This provision has been interpreted by the Committee against Torture in General Comment No. 2.[192] The Committee recognises the extraterritorial application of the CAT

---

[186] *Ibid.*, para 14.2.   [187] See the analysis of the *Al-Saadoon* case in Section 6.2.2.2.3.

[188] See Section 6.2.2.

[189] See likewise Gammeltoft-Hansen, *Access to Asylum*, 84–85; M. den Heijer, *Europe and Extraterritorial Asylum* (Hart Publishing, 2012), 136–141; V. Moreno-Lax, '(Extraterritorial) Entry Controls and (Extraterritorial) Non-refoulement in EU Law' in M. C. Foblets and P. De Bruycker (eds.), *The External Dimension(s) of EU Asylum and Immigration Policy* (Bruylant, 2011), 416–418.

[190] Articles 2(1), 5(1)(a), 5(2), 7(1), 11, 12, 13 and 16 CAT. See Nowak and McArthur, *The United Nations Convention against Torture* (Oxford University Press, 2008).

[191] Milanovic, *Extraterritorial Application of Human Right Treaties*, 33.

[192] Committee against Torture, General Comment No. 2, UN Doc. CAT/C/GC/2, 24 January 2008.

and applies the 'effective control' doctrine.[193] This renders it necessary to fathom precisely what is meant by 'control'. The Committee in its General Comment refers to individuals kept in a place of detention, but does not go so far as to say that 'jurisdiction' also amounts to control over individuals.[194] This would be contrary to the text of Article 2(1) CAT where the reference to the territory is clear. As such, an analysis of Article 2(1) CAT promotes a conclusion that it applies extraterritorially.[195] My recent conclusions regarding the ICCPR and its bearing on joint operations coordinated by Frontex outside the territory of the EU also apply to the CAT. However, in this case it is necessary to point out that the model of jurisdiction applied seems to be spatial rather than personal.

6.2.2.4.1 Non-Refoulement under the CAT The question now is whether Article 2(1) CAT affects the principle of non-refoulement as enshrined in Article 3 CAT. If we establish that Article 2(1) does affect the principle of non-refoulement in Article 3 CAT, that principle will have extraterritorial application. Two solutions to this question are proposed. The first solution relies on the literal meaning of the terms of these two provisions. Article 2(1) CAT obliges a State to prevent acts of torture in any territory under its jurisdiction. Article 3 CAT obliges a State not to return a person to another State where he or she would be in danger of being subjected to torture.[196] On this point, Wouters affirms that Article 2(1) CAT 'contains a general obligation on State parties to take all measures possible to prevent the occurrence of acts of torture in any territory under their jurisdiction'.[197] However, he states that Article 3 CAT 'is not meant to prevent acts of torture in the territory of a State party, but to prevent an individual from being subjected to torture after being expelled or returned by a State party to another State'.[198] Therefore, according to this first solution, the effect of Article 2(1) CAT on the principle of non-refoulement as enshrined in Article 3 CAT is excluded.

A second solution examines the concept of 'jurisdiction' which informs the CAT in its entirety (i.e. the actual control exercised by

---

[193] *Ibid.*, para 16. [194] Committee against Torture, General Comment No. 2, para. 16.
[195] See A. Boulesbaa, 'The Nature of the Obligations Incurred by States under Article 2 of the UN Convention against Torture' (1990) 12 *Human Rights Quarterly* 53, 80–82.
[196] Article 3 CAT states: 'No State Party shall expel, return ("refouler") or extradite a person to another State where there are substantial grounds for believing that he would be in danger of being subjected to torture.'
[197] Wouters, *International Legal Standards for the Protection from Refoulement*, 438.
[198] *Ibid.*.

a State outside its territory corresponds to its jurisdiction and triggers its responsibility). Accordingly, this concept of 'jurisdiction' applies to both Articles 2 and 3 (and every other article of the CAT). Both the preceding analysis of the meaning of 'jurisdiction' in human rights law and what is stated by the Committee against Torture in its General Comment No. 2 confirm this argument.[199] Although the former solution has regard for the ordinary meaning of the provisions, treaties must also be interpreted by looking at their context and purpose. In the light of this, the latter solution has to be preferred. Moreover, it has also been embraced by the Committee against Torture in the *Marine I* case.[200]

This particular case concerned a complaint by a Spanish citizen acting on behalf of 23 individuals of African and Asian origin whose vessel capsized on the high seas. When this occurred, there were 346 other migrants on board. The vessel was rescued by a Spanish military rescue tug and taken to the Mauritanian coast. Under an agreement between the Spanish and Mauritanian authorities, the migrants were allowed to dis-embark in Mauritania, and the individuals were screened. After screen-ing, part of the group was transferred to Guinea. Overall, the migrants either applied for asylum or were voluntarily repatriated. The alleged victims' asylum applications stated that they had left India due to fear of persecution as a result of the conflict in Kashmir. They refused voluntary repatriation and remained in detention under Spanish control in Mauritania. After beginning a hunger strike to protest about the poor detention conditions, they accepted the offer extended by the Spanish authorities to be transferred to other countries. At the time of their applications, they were still in detention. The complainant argued that Spain had acted in breach of several articles of the CAT, including Article 3, because if they were returned to India the alleged victims could be subject to torture. Although the Committee against Torture decided that the complainant lacked *locus standi*, it looked at the interpretation of 'jurisdiction' in relation to Article 2 CAT and other provisions.

In line with the second preferred solution outlined above, the Committee against Torture looked at the concept of 'jurisdiction' in relation to Article 2 CAT when there is an alleged breach of Article 3 CAT. Thus, the question of whether Article 2(1) CAT has an effect on the principle of non-refoulement as enshrined in Article 3 CAT is answered

[199] See Section 6.2.2.1.
[200] *J.H.A.* v. *Spain*. For commentary, Wouters and den Heijer, 'The *Marine I* Case: a Comment', 1.

in the affirmative. Furthermore, the Committee against Torture applied the 'actual control' doctrine to all provisions of the CAT. The Committee against Torture ruled that the personal model of jurisdiction applies to control over individuals in detention. Yet, importantly, the Committee against Torture also stated that the Spanish authorities 'maintained control over the persons on board the *Marine I* from the time the vessel was rescued and throughout the identification and repatriation process'.[201] This means that the criterion of control is not solely related to individuals in detention but it appears to be applicable in other situations (i.e. individuals on a rescued vessel taken to a place of safety).[202]

Finally, with regard to the extraterritorial application of the principle of non-refoulement, Article 3 CAT prevents a person being returned 'to another State'. Does the prevention of return 'to another State' only protect individuals who have crossed an international border? Can an individual be protected if he or she is in the State from which the threat derives? A literal reading of Article 3 CAT gives a negative answer to this question since 'return to another State' cannot be interpreted as return to the territory of the State in which the individual seeking protection finds oneself. However, it may be possible to consider a teleological interpretation of Article 3 CAT and point out that the CAT is intended to provide protection against torture.[203] For this reason, the interpretation of Article 3 CAT should depart from the literal meaning of 'to another State' and allow protection to be provided also when an individual has not crossed an international border.[204] The Committee against Torture dealt with this issue in its Conclusions and Recommendations on the periodic report of the United Kingdom on the measures taken to give effect to its undertakings under the CAT, as required by Article 19 CAT to all parties to the Convention. In its report, the United Kingdom stated that the CAT had limited application to the actions of the United Kingdom abroad and, in particular, that the CAT was not applicable to the actions of the United Kingdom in Afghanistan and Iraq. In this respect, the Committee against Torture stated as follows: first, it observed that the

---

[201] *J.H.A.* v. *Spain*, para 8.2. See also Committee against Torture, Concluding Observations on the United States of America, 26 July 2006, UN doc. CAT/C/USA/CO/2, para 20, emphasis added. See on this point, Wouters and den Heijer, 'The Marine I Case: a Comment', 9.

[202] See also Committee against Torture, *Sonko* v. *Spain*, Communication No. 368/2008, UN doc. CAT/C/47/D/368/2008, para 10.3.

[203] See the teleological interpretation by the ECtHR of Article 4 of Protocol No. 4 to the ECHR, Section 6.2.2.2.4.

[204] den Heijer, *Europe and Extraterritorial Asylum*, 135.

CAT applies to all territories where a State exercises effective control; second, with a focus on the principle of non-refoulement, the Committee against Torture recommended that Article 3 CAT should apply when a State transfers a detainee who is within a State's custody to the *de facto* or *de jure* custody of any other State.[205] The implication of this recommendation is that Article 3 CAT applies when an individual is transferred from the authorities of one State to the authorities of another State within the same territory. In other words, according to the Committee against Torture, an individual receives protection under Article 3 CAT even though he or she has not crossed an international border.[206]

6.2.2.5   Extraterritorial Application of the 1951 Refugee Convention

This section examines whether Article 33 of the 1951 Refugee Convention applies extraterritorially. A direct examination of the extra-territorial application of Article 33 of the 1951 Refugee Convention is necessary, since the Convention lacks a general provision concerning its *ratione loci* application, which renders it different to the other international treaties examined until now.

6.2.2.5.1 Methodological Considerations   As noted,[207] Article 31 VCLT states that a treaty should be interpreted in good faith in accordance with the ordinary meaning to be given to the terms of the treaty in their context and in the light of its object and purpose. If the meaning of a norm is clear when this rule of interpretation is applied, no further investigation is needed. However, Article 32 VCLT states that supplementary means of interpretation may be used to confirm the meaning of a norm resulting from the application of the rule of interpretation in Article 31 or to determine the meaning when interpretation pursuant to Article 31 leaves the meaning ambiguous or obscure or leads to a result which is manifestly absurd or unreasonable.[208] With these two provisions in mind, we now move to some methodological considerations.

---

[205] Committee against Torture, Conclusions and Recommendations: United Kingdom of Great Britain and Northern Ireland, 10 December 2004, CAT/C/CR/33/3, para 5(e).
[206] See also Nowak and McArthur, *The United Nations Convention Against Torture*, 199.
[207] Section 6.2.1.1.
[208] On the use of supplementary means of interpretation pursuant to Article 32 VCLT see Dörr and Schmalenbach, *Vienna Convention on the Law of Treaties: A Commentary*, 571.

The matter of the extraterritorial application of the principle of non-refoulement has been explored by Lauterpacht and Bethlehem.[209] The authors use the analogy of ICCPR and the ECHR to interpret the meaning of 'jurisdiction' in Article 33 of the 1951 Refugee Convention. Focusing their analysis on the case law of the Human Rights Committee and the ECtHR, they affirm that 'the reasoning in these cases support the more general proposition that persons will come within the jurisdiction of a State in circumstances in which they can be said to be under the effective control of that State'.[210] They use the analogy of the ICCPR and the ECHR in order to affirm the extraterritorial application of Article 33 of the 1951 Refugee Convention.[211] Similarly, Hathaway reflects on the fact that there are rights of the 1951 Refugee Convention not subject to a territorial or other level of attachment, including the principle of non-refoulement.[212] He suggests that 'in line with the views of both the European Court of Human Rights and the International Court of Justice, the duty to respect these rights inheres wherever a state exercises effective or de facto jurisdiction outside its own territory'.[213]

This approach has been criticised by Noll,[214] who has pointed out that, according to the VCLT, interpretation of a norm of a treaty requires in the first instance respect for the general rule of interpretation before turning to the supplementary means of interpretation.[215] Noll has observed that, according to Article 32 of the Vienna Convention, the *ratione loci* limitation of the ECHR and the ICCPR can only be used to determine the meaning when the primary interpretation leaves the meaning ambiguous or obscure or leads to a result which is manifestly absurd or unreasonable.[216] Noll's criticisms of the interpretations proffered by Lauterpacht and Bethlehem, and also those of Hathaway, must be shared since it is a position which respects the rule of interpretation of the VCLT. Accordingly, in my analysis (in contrast to the approach of

---

[209] Lauterpacht and Bethlehem, 'The Scope and Content of the Principle of Non-refoulement: Opinion'.

[210] *Ibid.*, para 67.   [211] *Ibid.*, paras 62–67.

[212] Hathaway, *The Rights of Refugees under International Law*, 339. On the structure of entitlement of the 1951 Refugee Convention, see Chapter 5, Section 5.3.5.1.

[213] Hathaway, *The Rights of Refugees under International Law*, 339. The same argument has been proferred by Hathaway together with Michelle Foster in *The Law of Refugee Status* (Cambridge University Press, 2014) and developed by Michelle Foster in her *International Refugee Law and Socio-Economic Rights: Refuge from Deprivation* (Cambridge University Press, 2007) in relation to socio-economic rights and the meaning of persecution.

[214] Noll, 'Seeking Asylum at Embassies', 542.   [215] *Ibid.*, 551.   [216] *Ibid.*, 552.

Lauterpacht and Bethlehem, and the approach of Hathaway), I look first at the wording, context and purpose of Article 33 of the Refugee Convention to interpret the norm. This interpretative exercise builds on the one I have already conducted in Section 6.2.1.1 concerning the application of Article 33 of 1951 Refugee Convention within the territory and at the borders. I use the meaning of 'jurisdiction' in the ICCPR and the ECHR as a supplementary means of interpretation pursuant to Article 32 VCLT. This is possible since the ICCPR and the ECHR are treaties *in pari materia* with the 1951 Refugee Convention as far as the prohibition of non-refoulement is concerned.[217] In the words of Linderfalk, 'by a treaty *in pari materia* we are to understand an instrument, the subject matter of which is identical – at least partly – with the subject matter covered by the treaty interpreted'.[218]

This approach may presuppose that there is an approximation of the concept of 'jurisdiction' in international human rights law (i.e. that 'jurisdiction' in the ECHR and the ICCPR must be treated similarly).[219] Such a solution has also been criticised by Noll. He is against setting a 'standard *ratione loci* delimitation of human rights treaties' since there are significant differences in the way each of the jurisdictional clauses of the human rights treaties is formulated.[220] Accordingly, Noll concludes: 'it is not correct to state that human rights treaty law is applicable *ratione*

---

[217] See likewise Noll, 'Seeking Asylum at Embassies', 552, note 39; Gammeltoft-Hansen, *Access to Asylum*, 91–92. On the legitimacy to use treaties *in pari materia* as a means of interpretation pursuant to Article 32 VCLT, see G. Haraszti, *Some Fundamental Problems of the Law of Treaties* (Akademiai Kiado Budapest, 1973), 148; I. A. Shearer, *Starke's International Law* (Butterworths, 1994), 438; F. Berman, 'Treaty Interpretation in a Judicial Context' (2004) 29 *Yale Journal of International Law* 315, 317; U. Linderfalk, *On the Interpretation of Treaties: The Modern International Law as Expressed in the 1969 Vienna Convention on the Law of Treaties* (Springer, 2007), 255–259.

[218] Linderfalk, *On the Interpretation of Treaties*, 255. As already indicated by Noll ('Seeking Asylum at Embassies', note 39), it is excluded that the ICCPR and the ECHR in connection with Article 31(1)(c), general rule of interpretation of the VCLT, can be used to establish the context for the purpose of the interpretation of Article 33 of the 1951 Refugee Convention since the signatory States to the 1951 Refugee Convention are not necessarily parties to the ICCPR and the ECHR: 'The context for the purpose of the interpretation of a treaty shall comprise ... (c) Any relevant rules of international law applicable in the relations *between the parties*' (emphasis added). See likewise N. Nathwani, *Rethinking Refugee Law* (Martinus Nijhoff, 2003), 76–77; Linderfalk, *On the Interpretation of Treaties*, 258–259; Dörr and Schmalenbach, *Vienna Convention on the Law of Treaties: A Commentary*, 566. *Contra*, M. Foster, *International Refugee Law and Socio-Economic Rights*, 75–76.

[219] On an 'integrated approach within human rights law', see den Heijer, *Europe and Extraterritorial Asylum*, 52.

[220] See den Heijer, *Europe and Extraterritorial Asylum*, 52.

loci wherever the jurisdiction of a state extends'.[221] In Noll's opinion, the jurisdictional clauses in the ICCPR and the ECHR are formulated differently and express different levels of attachment to territory, as explained above.[222] Nevertheless, an interpretation of relevant wording which takes into consideration the context and purpose of the provision, and the whole of each human rights treaty, as practiced in this chapter's analysis, leads to the conclusion that wherever a State exercises effective control, 'jurisdiction' is established and responsibility can be assessed.[223]

6.2.2.5.2 Application of Methodological Considerations

Earlier, Section 6.2.1.1 argued that pursuant to Article 31 VCLT, Article 33 of the 1951 Refugee Convention clearly applies within the territory and at the borders of the asylum State. Yet our analytical work must continue here, since this interpretation leaves the meaning ambiguous as to the application of Article 33 of the 1951 Refugee Convention beyond the borders. The interpretation of the ordinary meaning of the word 'return' in Article 33, along with the context, objective and purpose of the Convention, shows inconclusively that the presence of the individual within the territory of the country of asylum is not required for the provision to apply. Such a reading would mean that a State is responsible for a breach of the principle of non-refoulement if it apprehends a refugee outside its territory and returns him or her to a territory where the refugee could be at risk. In order to determine the meaning of Article 33 in this respect, recourse to the supplementary means of interpretation pursuant to Article 32 VCLT is necessary.

International human rights law will be used here as a supplementary means of interpretation. As noted previously, in human rights treaties 'jurisdiction' concerns the control that a State has over places or individuals. This has been confirmed by the jurisprudence of the ECtHR, the Human Rights Committee and the Committee against Torture in the judgments and decisions analysed above. A State exercises jurisdiction wherever its control is exercised, including outside its territory. Therefore, interpretation which uses human rights as a supplementary means of interpretation determines that Article 33 of the 1951 Refugee Convention applies when refoulement takes place outside the territory of a State.

---

[221] See *ibid.*   [222] Section 6.2.2.1.
[223] See Goodwin-Gill and McAdam, *The Refugee in International Law*, 248; Hathaway, *The Rights of Refugees under International Law*, 161; Cfr. Gammeltoft-Hansen, *Access to Asylum*, 82.

This methodological approach was used by the United Nations High Commissioner for Refugees (UNHCR) in its *amicus curiae* brief in the *Sale* case before the US Supreme Court.[224] While looking at the ordinary meaning of the terms of Article 33 of the 1951 Refugee Convention, the *amicus curiae* brief pointed out that, according to the VCLT, the 1951 Refugee Convention must be interpreted consistently with international law.[225] In this respect, the UNHCR referred first to the principle of non-refoulement without territorial limitation as customary international law.[226] Second, it referred to international human rights law which prohibits breaches of human rights by States acting outside their territory.[227] It referred to the jurisprudence of the Human Rights Committee and the European Commission on Human Rights establishing that there is 'jurisdiction' where a State exercises control, even in the territory of another State.[228] The UNHCR concluded that 'Article 33 is available wherever needed, and, thus, that Article 33 governs the behaviour of contracting States wherever they may act'.[229]

Further, in the *Sale* case, the majority of the US Supreme Court denied the extraterritorial application of Article 33 of the 1951 Refugee Convention.[230] Justice Blackmun dissented.[231] What was being examined was the practice of the US government of intercepting people on the high seas (i.e. outside US territory) and returning them, without screening, directly to Haiti, where they might be at risk of persecution. Although the US Supreme Court upheld the practice of interception and return mainly on the basis of national law, it also considered international law, in particular the protection afforded by Article 33 of the 1951 Refugee Convention. The Court interpreted the term 'return' as 'a defensive act of resistance or exclusion at a border rather than an act of transporting someone to a particular destination'.[232] Interpretation of Article 33 pursuant to Articles 31 and 33 VCLT clarified that the presence of the individual within the territory of the country is not required. The same was held by Justice Blackmun in his dissenting opinion.[233] Justice Blackmun also added:

[224] UNHCR, 'The Haitian Interdiction Case 1993 Brief Amicus Curiae' (1994) 6 *International Journal of Refugee Law* 85.
[225] *Ibid.*, 94.   [226] *Ibid.*   [227] *Ibid.*, 96.   [228] *Ibid.*   [229] *Ibid.*, 97.
[230] *Sale* v. *Haitian Centers Council*, 509 US 155 (1993).
[231] For an account of the facts and the law of the case with respect to the application of the principle of non-refoulement at the borders, see Section 6.2.1.1.
[232] *Sale*, para 182. See *contra*, Wouters, *International Legal Standards for the Protection from Refoulement*, 55.
[233] *Sale* v. *Haitian Centers Council*, 509 US 155 (1993), para 191.

Article 33 is clear not only in what it says, but also in what it does not say: it does not include any geographical limitation. It limits only where a refugee may be sent 'to', not where he may be sent from. This is not surprising, given that the aim of the provision is to protect refugees against persecution.[234]

In the Court's interpretation of Article 33(1) of the 1951 Refugee Convention, the majority in *Sale* construed Article 33(2) as an argument against the extraterritorial application of Article 33(1). Article 33(2) states:

The benefit of the present provision may not, however, be claimed by a refugee whom there are reasonable grounds for regarding as a danger to the security of the country in which he is, or who, having been convicted by a final judgment of a particularly serious crime, constitutes a danger to the community of that country.

The argument of the majority in *Sale* can be rendered as follows: if Article 33(1) were applicable outside the territory of the State, Article 33(2) could not be invoked since it requires that the refugee finds himself or herself within the State. The extraterritorial application of Article 33(1) would give dangerous refugees outside the territory of a State a benefit which dangerous refugees within the State would not have. Therefore, Article 33(1) should only apply to those refugees who are within the State.[235] The case concerned the application of Article 33(1) on the high seas rather than 'within the territory'. The dissenting opinion of Justice Blackmun expressed the counterargument that the decision of the signatories to the 1951 Refugee Convention to permit the deportation of dangerous refugees from within the territory of the State cannot be construed as being intended to allow the apprehension and return of non-dangerous refugees outside the territory of the State. The fact that a State can return dangerous refugees from within its territory but cannot return refugees who are outside its territory expresses the rationale of the 1951 Refugee Convention.[236] This latter argument takes into account the context, object and purpose of the 1951 Refugee Convention and must be endorsed. The absence of a territorial limitation in Article 33 of the 1951 Refugee Convention was affirmed by the Inter-American Commission on Human Rights, which heard the case and found the United States to be in breach of the principle of non-refoulement.[237]

---

[234] *Ibid.*, para 193.   [235] *Sale*, paras 179–180.   [236] *Ibid.*, paras 193–194.
[237] Inter-American Commission on Human Rights, *Haitian Centre for Human Rights v. United States of America*, Decision of the Commission as to the Merits of the Case 10–675, 13 March 1997, para 157.

As for the application of the principle of non-refoulement on the high seas, in the *Hirsi* case of 2012, the ECtHR ruled in favour of applying Article 3 ECHR to the high seas.[238] This is relevant to the present analysis of Article 33 of the 1951 Refugee Convention since, as stated above, the meaning of such a provision must be confirmed by using international human rights instruments.

The *European Roma Rights Centre* case, heard before the United Kingdom House of Lords, concerned the pre-clearance procedures of the British authorities at Prague Airport. Under these procedures, six Czech nationals of Roma origin, who were asylum seekers, were not allowed to leave the Czech Republic to enter the United Kingdom.[239] The House of Lords did not accept the application of Article 33 of the 1951 Refugee Convention to the case since the individuals interviewed at Prague Airport did not cross an international border, which is a requirement for the applicability of the norm. The House of Lords limited itself to examining the facts of the case, without engaging in a broader analysis of whether Article 33 of the 1951 Refugee Convention applies extraterritorially. In other words, the decision would have been different if the individuals screened under the pre-clearance procedures had crossed an international border to reach Prague Airport.

6.3   A Matter of EU Law

This section deals with the protection provided under EU law for violations of the principle of non-refoulement occurring at and beyond the EU borders. Here, our analysis must be framed by a further question: If Frontex or a Member State were to breach the principle of non-refoulement on the high seas in the context of a Frontex joint operation would such breach constitute an infringement of EU law?

The territorial application of EU law must be examined if we are then to succeed in investigating the territorial application of the principle of non-refoulement in the Charter of Fundamental Rights (EU Charter or Charter),[240] Articles 18 and 19(1) and the general principles of EU law.[241]

---

[238] See Section 6.2.2.2.4.
[239] For an account of the facts and the law of the case, see Section 6.2.1.1.
[240] Charter of Fundamental Rights of the European Union OJ 2010 No. C83, p. 1.
[241] On the extraterritorial application of the Charter in general, see V. Moreno-Lax and C. Costello, 'The Extraterritorial Application of the EU Charter of Fundamental Rights: From Territoriality to Facticity, the Effectiveness Model' in S. Peers, T. Hervey and Others (eds.), *The EU Charter of Fundamental Rights: A Commentary* (Hart/Beck, 2014).

There are two provisions in the TEU and in the Treaty on the Functioning of the European Union (TFEU) which deal with the territorial application of EU law. Article 52 TEU lists the territories of the Member States and affirms that EU law finds application in these territories. Article 355 TFEU, to which Article 52 TEU refers, includes further provisions on overseas countries and territories as well as territories with which Member States have special ties.[242] Accordingly, Articles 18 and 19(1) of the EU Charter and the principles of EU law, including the prohibition of refoulement, have effect within the territories of the Member States and at their borders.

The question is now whether EU law has effect extraterritorially (i.e. whether EU law applies outside the territories of the EU Member States). Should I find in favour of the extraterritorial application of EU law, the EU Charter and the general principles of EU law would apply accordingly.

The condition under which EU law applies extraterritorially is stated by the Court of Justice of the European Union (CJEU) in the case *Boukhalfa v. Germany*, which builds on previous case law on the freedom of movement of EU citizens.[243] The CJEU interpreted Article 227 EC (now Article 355 TFEU) as part of its adjudication in *Boukhalfa*. The case concerned the employment relationship of Ms Boukhalfa, a Belgian national who resided permanently in Algiers and was employed at the German Embassy in Algiers. The CJEU was asked whether the prohibition of discrimination based on nationality, stated both in primary and EU secondary law (regulations), applied in the case of Ms Boukhalfa, who was employed on the local staff of the German Embassy in Algiers under a contract subject to Algerian law. Germany refused to give Ms Boukhalfa the same treatment as local staff who were German nationals. The CJEU had to deal initially with the issue of the *ratione loci* application of EU law in order to see whether the prohibition of discrimination in EU law applies extraterritorially. After affirming the primarily territorial application of EU law derived from the Treaties and secondary legislation,[244] the CJEU referred to Article 227 TEC (now Article 355 TFEU) saying: 'that article does not, however, preclude Community rules from *having effects*

---

[242] See Case C-214/94 *Ingrid Boukhalfa v. Federal Republic of Germany* [1996] ECR I-2253; [1996] 3 CMLR 22, para 14: 'The geographical application of the Treaty is defined in Article 227' (now Article 355 TFEU).

[243] Among the previous cases, see Case 237/83 *SARL Prodest v. Caisse Primaire d'Assurance Maladie de Paris* [1984]ECR 3153, para 6; Case 9/88 *Mário Lopes da Veiga v. Staatssecretaris van Justitie* [1989]ECR 2989; [1991] 1 CMLR 217, para 15–16.

[244] *Boukhalfa*, para 13.

outside the territory of the Community ... as long as the employment relationship retains a sufficiently close link with the Community.[245] The CJEU has specified this 'sufficiently close link': it must be 'between the employment relationship, on the one hand, and the law of a Member State and thus the relevant rules of Community law, on the other'.[246] The CJEU found in favour of the extraterritorial application of EU law under this condition. Accordingly, it is possible to conclude that the EU Charter, including its Articles 18 and 19(1), and the general principle of EU law can apply outside the territory of the EU. However, it will be necessary to examine the existence of this condition on a case-by-case basis in respect of the legislation under examination.[247] If so, the EU Charter and the general principle of EU law will also apply. Notably, though, neither the concept of jurisdiction in general international law nor the one in international human rights law, analysed above, is sufficient to illustrate how EU law applies extraterritorially. As expressed by Moreno-Lax and Costello, the EU legal system poses 'autonomous requirements' to the *ratione loci* applicability of EU law and 'fundamental rights apply as a matter of EU constitutional obligation ... without any additional IHRL [international human rights law] jurisdictional criteria to be met'.[248]

There are two further arguments in favour of the extraterritorial application specifically of the EU Charter. First, Article 51 of the EU Charter, which establishes its area of application, does not impose any limitation on its geographical scope, as long as the EU respects international law in the exercise of its powers. Thus, it may be possible to maintain that the EU Charter has extraterritorial application and that the Member States, when they are implementing EU law, must respect it whenever they act.[249] Second, Article 52(3) of the EU Charter states that when one Charter right corresponds to a right guaranteed by the ECHR, the EU Charter right has the same meaning and the *same scope* as the right laid down in the ECHR. The protection provided by the ECHR is a minimum standard and the EU can provide greater protection. This is the case with Article 19(1) of the EU Charter which corresponds to

---

[245] *Ibid.*, para 14, emphasis added.   [246] *Ibid.*, para 15.

[247] See Moreno Lax, '(Extraterritorial) Entry Controls and (Extraterritorial) Non-refoulement in EU Law', 443; den Heijer, *Europe and Extraterritorial Asylum*, 193.

[248] Moreno-Lax and Costello, 'The Extraterritorial Application of the EU Charter of Fundamental Rights', 1660 and 1678.

[249] See likewise Moreno-Lax and Costello, 'The Extraterritorial Application of the EU Charter of Fundamental Rights', 1658.

Article 3 ECHR.[250] It is possible to maintain that the above scope also includes, as a minimum, the application *ratione loci* of the ECHR found by the ECtHR under Article 1 ECHR.[251] However, as we have noted, this argument must be qualified to the extent that not all features of international human rights law, including the concept of 'effective control' to establish jurisdiction, can be used in order to determine the applicability of the EU Charter.[252]

6.4 Conclusions

Our examination of the *ratione loci* application of non-refoulement has been animated by the need to establish which protection obligations against refoulement Frontex and Member State must respect in conducting joint operations at the EU's external borders. This has meant investigating the material space where joint operations are performed such as the Greek–Turkish borders, the central Mediterranean area and the sea between West Africa and the Canary Islands. This material space has emerged in our analysis as a juridical one in which a State is responsible for ensuring protection from return. Our examination has tried to clarify the link between juridical space and the territory of the State and has identified the actual control exercised on space and persons determinant in establishing jurisdiction. I have found that the principle of non-refoulement, as enshrined in Article 33 of the 1951 Refugee Convention, Article 7 ICCPR, Article 3 CAT and Article 3 ECHR, applies both within the territory of a State and at its borders. As to the extraterritorial application of non-refoulement, in human rights law 'jurisdiction' is concerned with the control which a State has over territory or persons. The pronouncements of the ECtHR, the Human Rights Committee and the Committee against Torture have not always confirmed this. However, the judgments and decisions affirm to a large extent that 'jurisdiction' under Article 1 ECHR, Article 2(1) ICCPR and Article 2(1) CAT is established by looking at the actual control exercised by a State over the territory of the third country or on the high seas. In some cases these decision-making bodies have established the personal model of jurisdiction – actual control over individuals. In the light of this, an examination of the relevant provisions and jurisprudence on the

---

[250] Chapter 5, Section 5.3.5.3.
[251] See also Costello, 'Courting Access to Asylum in Europe: Recent Supranational Jurisprudence Explored', 307.
[252] Cfr. Moreno-Lax and Costello, 'The Extraterritorial Application of the EU Charter of Fundamental Rights', 1660.

principle of non-refoulement has shown, first, that the ECtHR, with regard to Article 3 ECHR, has found that this provision applies extraterritorially where a State exercises *de jure* or *de facto* control over places or people. In particular, the ECtHR seemed in the *Al-Skeini* case to lean towards a personal model of jurisdiction. While the Court in *Al-Skeini* still required 'the exercise of some of the public powers normally to be exercised by a sovereign government', later case law seems to have made such a requirement less determinative. Thus, it seems possible to apply the personal model of jurisdiction to cases concerned with breaches of the principle of non-refoulement. The *Hirsi* case can be understood from this perspective, and it seems possible to conclude that Article 3 ECHR applies on the high seas by virtue of the *de facto* control exercised by the authorities of a State over individuals on board a vessel. Further, both Article 7 ICCPR and Article 3 CAT (in connection with Article 2 CAT) apply extraterritorially. The Human Rights Committee and the Committee against Torture have not yet specified whether control must be exercised over a place or over persons. Having established the extraterritorial application of the principle of non-refoulement in international human rights law, our analysis has determined that Article 33 of the 1951 Refugee Convention may apply wherever the State acts. This conclusion has been reached by using international human rights law as a supplementary means of interpretation pursuant to the VCLT. Finally, our examination has assessed the *ratione loci* application of the principle of non-refoulement as a matter of EU law. I have found that Articles 18 and 19(1) of the EU Charter, and the principle of non-refoulement as a general principle of EU law, apply at the borders and extraterritorially.

Frontex Saving Lives at Sea

7.1 Interaction of Protection Regimes

Frontex's surveillance operations, in which the Agency contributes at the EU's external sea borders to the task of preventing irregular migration to the EU, can also by necessity include search and rescue at sea operations. When surveillance operations involve the interception of unseaworthy vessels trying to cross the Mediterranean, this triggers the duty of the Member States involved to render assistance to persons in distress at sea.[1] The group of persons in distress may include individuals seeking protection who must not be returned to places where they may be at risk. The volume of those in need of rescue and assessment can be very significant: more than 24,400 migrants were rescued during November of 2014 in the context of Frontex's Joint Operation Triton which focused on the Central Mediterranean migrant route.[2] Such episodes of large-scale search and rescue prompt the question of whether Frontex, as part of its surveillance operations at the EU's external borders, should have a more proactive role in the protection of individuals crossing the Mediterranean Sea. In other words, should Frontex's role be limited to saving lives once it encounters persons in distress at sea in the context of its border control operations or should the Agency be entrusted with an increased involvement in search and rescue operations? This chapter will examine the legal problems related to this question (Section 7.5), but will first establish some necessary context through an examination of the interaction

---

[1] See R. Barnes, 'The International Law of the Sea and Migration Control' in B. Ryan and V. Mitsilegas (eds.), *Extraterritorial Immigration Control – Legal Challenges* (Martinus Nijhoff, 2010), 134. For an analysis of the international provisions concerning safeguarding of life at sea which focuses on the Mediterranean sea, see M. Di Filippo, 'Irregular Migration and Safeguard of Life at Sea. International Rules and Recent Developments in the Mediterranean Sea' in A. Del Vecchio (ed.), *International Law of the Sea: Current Trends and Controversial Issues* (Eleven International Publishing, 2014), 9.

[2] Frontex, '2400 migrants rescued off Libyan coast before Easter', www.frontex.europa.eu (accessed on 13 November 2015).

between the legal regime governing search and rescue at sea and the prohibition of refoulement (Sections 7.2, 7.3 and 7.4). Finally, conclusions on possible Frontex's contribution will be offered (Section 7.6).

7.2   Search and Rescue at Sea

The duty to render assistance to persons in distress at sea is part of customary international law to the extent that a ship in distress has a right of entry to any foreign port.[3] It does not cover search and rescue at sea performed on the high seas.[4] Yet to this limited extent, this duty under customary international law is binding on the EU and on its Member States. Notably, the duty to render assistance to persons in distress at sea is clearly enshrined in several international treaties. First, Article 98 of the United Nations Convention on the Law of the Sea[5] (UNCLOS) provides: 'every State shall require the master of a ship flying its flag . . . to render assistance to any person found at sea in danger of being lost'.[6] It also states: 'every coastal State shall promote the establishment, operation and maintenance of an adequate and effective search and rescue service regarding safety on and over the sea', and must cooperate with neighbouring States for this purpose.[7] Second, similar to UNCLOS, the International Convention for the Safety of Life at Sea[8] (the SOLAS Convention) provides: 'the master of a ship at sea which is in a position to be able to provide assistance on receiving a signal from any source that persons are in distress at sea, is bound to proceed with all speed to their assistance'.[9] It also provides that a State party to the SOLAS Convention

---

[3] Barnes, 'The International Law of the Sea and Migration Control', 134; P.C. Jessup, *The Law of Territorial Waters and Maritime Jurisdiction* (G.A. Jennings Co., 1927), 207–208; R. R. Churchill and A. V. Lowe, *The Law of the Sea* (Manchester University Press, 1999), 63; J. E. Noyes, 'Ships in Distress' in *Max Planck Encyclopedia of Public International Law* (Oxford University Press, 2007), paras 11–12.

[4] The duty to render assistance to persons in distress at sea may constitute an international obligation based on the general principle of law of elementary considerations of humanity. For this argument, it is useful to refer to *The Corfu Channel Case* (Judgment), ICJ Reports 1949, p. 22 and *The M/V Saiga* ITLOS Case No 2, ICGJ 336 (ITLOS 1999), para 155. The author wishes to thank Professor Yoshifumi Tanaka for drawing his attention to this argument.

[5] 1982 United Nations Convention on the Law of the Sea (1833 UNTS 3).

[6] Article 98(1) UNCLOS.   [7] Article 98(2) UNCLOS.

[8] 1974 International Convention for the Safety of Life at Sea (1184 UNTS 277). Chapter V of the SOLAS Convention was amended in 2004.

[9] 1974 International Convention for the Safety of Life at Sea (1184 UNTS 277), Chapter V, Regulation 33(1).

is obliged to 'ensure that necessary arrangements are made for distress communication and co-ordination in their area of responsibility and for the rescue of persons in distress at sea around its coast'.[10] Third, the International Convention on Maritime Search and Rescue[11] (the SAR Convention) establishes an international system to coordinate search and rescue operations. Although both the UNCLOS and the SOLAS Convention include provisions on this matter, the SAR Convention was established to fill in gaps in the assistance given to persons in distress at sea. The SAR Convention provides for the coordination of search and rescue services and for cooperation between States that are party to the Convention,[12] as well as for establishing search and rescue areas for which each State is responsible.[13]

UNCLOS has been ratified by the EU and all its Member States.[14] However, specifically on the matter of the duty to render assistance to persons in distress at sea, the EU has not made any declaration specifying that the duty to render assistance governed by UNCLOS under Article 98 is a matter in respect to which competence has been transferred to the EU by its Member States, which are also party to UNCLOS.[15] Thus, all Member States, but not the EU, are under the obligation to render assistance to persons in distress at sea under UNCLOS. Further, the EU itself is not a member of the International Maritime Organisation (IMO) and has not acceded to the SOLAS Convention or the SAR Convention. However, the majority of the Member States are parties to the SOLAS Convention and the SAR Convention.[16] In sum, the duty to render

---

[10] *Ibid.*, Regulation 7(1).

[11] 1979 International Convention on Maritime Search and Rescue (1405 UNTS 119). Chapters 2–4 of the SAR Convention were amended in 2004.

[12] 1979 International Convention on Maritime Search and Rescue (1405 UNTS 119), Annex, Chapters 2 and 3.

[13] For an overview of the safety regime at sea, Z. Kopacz, W. Morgas and J. Urbanski, 'The Maritime Safety System: Its Main Components and Elements' (2001) 54 *The Journal of Navigation* 199, 199–204, 208–209. On the search and rescue areas and the relations between Mediterranean States, see S. Trevisanut, 'Search and Rescue Operations in the Mediterranean: Factor of Cooperation or Conflict?' (2010) 25 *The International Journal of Marine and Coastal Law* 523.

[14] See the status of the UNCLOS, www.treaties.un.org (accessed 13 November 2015).

[15] Article 5(1) of Annex IX of the UNCLOS. For the competence that the Member States have transferred to the EU under the Treaties in matters governed by the UNCLOS, see 'United Nations Convention on the Law of the Sea: Declarations made upon signature, ratification, accession or succession or anytime thereafter', www.un.org/Depts/los/convention_agreements/convention_declarations.htm (accessed 13 November 2015).

[16] All Member States except Austria, the Czech Republic and Hungary have ratified the SOLAS Convention; all Member States except Austria, the Czech Republic and Slovakia

assistance to persons in distress at sea is only a limited obligation under customary international law and the EU is not bound by such duty under any of the international treaties analysed above dealing with the matter. Therefore, only the Member States are under such obligation.

7.3   Interaction with the Principle of Non-Refoulement

Interaction between the legal regime governing search and rescue at sea and the principle of non-refoulement can arise when a specific place of disembarkation must be determined. For instance, the issue may become important in a surveillance operation coordinated by Frontex on the high seas if a Member State vessel involved in this Frontex-led operation patrols the margins of Libyan territorial waters and identifies a boat in distress in Libyan territorial waters. It is well known that Libya is a country in which human rights are not respected.[17] Yet, in immediate terms, by informing the Libyan authorities the Member State could ensure rapid disembarkation in Libyan territory and an immediate intervention to save lives. The question is whether a Member State can circumvent its human rights law obligations, specifically the principle of non-refoulement, and justify its actions by claiming that it is complying with the legal regime governing search and rescue at sea.

The binding Annex to the SAR Convention states that rescue involves an 'operation to retrieve persons in distress, provide for their initial medical or other needs and *to deliver them to a place of safety*'.[18] The abiding issue to determine here is, what constitutes 'a place of safety' for individuals seeking protection?

The Maritime Safety Committee of the IMO has issued Guidelines on the treatment of persons rescued at sea (IMO Guidelines).[19] The Maritime Safety Committee is a technical body of the IMO which is contributed to by 'governments of those nations having an important interest in maritime safety'.[20] It has 'the duty of considering any matter

---

have ratified the SAR Convention. See the status of the SOLAS and the SAR Conventions, www.imo.org (accessed 13 November 2015).

[17] See Amnesty International, 'Amnesty International Report 2014/2015 – The State of the World's Human Rights', 229; and the ruling of the European Court of Human Rights (ECtHR) in the *Hirsi* case, in particular, paras 123–131.

[18] SAR Convention Annex, para 1.3.2.

[19] Maritime Safety Committee, Resolution 167(78), 20 May 2004, Guidelines on the treatment of persons rescued at sea, MSC 78/26/Add. 2, Annex 34.

[20] Convention on the International Maritime Organization, 1948, 289 UNTS 3, Article 28(a).

within the scope of the Organisation and concerned with . . . salvage and rescue'.[21] The IMO Guidelines define a 'place of safety' as follows:

> a location where rescue operations are considered to terminate. It is also a place where survivors' safety of life is no longer threatened and *where their basic human needs (such as food, shelter and medical needs) can be met.* Further, it is a place from which transportation arrangements can be made for the survivors' next or final destination.[22]
>
> An assisting ship should not be considered a place of safety based solely on the fact that the survivors are no longer in immediate danger once on board the ship.[23]

This definition of 'place of safety' means that the persons rescued at sea must no longer be in danger, and it focuses on their basic human needs. The place of safety must be in the territory of a coastal State. With regard to individuals seeking protection, the IMO Guidelines state:

> the need to avoid disembarkation in territories where the lives and freedoms of those alleging a well-founded fear of persecution would be threatened is a consideration in the case of asylum-seekers and refugees recovered at sea.[24]

A place of safety for asylum seekers is not only a location where their basic human needs are met. The place of disembarkation must also guarantee protection against refoulement. In several documents, the United Nations High Commissioner for Refugees (UNHCR) identifies the 'place of safety' as the 'next port of call' (i.e. the first port in a State that is a party to the SAR Convention at which the ship calls after rescuing the persons in distress at sea).[25] The UNHCR has also specified that the 'next port of call' must be a place where persons are not at risk of persecution.[26] The practice of disembarkation at the next port

---

[21] *Ibid.,* Article 29(a).
[22] Maritime Safety Committee, Resolution 167(78), 20 May 2004, Guidelines on the treatment of persons rescued at sea, MSC 78/26/Add. 2, Annex 34, para 6.12.
[23] *Ibid.,* Annex 34, para 6.13.   [24] *Ibid.,* para 6.18.
[25] See e.g. UNHCR Executive Committee Conclusion No 23 (XXXII), para 3.
[26] UNHCR, 'Background Note on the Protection of Asylum-seekers and Refugees Rescued at Sea' (Final version, including Annexes) 18 March 2002, www.unhcr.org (accessed 13 November 2015). For a similar view, see A. Fischer-Lescano, T. Löhr and T. Tohidipur, 'Border Controls at Sea: Requirements under International Human Rights and Refugee Law' (2009) 21 *International Journal of Refugee Law* 256, 290; and V. Moreno-Lax, 'Seeking Asylum in the Mediterranean: Against a Fragmentary Reading of EU Member States' Obligations Accruing at Sea' (2011) 23 *International Journal of Refugee Law* 174, 198–199.

of call has not yet been consolidated into a norm of customary international law.[27]

The SAR Convention has no rule specifying where the place of disembarkation must be, but leaves the States that are party to the Convention to arrange for disembarkation.[28] It also states that it is a 'primary responsibility' of the State responsible for the search and rescue region to arrange cooperation between States to ensure disembarkation in a place of safety.[29]

The interaction between the legal regime governing search and rescue at sea and human rights law was dealt with by the ECtHR in the *Hirsi* case, outlined and analysed previously.[30] In this case, the ECtHR ruled that Italy could not circumvent its obligations under the European Convention on Human Rights by claiming that it acted in the context of a search and rescue at sea operation.

7.4   EU Sea External Borders Regulation

In previous chapters, I analysed the EU Sea External Borders Regulation and provisions on the principle of non-refoulement enshrined therein.[31] We must now turn specifically to the interaction of the search and rescue regime and the prohibition of non-refoulement under the Regulation. The Regulation supersedes the EU 'Guidelines for search and rescue situations and for disembarkation in the context of sea border operations coordinated by [Frontex]' which were issued to provide better coordination between Member States for rescuing people in distress at sea (EU Search and Rescue guidelines).[32] The EU Search and Rescue guidelines were the second part of the Annex to the Sea External Borders Decision

---

[27] R. Barnes, 'Refugee Law at Sea' (2004) 53 *The International and Comparative Law Quarterly* 47, 63.

[28] SAR Convention Annex, para 3.1.9.   [29] *Ibid.*

[30] For a fuller account of the case, see Chapter 6, Section 6.2.2.2.4. Specifically, on the interaction between the legal regime governing search and rescue at sea and human rights law, see Chapter 6, Section 6.2.2.

[31] Regulation (EU) 656/2014 of the European Parliament and of the Council of 15 May 2014 establishing rules for the surveillance of the external sea borders in the context of operational cooperation coordinated by the European agency for the management of operational cooperation at the external borders of the Member States of the European Union OJ 2014 No. L189, p. 93. See Chapter 5, Section 5.3.6.

[32] Council Decision 2010/252/EU of 26 April 2010 supplementing the Schengen Borders Code as regards the surveillance of the sea external borders in the context of operational cooperation coordinated by the European agency for the management of operational cooperation at the external borders of the Member States of the European Union OJ 2010 No. L111, p. 20.

and, according to Article 1 of the Decision, they were not binding. However, the first part of the Annex, which set out rules for sea border operations, was binding. In 2012, in the *European Parliament v. Council of the European Union* case, the Court of Justice of the European Union (CJEU) stated that the rules in the second part of the Annex must be considered essential and intended to produce legal effects. The CJEU came to this conclusion by observing that, pursuant to Article 1 of the Sea External Borders Decision, the second part of the Annex, together with the first part, must be included in the operational plan drawn up for each operation coordinated by Frontex. The operational plan establishes the conditions for Frontex's operations and must be complied with. Therefore, according to the CJEU, what is part of the operational plan, including the second part of the Annex, has a legal effect.[33] With the adoption of the EU Sea External Borders Regulation, the legally binding nature of the measure concerning surveillance, rescue at sea and disembarkation in the context of Frontex's joint operations is beyond doubt. As with the EU Search and Rescue guidelines, under the EU Sea External Borders Regulation the operational plan is the document which must contain measures to be taken in case of rescue at sea situations and disembarkation.[34] Article 9(1) of the Regulation reiterates the Member States' search and rescue obligations noted above and it states that such obligations must be extended to any EU Member State's participating units during a joint sea operation. Pursuant to the same provision, a joint sea operation's operational plan must contain provisions determining how Member States deal with the search and rescue situation, in accordance with international law.[35] For our purposes, the Regulation clarifies the relation between disembarkation and protection against refoulement.

---

[33] Case C-355/10 *European Parliament v. Council of the European Union*, judgment of 5 September 2012; [2013] 1 CMLR 1, paras 80–81. On the operational plan for Frontex's joint operations, see Chapter 3, Section 3.3.

[34] EU Search and Rescue guidelines, para 2.1. The inclusion in the operational plan of the joint operation of measures to be taken in case of rescue at sea were not explicitly stated in the Annex to the Decision. Only measures on disembarkation were included. However, this limitation of the measures to apply exclusively in the context of Frontex's joint operations could be logically deduced from the scope of the Decision (surveillance of the sea external borders in the context of operational cooperation coordinated by [Frontex]). For this argument applied to the drafting of the EU Sea External Borders Regulation, see S. Carrera and L. den Hertog, 'Whose Mare? Rule of Law Challenges in the Field of European Border Surveillance in the Mediterranean' *CEPS Paper* No. 79/ January 2015, 12. On the operational plan in the EU Sea External Borders Regulation see Article 1(8) and Recital (17) of the Regulation.

[35] Article 9(2) of the EU Sea External Borders Regulation.

Among the modalities for disembarkation, in case of a search and rescue situation, a 'place of safety' must be identified and 'disembarkation of the rescued persons is carried out rapidly and effectively'.[36] Under the Regulation, disembarkation may take place either in the territory of a third country from which the vessel is assumed to have departed or in the territory of the host Member State, in accordance with the Member State's international law obligations.[37] In identifying the 'place of safety', the encompassing definition of non-refoulement enshrined in Article 4 of the Regulation must be taken into account together with the general situation of the third country where disembarkation takes place: 'the assessment shall be based on information derived from ... other Member States, Union bodies, offices and agencies, and relevant international organisations'.[38] Further, under Article 4(3) of the Regulation, in case of rescue (as of interception), a disembarkation procedure which has been defined as 'maritime asylum procedure' is established.[39]

In summary, when compared with the earlier EU Search and Rescue guidelines, the EU Sea External Borders Regulation better frames and defines the interaction between the search and rescue regime and the principle of non-refoulement, especially when rescuees are disembarked in third countries.[40] With this analysis in mind, we now turn to examine Frontex's present involvement in search and rescue at sea, along with some considerations pertaining to the Agency's future role.

7.5   Greater Involvement for Frontex in Search and Rescue Operations?

A large volume of diffuse pressure and disappointment stems from public opinion concerning the death toll of migrants departing from North

---

[36] Article 10(1)(c).

[37] See Article 10(1) and (2) as well as Recital (16) of the EU Sea External Borders Regulation.

[38] Article 4(2) of the EU Sea External Borders Regulation. See also the definition of 'place of safety' given in the Regulation: Article 2(12).

[39] S. Peers, 'New Rules on Maritime Surveillance: Will They Stop the Deaths and Push-backs in the Mediterranean?' – Statewatch Analysis, February 2014, www.statewatch.org (accessed 13 November 2015).

[40] For an overview of the still controversial issues concerning search and rescue at sea, see Di Filippo, 'Irregular Migration and Safeguard of Life at Sea', 15–23; A. Klug, 'Strengthening the Protection of Migrants and Refugees in Distress at Sea through International Cooperation and Burden-sharing' 26 (2014) *International Journal of Refugee Law* 48, 51–54.

Africa and attempting to cross the Mediterranean.[41] This feeling has been exacerbated by recent humanitarian tragedies off the Italian island of Lampedusa. On this point, Thomas Spijkerboer has argued that 'increased controls have led to the loss of more lives, and given this, it is foreseeable that further tightening of the external borders, as envisaged by the Member States and the EU, will intensify this trend'.[42] Thus, questions have been raised about whether Frontex should be more urgently and exclusively involved in search and rescue at sea operations and participate more fully in a protection-sensitive management of the EU borders.[43]

The problems related to these questions are best investigated by closely examining two maritime operations which included, to different extents, search and rescue situations: the Italian Navy-led operation Mare Nostrum and Frontex's Joint Operation Triton. The Mare Nostrum operation was launched in October 2013 and was halted in October 2014. Its focus was on security, combatting illegal activities such as trafficking and, importantly, search and rescue in an operational area in the Strait of Sicily of around 70, 000 square kilometres. In one year of activity, 421 operations were conducted and 150, 810 migrants rescued.[44] The Mare Nostrum operation had a large effect on public opinion and captivated the media's attention since it constituted an immediate intervention to stop the loss of lives in the Strait of Sicily (In October 2013, 300 people had just died in one of the refugee disasters near the coast of Lampedusa).[45] The costs of the operation were initially put at 1.5 million euros per month, projected to reach 9.5 million euros per month.[46] Only

---

[41] Amnesty International, ' "Frontex Plus" must focus on search and rescue at sea', www .amnesty.eu (accessed 13 November 2015).

[42] T. Spijkerboer, 'The Human Costs of Border Control' (2007) 9 *European Journal of Migration and Law* 127, 127.

[43] The term 'protection-sensitive management' was used at the Expert Roundtable convened by UNHCR in November 2008 to explore practical ways to operationalise refugee and human rights protection in the context of entry control and border management. 'Protection-sensitive entry systems' refers to 'activities beyond immediate measures at the border of a State's territory into an entry management strategy' and includes measures on the high seas: '*10-Point Plan Expert Roundtable No. 1, Controlling Borders while Ensuring Protection*' 20–21 November 2008, Geneva, 1.

[44] Ministero della Difesa, 'Mare Nostrum Operation', www.marina.difesa.it (accessed 13 November 2015).

[45] BBC, 'Italy boat sinking: Hundreds feared dead off Lampedusa', www.bbc.com (accessed 13 November 2015).

[46] *The Economist*, 'Italy's illegal immigrants: Tidal wave', www.economist.com (accessed 13 November 2015).

one month of operations was covered by EU funding derived from the External Borders Fund during November 2013.[47] The Mare Nostrum operation ceased in October 2014 during the Italian Presidency of the Council of the European Union, and Frontex's Joint Operation Triton was launched in November 2014. Frontex's operation was granted a more limited capacity (although it has been recently expanded). Monthly operational costs were set at 2.9 million euros with an additional increase of 26.25 million euros for 2015. Triton's operational area, initially not extending beyond 30 nautical miles from the Italian coast, stretch today 138 nautical miles south of Sicily.[48] The initiative was launched amid an 'authority struggle' between Frontex and the Italian Navy concerning how the migrant-crossing emergency in the Mediterranean should be managed, and the debate revolved around whether Triton's focus could exclusively be on search and rescue, like Mare Nostrum, thus constituting a continuation of this earlier operation.[49] A document issued by Frontex's Operations Division of the Joint Operations Unit – 'JO EPN-Triton to better control irregular migration and contribute to SAR in the Mediterranean'[50] – addresses the issue in terms which are worth scrutinising. From the outset, in its very title, the document states that Joint Operation Triton will 'contribute' to the search and rescue activities of the Member States in the Mediterranean. The body of the document notes that the specific outcome of the operation is 'early detection as *contribution* to national MS SAR [Member State search and rescue] obligations; and that objectives of the operations are 'effective border control and *contribution* to saving lives'.[51] Thus, the document asserts

---

[47] Data available from Sergio Carrera and Leonhard den Hertog after interview at the Commission, DG Home Affairs: Carrera and Hertog, 'Whose Mare?', 3.

[48] See Frontex, 'Frontex expands its joint operation Triton, www.frontex.europa.eu, and EUobserver; 'Frontex mission to extend just beyond Italian waters', www.euobserver.com /justice/125945 (both accessed 13 November 2015).

[49] For an account of the political debate at the EU level, see Carrera and Hertog, 'Whose Mare?', 5–10.

[50] Frontex, Operations Division – Joint Operations Unit, 'Concept of reinforced joint operation tackling the migratory flows towards Italy: JO EPN-Triton to better control irregular migration and contribute to SAR in the Mediterranean Sea', 28 August 2014, Reg. No 2014/JOU Limited. 'EPN' stays for European Patrols Network. Since many authorities in each EU Member State were engaged in marine surveillance, the EPN was created to reduce overlaps in the operations and to reduce duplicated effort by way of a multi-agency approach. EPN operations are complementary to Frontex's sea operations and are effective in the Western and Central Mediterranean region. See Frontex, 'Operations-Sea', www.frontex.europa.eu (accessed 13 November 2015).

[51] Frontex, Operations Division – Joint Operations Unit, 'Concept of reinforced joint operation tackling the migratory flows towards Italy', 1, 7 and 12.

that Joint Operation Triton is not a search and rescue operation but that it complements the search and rescue operations conducted by Member States in accordance with their international obligations.

In order to assess whether the content of this document constitutes a correct interpretation of international and EU legislation on this matter, we should consider several complications. The international obligations on search and rescue bind the Member States but do not pertain directly to the EU since it is not party to the SAR and the SOLAS Convention.[52] Also, the EU Sea External Borders Regulation establishes the rules applying to search and rescue situations and disembarkation only in the context of surveillance operations coordinated by Frontex. The Regulation is clear on this point: Articles 9(2) and 10(1) establish that any search and rescue measure is included in the operational plan of the surveillance operation coordinated by Frontex. Although such an inclusion was deducible from the scope of the Regulation, the insertion probably sought to provide reassurance for those Member States which were reluctant to conclude the negotiation on the adoption of the Regulation.[53] Accordingly, the provisions of the Regulation concerning search and rescue will apply only when Member States take part in Frontex's surveillance operations, leaving them otherwise free to organise search and rescue operations themselves as per their international obligations. A second factor to consider is that pursuant to Article 9(3) of the Regulation, the sea operation must be resumed when the search and rescue situation has been concluded which indicates the incidental element of the search and rescue situation with respect to the main surveillance operation. Thirdly, according to the Recital of the Regulation, 'border surveillance ... extends to ... arrangements intended to address situations such as search and rescue *that may arise during a border surveillance operation at sea*'.[54] Cumulatively, these three points of detail indicate the extent to which Frontex's involvement in search and rescue operations is 'necessarily coincidental' with Frontex's surveillance operations.[55] Simultaneously, Frontex's

---

[52] See Section 7.2 above.   [53] See Carrera and Hertog, 'Whose Mare?', 12.

[54] Recital (1) of the EU Sea External Borders Regulation. Emphasis added.

[55] The CJEU in the Case C-355/10 *European Parliament v. Council of the European Union*, judgment of 5 September 2012 did not clarify whether interception, disembarkation and search and rescue – as defined in the then in force Council Decision 2010/252/EU – fall within the concept of surveillance. The Advocate General Mengozzi included interception within the concept of surveillance but did harbour some doubts about whether disembarkation and search and rescue can be also included: paras 59–60. See J. Rijpma, 'The Patrolling of the European Union's External Maritime Border: Preventing the Rule of Law from Getting Lost at Sea' in A. Del Vecchio (ed.), *International Law of the Sea: Current Trends and Controversial Issues* (Eleven International Publishing, 2014), 97.

involvement in search and rescue operations permits Member States to obey their search and rescue obligations when they are jointly operating with other Member States in the context of surveillance operations under Frontex's auspices: 'during a border surveillance operation at sea, a situation may occur where it will be necessary to render assistance to persons found in distress. The obligation ... should be fulfilled by Member States in accordance with the applicable provisions of international instruments'.[56] Hence, Frontex's involvement is 'exclusively instrumental' to the search and rescue activities of the Member States. The argument has been advanced that the possibility of an exclusive Frontex search and rescue operation should not be ruled out since search and rescue still appears as part of Frontex's mandate in the EU Sea External Borders Regulation.[57] In political debates, such as the one on the transition from the Mare Nostrum operation to the Triton operation, concern has been voiced that 'rule of law frameworks can thereby also be used as a forceful argument to refrain from taking action'.[58] While it is recognised that not only legal reasons but also political considerations may have led to the closure of Mare Nostrum and the launching of Frontex's border surveillance operation in its place, respect of the rule of law must still be the priority. The preceding analysis of the provisions of the EU Sea External Borders Regulation shows that an exclusive Frontex-led search and rescue operation is not permissible under the law. Moreover, as seen above, search and rescue is not an EU competence since the EU is not party to any relevant treaty on the subject and has not made any declarations in this respect to the UNCLOS.[59]

Thus, an analysis of the legal framework concerning the mandate of the Agency and the competence of the EU prompts a negative reply to the question of whether Frontex should be more involved in search and rescue operations in the Mediterranean. Currently, operations exclusively focused on search and rescue can be only conducted by Member States, as the case of Mare Nostrum has shown. Surveillance operations at sea under Frontex's auspices may include search and rescue measures when the situation occurs. However, in view of the legal setting, the Member States are the correct recipients of the political pressure calling for an intensification of rescue at sea in the Mediterranean rather than Frontex. Yet, a salutary reminder is also necessary: Frontex's joint operations nonetheless provide the legal setting in which Member

---

[56] Recital (15) of the EU Sea External Borders Regulation.
[57] Carrera and Hertog, 'Whose Mare?', 9–10.   [58] *Ibid.*, 10.
[59] See likewise Rijpma, 'The Patrolling of the European Union's External Maritime Border', 96.

States incur the most stringent obligations to respect the rules on surveillance, interception, search and rescue, as well as disembarkation and non-refoulement which are appositely formulated by the EU legislator in the EU Sea External Borders Regulation. Notably, this latter instrument was adopted to clarify the legal intricacies of the regime of surveillance at sea established by the previously adopted SOLAS and SAR Conventions.

7.6 Conclusions

The international and EU legal instruments analysed above show that protection from refoulement and the legal regime governing search and rescue at sea are 'interlocked'.[60] With regard to disembarkation, the legal regime governing search and rescue at sea is respected only when the principle of non-refoulement is observed.[61] As stated, the obligation to render assistance to persons in distress at sea is part of customary international law only to a limited extent. Further, the practice of not disembarking persons in a place where they are at risk of persecution is not yet part of customary international law, and thus there is no obligation under customary international law which is binding on the EU and its Member States in this respect. Hence, with regard to the principle of non-refoulement, it appears that only the Member States that are party to the international agreements on search and rescue at sea, in particular the SAR Convention, are bound by an obligation to disembark asylum seekers rescued at sea at a place where they are not at risk. Unlike its Member States, the EU, party to neither the SAR nor the SOLAS Convention, does not have search and rescue obligations which pertain directly to it. Nor has the EU made any declaration of competence with regard to the duty to render assistance to persons in distress at sea under the UNCLOS. A clarification of the legal framework pertaining to surveillance, search and rescue at sea, disembarkation, and non-refoulement emerged with the adoption of the EU Sea External Borders Regulation which superseded a Decision on the same matters. Provisions of the Regulation apply to Member States when they take part in Frontex's joint operations at sea. Protection from refoulement and disembarkation in third countries are stated in the Regulation to

---

[60] See Fischer-Lescano, Löhr and Tohidipur, 'Border Controls at Sea', 291; G. S. Goodwin-Gill, 'The Right to Seek Asylum: Interception at Sea and the Principle of Non-refoulement' (2011) 23 *International Journal of Refugee Law* 443, 452.
[61] Fischer-Lescano, Löhr and Tohidipur, 'Border Controls at Sea', 291.

a greater extent than they were previously in the EU Sea External Borders Decision. At the same time, the Regulation rules out the possibility of conducting joint operations coordinated by Frontex with an exclusive focus on search and rescue. This is due to the way Frontex's mandate is drafted in the Regulation and is also due to the lack of EU competence in this respect.

The EU, Frontex and Non-Refoulement

Constructing Scenarios

8.1 Potential Triggers of EU and Member State Responsibility

Previous chapters have emphasised that decisions made at the operational level of Frontex's joint operations constitute the most important and open avenue of legal risk regarding potential violations of the principle of non-refoulement by Member States' border guards. The most urgent sources of legal vulnerability arise not from the implementation of EU legislation on external border control but from the way each joint operation is planned.

When border control and border surveillance are carried out under Frontex's auspices, third-country nationals may be sent back to territories where they could be at risk of persecution, torture or other ill treatment, in breach of the principle of non-refoulement. According to the 'organic model' of attribution of responsibility, any such breaches contain the potential to trigger the responsibility of the EU and its Member States when participating in joint operations. Provided the other conditions for responsibility are fulfilled, under the 'organic model' of attribution the responsibility of the EU and its Member States is established when the acts giving rise to claims of responsibility can be attributed to the organs of the EU or to the organs of the Member States.

Besides incurring the status of an internationally wrongful act, such violations would also constitute an infringement of EU law to the extent that EU law prohibits refoulement.[1] Specifically, under Article 263 of the Treaty on the Functioning of the European Union (TFEU), the Court of Justice of the European Union (CJEU) 'shall also review the legality of acts of bodies, offices or *agencies* of the Union intended to produce legal effects vis-à-vis third parties'.[2] In this respect, in the action brought by the European Parliament to annul the Sea External

---

[1] See Chapter 5 in this respect.   [2] Emphasis added.

Borders Decision,[3] the CJEU ruled that the operational plan drawn up for each operation coordinated by Frontex has binding legal effect and must be complied with.[4] Therefore, the CJEU could review the legality of an operational plan in order to assess its compliance with the principle of non-refoulement under EU law. Additionally, under the European Charter of Fundamental Rights (EU Charter) and the general principles of EU law, Member States, when implementing EU law, and Frontex must comply with the principle of non-refoulement.[5]

This chapter examines the circumstances in which the EU and its Member States may incur responsibility under international law for violations of the principle of non-refoulement in Frontex's joint operations. Its focus will be on specific situations in which Member States act together in joint operations under the coordination of Frontex. Aspects of this specific legal setting that are insufficiently safeguarded regarding breaches of the principle of non-refoulement by the EU and its Member States will be analysed (Section 8.2). Conclusions will follow these scenarios and this analysis (Section 8.3). This examination offers indications of the extent to which the EU and its Member States may be responsible and how violations of the principle may be avoided by Frontex. In identifying the specific situations which may lead to violations of the principle of non-refoulement, I do not include misconduct by border guards acting in the context of a joint operation. 'Misconduct' means that a border guard does not comply with the instructions

---

[3] The Sea External Borders Decision (Council Decision 2010/252/EU of 26 April 2010 supplementing the Schengen Borders Code as regards the surveillance of the sea external borders in the context of operational cooperation coordinated by the European agency for the management of operational cooperation at the external borders of the Member States of the European Union OJ 2010 No. L111, p. 20) has been annulled by the Court of Justice of the European Union in its judgment of 5 September 2012 (Case C-355/10) and replaced by Regulation (EU) 656/2014 of 15 May 2014 of the European Parliament and of the Council establishing rules for the surveillance of the external sea borders in the context of operational cooperation coordinated by the European agency for the management of operational cooperation at the external borders of the Member States of the European Union OJ 2014 No. L189, p. 93 (hereafter Sea External Border Regulation). For an analysis of the case before the Court of Justice of the European Union which led to the annulment of the Decision, the Sea External Borders Regulation and the legal regime of search and rescue at sea, see Chapter 7, Section 7.4.

[4] Case C-355/10 *European Parliament* v. *Council of the European Union*, judgment of 5 September 2012; [2013] 1 CMLR 1, para 82. On the 'operational plan', see J. Rijpma, 'Building Borders: The Regulatory Framework for the Management of the External Borders of the European Union' (DPhil thesis, European University Institute, 2009), 272; and Chapter 3, Section 3.3.

[5] See Chapter 5.

rendered by the host Member State pursuant to the operational plan of the joint operation.

8.2   Joint Operations at Sea

'Joint Operation Hermes Extension 2011' concerned coordinated sea border activities to control irregular migration flows from Tunisia towards the south of Italy. This operation was hosted by Italy. The Member States participating in the operation were Austria, Belgium, France, Germany, Greece, Hungary, the Netherlands, Poland, Portugal, Romania and Spain. Switzerland, an associated country, also took part in the joint operation. The operational plan for Joint Operation Hermes Extension 2011 states that joint operations at sea under the auspices of Frontex focus on 'the common effort to carry out border surveillance to ensure that persons attempting to cross the external borders undergo the border control as required by the Schengen Borders Code'. Among these joint operations' objectives is the imperative to 'facilitate effective cooperation with relevant third countries in Frontex-coordinated operational activities at the EU external borders'.[6]

In the Sea External Borders Regulation three situations which may lead to violations of the principle of non-refoulement are listed: (1) intercepting a vessel, ordering the vessel to modify its course outside territorial waters or the contiguous zone and escorting the vessel until it is heading on such course; (2) conducting a vessel to a third country; and (3) handing over the vessel or the persons on board the vessel to the authorities of a third country.[7] These situations will receive scrutiny in my ensuing analysis.

Interception at sea consists of any action which prevents a vessel from pursuing its course towards the territory of any State. It may take place under various legal regimes. First, interception may take place in the territorial waters of a Member State, as coastal Member States have full sovereignty to intercept vessels unless the right of innocent passage applies. In Frontex's joint operations, authorisation to intercept is only necessary when it is carried out in the territorial waters of a Member State that is not taking part in the joint operation.[8] Second, interception may take place in the contiguous zone, since a coastal Member State can exercise control in order to prevent the infringement of border controls

---

[6] EPN Programme Ref: 2011/OPS/10, Operational Plan, Joint Operation EPN Hermes Extension 2011, 3.
[7] Sea External Borders Regulation, Articles 6 and 7.   [8] *Ibid.*, Article 8.

by vessels coming from the high seas and heading towards its land territory. Third, interception may take place on the high seas when there are reasonable grounds for assuming that a vessel is without nationality, as with many vessels carrying migrants, or when there is an agreement between a Member State and a third country which allows the Member State to intercept such a vessel on the high seas if it is flying the flag of the relevant third country. Fourth, interception may take place in the territorial waters of a third country. For instance, Frontex's joint operation 'Hera 2006' consisted of sea surveillance of the area between West Africa and the Canary Islands. The operation was carried out in the territorial waters of Senegal and Mauritania by virtue of an agreement between Spain and those countries. The outcome of the operation was the interception of migrant vessels close to the African coast and their diversion to prevent them crossing the EU's external borders.

As earlier chapters revealed,[9] the rules of general international law in this respect concern the legality of Member States' actions in these different legal regimes and do not apply for establishing jurisdiction in human rights law when an action takes place outside the territory of a Member State. The following section looks at the connection between the possible violations of the principle of non-refoulement and the issue of jurisdiction, applied to specific scenarios of Frontex's joint operations.

8.2.1   The Principle of Non-Refoulement

Situation (1) – intercepting a vessel, ordering it to modify its course outside the territorial waters or the contiguous zone and escorting it until it is heading on such a course – does not in itself constitute a breach of the principle of non-refoulement. The course of action terminates with pushing the intercepted vessel out into the open sea, which does not necessarily expose the people on the vessel to the risk of persecution, torture or other ill treatment. There will only be refoulement if, once pushed out to the open sea, the vessel is forced to return to a place where the people on board are at risk of persecution or where they can be indirectly refouled.[10] Further, a joint operation at sea may coincide with

---

[9] See Chapter 6, Section 6.2.2.2.1.

[10] M. den Heijer notes that forcing refugees back into open sea may entail: (i) a violation of the principle of non-refoulement if 'the vessel has no other option than to return to a country where . . . the principle of non-refoulement is not respected'; and (ii) that 'the State may be under a positive obligation to allow entry to the vessel or at least to render assistance if not to do so would put the lives of the passengers in danger'. See M. den Heijer, 'Europe Beyond

a search-and-rescue operation.[11] In this case, the issue of disembarkation is relevant and the obligation to observe the principle of non-refoulement applies when identifying a place of safety.[12]

Conversely, in situation (2) – conducting a vessel to a third country – and situation (3) – handing over a vessel or a person on board a vessel to the authorities of a third country – the action terminates in the juridical sphere of the third country. If the third country is a place where a person may be at risk, the prohibition of refoulement is triggered. Since situation (1) does not necessarily constitute a breach of the principle of non-refoulement, my analysis will focus on situations (2) and (3).

As evidenced in my analysis of the case law on interception at sea,[13] a state exercises jurisdiction only if it exercises control over an intercepted vessel or over the people on board the vessel. Therefore, in situations (2) and (3), a Member State may be responsible for a breach of the principle of non-refoulement (provided the other conditions for responsibility are fulfilled) if it exercises control over the intercepted vessel or over the people on board the vessel so that the people can be considered to be under the State's jurisdiction. In connection with this, closer scrutiny of some cases where jurisdiction has been established is warranted.

A first scenario to consider, common to both situations (2) and (3), is when an act of interception consists of stopping, boarding and searching a vessel, before conducting the vessel to a third country or handing it over to the authorities of a third country. In the *Medvedyev and Others v. France* case,[14] in which French authorities boarded and searched a vessel flying the Cambodian flag in the context of an operation against international drug trafficking, the European Court of Human Rights (ECtHR) stated that France's jurisdiction required France to have 'full and exclusive control' over the vessel and its crew 'in a continuous and

---

Its Borders: Refugee and Human Rights Protection in Ext raterritorial Migration Control' in B. Ryan and V. Mitsilegas (eds.), *Extraterritorial Immigration Control: Legal Challenges* (Martinus Nijhoff, 2010), 189 and also V. Moreno-Lax, 'Seeking Asylum in the Mediterranean: Against a Fragmentary Reading of EU's Member States Obligations Accruing at Sea' (2011) 23 *International Journal of Refugee Law* 174, 193.

[11] See Chapter 7, Section 7.1.   [12] See Chapter 7, Section 7.3.

[13] See in Chapter 6, *Sale v. Haitian Centers Council*, 509 U.S. 155 (1993); *Medvedyev v. France* App No. 3394/03 (ECtHR, 29 March 2010); *Hirsi Jamaa and Others v. Italy* App No. 27765/09 (ECtHR, 23 February 2012); and, Committee against Torture, *J.H.A. v. Spain*, Communication No. 323/2007, UN doc. CAT/C/41/D/323/2007.

[14] See also *Xhavara v. Italie et Albanie* App No. 39473/98 (Commission Decision, 11 January 2001).

uninterrupted manner until they were tried in France'. Thus, jurisdiction
is established when an act of interception amounts to stopping, boarding
and searching a vessel.

It becomes more difficult to assess whether jurisdiction is established
when interception consists of escorting an intercepted vessel without any
physical contact with it and/or the people on board. In the *Marine I*
case,[15] the Committee against Torture stated that Spain maintained
control over the individuals on board the Marine I 'from the time the
vessel was rescued and throughout the identification and repatriation
process' in North Africa. The rescue operation carried out by Spain
consisted of *towing* the vessel in distress to the African coast: it entailed
physical control and closer contact than merely escorting the vessel.
Thus, a lack of physical contact with a vessel, as when simply escorting
a vessel, may be an obstacle to establishing jurisdiction. The same consideration applies to interceptions which merely consist of verbally
persuading an intercepted vessel to change its course.[16]

Additionally, handing over a vessel or a person on board a vessel to the
authorities of a third country appears to mean there is the necessary
control for establishing jurisdiction. In *Hirsi* v. *Italy*,[17] the ECtHR stated:
'in the period between boarding the ships of the Italian armed forces and
being handed over to the Libyan authorities, the applicants were under
the continuous and exclusive de jure and de facto control of the Italian
authorities'. Although in this case the individuals were transferred to
Italian vessels and were, accordingly, under Italy's control, arguably the
very fact of being able to hand over individuals to a third country's
authorities presupposes control over them.

8.2.2   Frontex and the EU

As confirmed in a preceding chapter,[18] under international law a host
Member State is responsible for the actions of its border guards and of
guest officers seconded by other Member States in a joint operation.
Thus, if in the context of a joint operation at sea hosted by Member

---

[15] *J.H.A.* v. *Spain*.
[16] den Heijer, 'Europe Beyond Its Borders', 189; T. Gammeltoft-Hansen, *Access to Asylum: International Refugee Law and the Globalisation of Migration Control* (Cambridge University Press, 2011), 133; A. Klug and T. Howe, 'The Concept of State Jurisdiction and the Applicability of the Non-refoulement Principle to Extraterritorial Interception Measures' in Ryan and Mitsilegas (eds.), *Extraterritorial Immigration Control*, 94.
[17] *Hirsi*.   [18] See Chapter 4, Section 4.3.1.4.

State X, guest officers from Member States Y and Z commit acts which amount to breaches of the principle of non-refoulement – for instance, if they hand over persons on board an intercepted vessel to the authorities of third country A, where it is well known that torture takes place, as a means of preventing the intercepted persons from crossing the EU's external borders – Member State X may be responsible for breaching the principle of non-refoulement. This does not exclude the possibility of Member States Y and Z being jointly responsible with Member State X for the same breach.[19]

Furthermore, once it is established that Member State X has committed a breach of the principle of non-refoulement in a joint operation at sea, it is possible to establish whether the EU, acting through Frontex, has derivative responsibility for aiding or assisting Member State X in committing the internationally wrongful act. I will consider in particular the aid or assistance that Frontex provides by coordinating joint operations. Two requirements must be fulfilled for the EU, via Frontex, to be indirectly responsible for a breach of the principle: (a) there must be a clear link between the refoulement and the coordination of the operations; and (b) there must be knowledge of the fact that the act of refoulement has been committed by means of the contribution of Frontex's coordination.[20]

Concerning the existence of a clear link, Frontex's coordination of an operation need not be essential to the refoulement, but it must contribute to it. The existence of a clear link between an act of refoulement committed by a border guard of Member State X (or a guest officer from Member State Y whose act is attributed to Member State X) and Frontex's coordination may be envisaged in the following situation. Frontex's Executive Director, the host Member State and the Member States participating in a joint operation draw up an operational plan which explains the mission of the operation and how it will be carried out. Specifically, the operational plan includes the names of the third countries participating in the operation and the operational details for specific acts of interception.[21] In this respect, Frontex's involvement includes coordinating the border control activities of both Member States and third countries. If the operational plan includes courses of action such as the two identified above where violations of the principle of non-refoulement may occur (conducting a vessel to a third

---

[19] See Chapter 4, Section 4.4.1.   [20] See Chapter 4, Section 4.4.3.

[21] The participation of a third country in a joint operation may result from a working arrangement between Frontex and the third country in question or from a bilateral agreement between a Member State and the third country in question.

country and handing over a vessel or persons on board a vessel to the authorities of a third country), and if it is well known that the third country does not respect human rights or practises indirect refoulement, a clear link is established via this legal avenue. Concerning the second require-ment (i.e. having knowledge of the fact that the act of refoulement would be committed under Frontex's coordination), it is again the operational plan which shows whether Frontex possesses prior knowledge that the action of refoulement could be committed in connection with its contribu-tion of coordinating the activities of the Member States and the third country involved in the joint operation. Here, it may be difficult to estab-lish a close connection with the victim of the violation.

The need for further work to rid this legal setting of any avenues of uncertainty is reflected in the fact that information concerning the invol-vement of third countries in the implementation of the operational plan and the specific acts of interception of persons at sea in joint operations is not accessible. In response to my request to Frontex in December 2012 for access to the operational plans of Joint Operation Hera 2011 and Joint Operation Hermes Extension 2011, Frontex decided not to disclose the relevant text. In its reasoning, Frontex stated such disclosure would under-mine the protection of the public interest with regard to public security in Member States.

Joint operations taking place in the territorial waters of a third country demand separate consideration. As noted, such joint operations require an agreement between a Member State and the third country in whose territorial waters the joint operation takes place. Under such agreements, personnel of the third country are present on board the Member State's vessel and are responsible for deciding on the return of intercepted persons. In Joint Operation Hera, which was carried out in the territorial waters of Senegal and Mauritania, a law-enforcement officer of one of the two third countries was always present on board the Spanish vessel and was always responsible for the diversion of intercepted vessels.[22] It could be argued that the presence of a law-enforcement officer of the third country on board the Member State's vessel, and his power to decide on the diversion of intercepted vessels, interrupts the chain of responsibility. This would mean that the third country, and not the Member State hosting the joint operation, would be responsible for a breach of the principle of non-refoulement. This argument can only be accepted to

---

[22] Frontex, 'Hera 2008 and Nautilus 2008 Statistic', www.frontex.europa.eu (accessed 13 November 2015).

a limited extent. It is true that the exercise of law-enforcement power by third-country officers on board the Member State's vessels seems to exclude the idea that the third-country officers are placed at the disposal of the host Member State or that their acts constitute the exercise of the governmental authority of the host Member State. As emphasised previously,[23] only if these requirements are met will the acts of the third-country officers be considered the acts of the host Member State, according to Article 6 of the Articles on State Responsibility (ASR).[24] However, this does not exclude the derivative responsibility of the host Member State for aiding or assisting the third-country officers in diverting the intercepted vessels if, as a consequence of the diversion, there is a breach of the principle of non-refoulement.[25] Also, in this situation the derivative responsibility of the EU, via Frontex, remains unchanged, to the extent that Frontex aids or assists the third country in committing a breach of the principle of non-refoulement. Therefore, my existing arguments concerning the identification of a clear link between refoulement and the coordination of the operations also apply in this case.

8.3 Joint Operations on Land

8.3.1 In EU Territory

Joint operations at land borders are generally implemented in EU territory. The basic concept of a joint operation is to deploy guest officers (border guards from a Member State other than the Member State hosting the joint operation) and 'additional technical means' from Member States to other Member States at the external borders of the EU, in order to 'intensify border security and tackle the phenomenon of illegal migration'.[26]

Border guards of the home Member State and guest officers carry out border checks and border surveillance. 'Border checks' are controls performed 'at border crossing points, to ensure that persons ... [are] authorised to enter the territory of the Member States'.[27] 'Border surveillance' consists of controlling the borders 'between border crossing points

---

[23] See Chapter 4, Section 4.3.2.   [24] UN Doc. A/Res/ 56/83 (12 December 2001).

[25] See likewise M. den Heijer, *Europe and Extraterritorial Asylum* (Hart Publishing, 2012), 257.

[26] Joint Operation Neptune 2010, Warsaw, 10 February 2010, 9.

[27] Regulation (EC) 562/2006 establishing a Community Code on the rules governing the movement of persons across borders (Schengen Borders Code) OJ 2006 No. L105, p. 1 (hereinafter SBC), Article 2(10).

and the surveillance of border crossing points outside the fixed opening hours, in order to prevent persons from circumventing border checks'.[28] At border crossing points, border guards of the host Member States (and not guest officers) can lawfully refuse entry to the territories of the Member States to third-country nationals who do not fulfil the entry conditions for reasons such as non-possession of a valid visa or a residence permit.[29] However, such refusal of entry is not lawful with respect to third-country nationals who claim asylum.[30] Surveillance between border crossing points entails the apprehension of third-country nationals who attempt to cross EU borders irregularly. If, upon apprehension, a third-country national expresses a wish to claim asylum, this will trigger the asylum procedure according to the domestic law of the host Member State. This procedure at the EU borders (and upon apprehension within EU territory) reflects the international and EU legal obligation for States to respect the principle of non-refoulement within the territory of the State and at its borders. If the principle of non-refoulement is not respected, the host Member State will be responsible for the refoulement. It is worth recalling from the previous chapters that, together with the host Member State, a Member State seconding guest officers may also be responsible for an internationally wrongful act of refoulement committed at the borders or within EU territory because of its aid or assistance given in the context of a joint operation. However, unless it is possible to establish, from the planning of a joint operation, that there is a clear link between the refoulement and the coordination of the operations, and that there is knowledge of the fact that the act of refoulement has been committed by means of the contribution of Frontex's coordination, it will be difficult to establish the responsibility of the EU, via Frontex.

8.3.2   Outside EU Territory

Although joint operations at the land borders are generally implemented in EU territory, two situations which do not wholly take place within EU territory can be identified.

The first situation derives from the fact that the EU's external borders are not only protected by human resources but also by technical means such as radar or thermo-visors. These technical means are deployed in the territory of the Member State hosting an operation and are used to

---

[28] Article 2(11) SBC.   [29] Article 10(10) SBC.   [30] Article 13 SBC.

identify third-country nationals who are approaching the EU's external borders but who are still in the territory of a neighbouring third country.

The second situation is hypothetical. It consists of the deployment of Member States' border guards in the territory of a third country as part of a Frontex joint operation to intensify border surveillance with the goal of intercepting third-country nationals trying to cross the EU's external borders irregularly. In other words, this would be a situation in which the Member States' border guards exercise law-enforcement power in the territory of a third country with the consent of that third country. As confirmed by Jozsef Bali, head of the Land Border Operations Division at Frontex, this situation is not yet part of Frontex's practice.[31] However, I submit that its feasibility cannot be excluded since it is already the practice of individual Member States to deploy personnel in the territory of third countries to prevent the onward passage of irregular migrants. Notably, the *European Roma Rights Centre* case[32] concerned the deployment of British personnel at Prague Airport to screen passengers and control entry permission to the United Kingdom at a time when the Czech Republic was not yet an EU Member State. This screening was based on an agreement between the United Kingdom and the Czech Republic. In future, Frontex could endorse such agreements between Member States and third countries and use them as a basis for joint operations. Furthermore, the Frontex Regulation provides that Frontex may deploy its liaison officers in third countries as part of the cooperation networks of immigration liaison officers of the Member States.[33] Their task consists of 'establishing and maintaining contact with the competent authorities of the third country ... with a view to contributing to the prevention of and fight against illegal immigration and the return of illegal migrants'.[34] Therefore, Frontex is empowered to place personnel

---

[31] Jozsef Bali, head of the Land Border Operations Division (now Land Border Sector) at Frontex: interview conducted at Frontex's headquarters, 8 November 2012.

[32] *European Roma Rights Centre and Others v. the Immigration Officer at Prague Airport and the Secretary of State for the Home Department* [2003] EWCA Civ 666, Court of Appeal (Civil Division), 20 May 2003, and *Regina v. Immigration Officer at Prague Airport and Another, Ex parte European Roma Rights Centre and Others* [2004] UKHL 55, House of Lords, 9 December 2004.

[33] See Council Regulation (EC) 377/2004 of 19 February 2004 on the creation of an immigration liaison officer network OJ 2004 No. L64, p. 1.

[34] Council Regulation (EC) 2007/2004 of 26 October 2004 establishing a European agency for the management of operational cooperation at the external borders of the Member States of the European Union OJ 2004 No. L349, p. 1 as amended by Regulation (EC) 863/2007 of the European Parliament and the Council of 11 July 2007 establishing a mechanism for the creation of Rapid Border Intervention Teams and amending Council

in a third country's territory. These personnel, besides collecting information for operational use, are also tasked with establishing the identity of third-country nationals and facilitating their return in their country of origin.[35] What these personnel currently lack is law-enforcement power (i.e. the power to intercept migrants trying to enter EU territory).[36]

8.3.2.1   Deployment of Technical Means

Once a group of third-country nationals is seen approaching EU borders, this information is passed to the third-country authorities. On the basis of this information, the third country can decide to apprehend the people on its own soil. According to Jozsef Bali, head of the Land Border Operations Division at Frontex, it is possible to transmit the information on the basis of bilateral cooperation between the host Member State, where the radar is deployed, and the third country. When Frontex coordinates a joint operation involving a host Member State and a third country, it also coordinates the transmission of information.

Regarding the extent to which such conduct may constitute a breach of the principle of non-refoulement, the following distinctions must be considered. The apprehension of individuals in the territory of third country A by the authorities of third country A does not breach the principle of non-refoulement. What is relevant is what happens to those individuals once they are apprehended. There will be a breach of the principle of non-refoulement if third country A returns the apprehended individuals to third country B, where they can be exposed to persecution, torture and other ill treatment. This book has focused its scrutiny exclusively on the possible responsibilities of the EU and its Member States regarding non-refoulement; and for this reason no punitive speculation will be made concerning the liability of third country A. However, it certainly falls within the scope and intent of this book to establish whether the host Member State that transmitted the information may

---

Regulation (EC) 2007/2004 as regards that mechanism and regulating the tasks and powers of guest officers OJ 2007 No. L199, 30 and by Regulation (EU) 1168/2011 of the European Parliament and the Council of 25 October 2011 amending Council Regulation (EC) 2007/2004 establishing a European agency for the management of operational cooperation at the external borders of the Member States of the European Union OJ 2011 No. L304, p. 1 (hereinafter the Frontex Regulation), Article 14(4).

[35] Council Regulation (EC) 377/2004 of 19 February 2004 on the creation of an immigration liaison officer network OJ 2004 No. L64, p. 1, Article 1(3).

[36] See the rejection by Tunisian authorities of Italy's offer to deploy its personnel to stop migrants heading towards Italy, www.nytimes.com (accessed 13 November 2015).

be responsible for refoulement committed by third country A as a result of receiving such information.

In order to establish the derivative responsibility of a host Member State, or of the EU via Frontex, it is necessary to establish: (1) a clear link between the transmission of information about the third-country nationals attempting to cross the EU's borders and the refoulement committed by the third country A; and (2) that refoulement is committed because of the contribution of the transmission of the information.

Once the information has been transmitted, the host Member State does not know with certainty whether the individuals concerned will be apprehended and, subsequently, *refouled*. There would be derivative responsibility if: (i) there was a well-established practice by the authorities of third country A to apprehend individuals whenever they receive information and subsequently to *refoul* them; and (ii) the host Member State were aware of that practice.[37] However, in this latter case, it may be difficult to establish a close connection with the victim of the breach. The same reasoning applies to the assessment of the derivative responsibility of the EU for coordinating the deployment of technical means in the territory of the host Member State.

8.3.2.2 Member States' Border Guards in the Territory of a Third Country

The second (hypothetical) situation with regard to joint operations on land now warrants consideration. (Recall that this involves the deployment of Member States' border guards in the territory of a third country with the aim of intensifying border surveillance and intercepting third-country nationals trying to cross the EU's external borders irregularly.) The deployment of border guards in the territory of a third country requires an agreement between the Member State deploying the border guards and the third country receiving them. Arguably, a Member State can enter into such an agreement with regard to its own personnel. The deployment of border guards from other Member States participating in the same joint operation would require different arrangements, probably an agreement for each Member State. The fact that Frontex does not have international legal personality, and the fact that no EU personnel act in joint operations, because of the limited EU competence analysed above,[38] excludes Frontex entering into such an agreement. In my

---

[37] See the *M.S.S.* case as analysed in Chapter 4, Section 4.4.4.
[38] See Chapter 2, Section 2.2.

analysis, I will consider the hypothesis that Member State X, which hosts a joint operation, has a bilateral agreement with third country Z, and that only border guards from Member State X are deployed in the territory of third country Z.

8.3.2.3   The Principle of Non-Refoulement

The interception of third-country nationals in foreign territory may constitute a breach of the principle of non-refoulement. Individuals may be intercepted by the border guards of Member State X deployed in third country Z; these individuals may be stopped and their onward passage may be refused. If the intercepted individuals are nationals of third country Z, or if they have their habitual residence in third country Z (and if in third country Z they can said to be at risk), the 1951 Refugee Convention does not apply.[39] This is because Article 33 of the 1951 Refugee Convention only applies to persons who have crossed an international border. Accordingly, in respect to this international instrument, there is no breach of the principle of non-refoulement. Conversely, this situation may invoke the application of the ECHR,[40] the International Covenant on Civil and Political Rights (ICCPR)[41] and the Convention against Torture (CAT),[42] since these instruments do not require an individual to have crossed an international border, so a breach of the principle of non-refoulement may be triggered in this case.

8.3.2.4   Jurisdiction in Third-Country Territories

The case law of the ECtHR, particularly after the *Al-Skeini* judgment, has stated that the exercise of authority and control over individuals by the authority of a state in the territory of a third country is capable of creating a jurisdictional link between the individual and the state.[43] The personal

---

[39] See *Regina* v. *Immigration Officer at Prague Airport*. See den Heijer, *Europe and Extraterritorial Asylum*, 132.

[40] 1950 European Convention for the Protection of Human Rights and Fundamental Freedoms (213 UNTS 222). See *Al-Saadoon and Mufdhi* v. *United Kingdom* App No. 61498/08 (ECtHR, 2 March 2010).

[41] 1966 International Covenant on Civil and Political Rights (999 UNTS 171). See *Arshdin Israil* v. *Pakistan*, Communication No. 2024/2011, UN doc. CCPR/C/103/D/2024/2011.

[42] 1984 Convention against Torture and Other Cruel, Inhuman or Degrading Treatment or Punishment (1465 UNTS 85). See Committee against Torture, UK, CAT/C/CR/33/3, 10 December 2004. See den Heijer, 'Europe and Extraterritorial Asylum', 135.

[43] *Al-Skeini and Others* v. *The United Kingdom* App No. 55721/07 (ECtHR, 7 July 2011). See also *Ocalan* v. *Turkey* App No. 46221/99 (ECtHR, 12 May 2005); and, *Al-Saadoon and Mufdhi* v. *United Kingdom* App No. 61498/08 (ECtHR, 2 March 2010).

model of jurisdiction identified by the ECtHR in *Al-Skeini* requires a spatial connection of some kind with the territory in which the breach occurs, since jurisdiction is only established when a State's agents have assumed the exercise of 'public powers'. This requirement seems not to be determinant anymore to establish jurisdiction, after the ruling by the ECHR in the cases *Hassan* and *Jaloud*.[44] The threshold of control over individuals is quite high, since it entails physical control. Notably, in the *Al-Skeini* case the jurisdictional link was established when individuals were killed.[45]

The Human Rights Committee stated that jurisdiction is established 'wherever' breaches of rights under the ICCPR occur and that what is important is 'the relationship between the individual and the State'.[46] The case in which this principle was affirmed by the Human Rights Committee concerned the apprehension and detention of individuals. The threshold of control in the decision of the Human Rights Committee is also physical control. Unlike the ECtHR and the Human Rights Committee, the Committee against Torture in its General Comment No. 2 stated that jurisdiction is established when individuals are kept in a place of detention; but it did not go so far as to say that jurisdiction is established through control over individuals. The distinction between detention and control is meaningful. If we apply the above-mentioned General Comment of the Committee against Torture to instances when border guards potentially carry out interception of individuals and refuse their onward passage, jurisdiction is not established unless the intercepted individuals are constrained in a place of detention. An additional factor is that according to Article 33 of the 1951 Refugee Convention a State will breach the principle of non-refoulement if it apprehends a refugee outside its territory and returns this individual to a territory where he or she could be at risk. In the words of the United Nations High Commissioner for Refugees' *amicus curiae* brief: 'Article 33 is available wherever needed, and, thus ... Article 33 governs the behaviour of contracting States wherever they may act.'[47] The absence of a territorial restriction under Article 33 of the 1951 Refugee Convention has also been

---

[44] *Hassan v. United Kingdom*, Application No. 29750/09 (ECtHR, 16 September 2014); *Jaloud v. The Netherlands*, Application No. 47708/08 (ECtHR, 20 November 2014).
[45] See Chapter 6, Section 6.2.2.2.1.
[46] Human Rights Committee, *De Lopez v. Uruguay*, Communication No. 52/1979, UN doc. CCPR/C/13/D/52/1979 (1981), para 12.2.
[47] UNHCR, 'The Haitian Interdiction Case 1993 Brief Amicus Curiae' (1994) 6 *International Journal of Refugee Law* 85, 97.

stated by the Inter-American Commission on Human Rights.[48] In summary, the principle of non-refoulement applies extraterritorially when agents of a state exercise physical control over individuals, including in the territory of a third country. Only the Committee against Torture has stated that jurisdiction is established by virtue of the control exercised over places where people are kept in detention.

In applying this to our core scenario presently – where individuals are intercepted by the border guards of a Member State deployed in the territory of a third country in order to refuse their onward passage – the control exercised may be insufficient to establish jurisdiction. This will be the case if the border guards do not exercise physical control over the intercepted individuals but only prevent them from reaching the border of the Member State, for example, by carrying out migration interviews.[49]

8.3.2.5 Frontex and the EU

I have examined the permutations of a case in which border guards deployed in a third-country territory are the border guards of a Member State hosting a joint operation. In this situation the host Member State would be exposed to very high likelihoods of incurring responsibility and breaching the principle of non-refoulement via its border guards. On the question of the EU's responsibility via Frontex, the existence of a clear link between an action of refoulement and Frontex's coordination pertains most directly to the operational plan for the joint operation. It is unlikely that Frontex would deploy European Border Guard Teams in the territory of a third country in which human rights violations occur.[50] It is more likely that breaches of the principle of non-refoulement would be incurred if individuals are taken from the third country where they are intercepted to another third country which violates human rights. In this last case, in order to establish the clear link, the name of the third country to which the individuals are taken must appear in the operational plan. Only this degree of explicitness would establish a clear link between a breach of the principle of non-refoulement and Frontex's coordination.

---

[48] Inter-American Commission on Human Rights, *Haitian Centre for Human Rights* v. *United States of America*, Decision of the Commission as to the Merits of the Case 10–675, 13 March 1997, para 157.

[49] See likewise Gammeltoft-Hansen, *Access to Asylum*, 132.

[50] But note that Frontex is planning to enter into a working arrangement with Lybia in the future: Frontex, www.frontex.europa.eu (accessed 13 November 2015).

8.4 Conclusions

In order to analyse the legal setting of Frontex's joint operations – scrutinising potential legal triggers regarding the principle of non-refoulement – specific situations have been identified in which Member States act together under the coordination of Frontex. A border guard commits a violation of the principle of non-refoulement if this border guard returns an individual to a place where he may be exposed to persecution, torture or other ill treatment provided that the border guard exercises sufficient physical control over the individual to establish jurisdiction. These two conditions are met in the following situations:

(I) In joint operations at sea, conducting a vessel to a third country and handing over the vessel to the authorities of a third country can entail refoulement, depending on the destination in question. Jurisdiction is established when an interception amounts to stopping, boarding and searching a vessel and handing over the vessel to the authority of a third country. The derivative responsibility of the EU may be established when Frontex's coordination of a joint operation involves both Member States and third countries.

In the context of joint operations in the territorial waters of a third country and involving the exercise of law-enforcement power by third-country officers on board a Member State's vessels, the host Member State may incur derivative responsibility for a breach of the principle of non-refoulement by aiding and assisting the third-country officers. The EU may also incur derivative responsibility through Frontex, in so far as it aids or assists third-country officers by coordinating a joint operation.

(II) In joint operations on land, a Member State hosting a joint operation can incur responsibility for breaches of the principle of non-refoulement at the borders or within the territories of the EU when border control and border surveillance are carried out. It is also possible that a Member State deploying border guards in such a joint operation may incur derivative responsibility.

In addition, it is possible to envisage a host Member State incurring responsibility in a hypothetical situation in which the Member State's border guards are deployed in a Frontex joint operation to the territory of a third country to intercept third-country nationals trying to cross the EU's external borders irregularly.

9

General Conclusions

9.1   The Process of Embedding the EU/Frontex's Border Control and Surveillance in a Fundamental Rights Milieu

Our conclusion begins by appraising the protection obligations of human and refugee rights incumbent upon Frontex and the EU, and by considering future developments. Thereafter, the chapter looks closely at the more technical legal elements which constitute the findings of this study and it brings together recommendations for addressing the persistent areas of contradiction or potential risk pertaining to the Agency's legal setting that has been identified in the course of this work.

The preceding chapters have shown that there are many provisions in the EU treaties which state the commitment of the EU to the respect of human rights when it acts internally and in its relationship with the outside world.[1] The Charter of Fundamental Rights of the European Union (EU Charter) is the catalogue of fundamental rights which should inform the EU's action. Complementing this obligation, although with a different legal value, we have studied the role of the European Convention for the Protection of Human Rights (ECHR) and the other international human rights treaties.

The EU's commitment to respect for human rights is definitely put to the test when the EU takes action to prevent or reduce irregular migration to the EU's territories. The EU must currently manage several 'domestic' issues while engaging in the delicate enterprise of finding a balance between protection of those individuals who may face persecution, torture and other ill treatment if sent back to third countries, in compliance with the principle of non-refoulement, and preventing unauthorised migrant-entry. The political pressure to adopt measures designed to discourage third-country nationals from embarking on any journey towards the EU's territory is growing exponentially. Claims abound that the social (and physical) security of the EU's citizenry is

---

[1]   See Chapter 1 and Chapter 5.

threatened by those who cross the EU's external borders irregularly. Thus, building barriers, both physical and legal, is increasingly seen as a viable solution. Notably, in June 2015, Hungarian Prime Minister Viktor Orbán ordered the building of a fence to prevent Kosovars passing through Serbia to reach Hungary.[2] At the EU level, an emphasis on the importance of having tighter border controls is evident. The 'Smart Border' Package proposal by the European Commission in 2013 and the adoption in the same year of the European Border Surveillance System (Eurosur) are telling examples in this respect.[3]

Frontex has had to operate within, and be shaped by, this difficult political and social climate. There is an enduring 'fabric of legal complexity' which affects the Agency, examined in Chapter 3, and this carries broad consequences because of the way Frontex has been entrusted by the EU with a leading role in the performance of border control and surveillance operations conducted by EU Member States. Accordingly, its actions may trigger the responsibility of the EU should violations of human rights and refugee rights be committed. When Frontex personnel began the Agency's work in 2004, the legal instrument establishing Frontex's mandate contained only one reference concerning fundamental rights and refugee rights.[4] The border guard culture was strong among the people working in Warsaw, where Frontex has its headquarters, and

---

[2] Euractive, 'Hungary to Build Fence at Serbia Border', www.euractiv.com (accessed 13 November 2015). The same choice was made by Greece in 2012 at the borders with Turkey in the region of Orestiada to prevent the border crossing of migrants coming originally from North Africa and Afghanistan. In 2014, also working at the borders with Turkey, Bulgaria adopted the same approach to curbing the number of migrants coming primarily from Syria (Euobserver, 'Greeks build fence to ward off asylum seekers' at euobserver.com/justice/115161; Reuters, 'Bulgaria's fence to stop migrants on Turkey border nears completion', www.reuters.com (both accessed 13 November 2015)).

[3] The 'Smart Borders' Package consists of the Entry/Exit System and of the Registered Traveller Programme proposed by the European Commission in February 2013: European Commission, 'Proposal for a Regulation of the European Parliament and of the Council establishing an Entry/Exit System (EES) to register entry and exit data of third-country nationals crossing the external borders of the Member States of the European Union' and 'Proposal for a Regulation of the European Parliament and of the Council establishing a Registered Traveller Programme', COM (2013) 95 final. For an analysis of the 'Smart Borders' Package, see C. Jones, 'Smart borders: fait accompli?', Statewatch Analysis, www.statewatch.org (accessed 13 November 2015). On Eurosur, Regulation (EU) No 1052/2013 of the European Parliament and of the Council of 22 October 2013 establishing the European Border Surveillance System (Eurosur) OJ 2013 No. 295, p. 11.

[4] Council Regulation (EC) 2007/2004 of 26 October 2004 establishing a European agency for the management of operational cooperation at the external borders of the Member States of the European Union OJ 2004 No. L349, p. 1, Preamble (22).

at the borders in Frontex's joint operations. However, as the Agency's activities have progressed, Frontex personnel (and personnel deployed by Member States) increasingly had to face that the process of performing border control and surveillance brings concerns about human rights and refugee rights to the forefront. There is now a greater consciousness of how Frontex's work and decision-making can heavily affect third-country nationals' lives. In the words of the Parliamentary Assembly of the Council of Europe:

> When Frontex was established, its role was seen primarily in terms of border control and migration management. Once it began to operate, it became clear that there were many human rights implications attached to its work and that it was ill-equipped to tackle them. This was particularly the case when intercepting irregular migrants, asylum seekers and refugees at borders or at sea, and also during return operations involving irregular migrants and rejected asylum seekers.[5]

The adoption of the 'new' Frontex Regulation in 2011 which contained more provisions about the respect of fundamental rights, and entrusted the Agency and the Member States participating in joint operations with more obligations in this respect, was clear evidence of this developing consciousness. On this point, the United Nations High Commissioner for Refugees (UNHCR) on the proposal for the new Regulation by the European Commission in 2010 observed: 'although Frontex does not have a protection mandate, its activities should nonetheless be carried out consistently with the EU *acquis communautaire*, including its measures on asylum'.[6] The new Regulation has begun the process of addressing shortcomings, and it includes the planning of a Fundamental Rights Strategy whereby 'respect and promotion of fundamental rights are unconditional and integral components of effective integrated border management'; the drafting of a Code of Conduct and Common Core Curricula for border guards 'to promote ... the respect of fundamental rights ...'; the creation of a Consultative Forum to look after the development and implementation of the previous two instruments and the

---

[5] Parliamentary Assembly of the Council of Europe, 'Frontex: Human Rights Responsibilities', Resolution 1932(2013) Final version, para 2.
[6] UNHCR, 'UNHCR's observations on the European Commission's proposal for a Regulation of the European Parliament and the Council amending Council Regulation (EC) No 2007/2004 establishing an European Agency for the Management of Operational Cooperation at the External Borders of the Member States of the European Union (FRONTEX)', COM(2010)61 final, 2–3.

appointment of a Fundamental Rights Officer.[7] This now requires greater refinement and implementation. Thus far, what we have witnessed with respect to Frontex and the making of its activities at the external borders of the EU is a slow process according to which Frontex has moved from a 'pure border guard culture' to a 'fundamental rights culture'. In other words, Frontex is catching up with a fundamental rights culture which was to some extent missing at the start of its activities. This indicates that in its development of a common policy on border control the EU may be capable of living up to the relevant international law obligations to which it has subscribed. The process of reforming Frontex's preparedness and capacity to deal with fundamental rights compliance requires the common effort of EU institutions, Member States, Council of Europe, UNHCR, NGOs, civil society as well as Frontex itself. Notably, in this connection, the action brought by the European Parliament against the Council of the EU seeking the annulment of Council Decision 2010/252/EU on the surveillance of the sea external borders led to the adoption of the Sea External Borders Regulation which, in replacing the previous legal instrument, included clearer legal measures on non-refoulement, disembarkation, and search and rescue.

This process of developing Frontex's fundamental rights preparedness and capacities provides a fitting context for my study which has tried to contribute to the creation of a more comprehensive awareness of the risks of possible human rights and refugee rights violations (in particular of the principle of non-refoulement) in the context of Frontex's joint operations.

9.2 The Contribution of This Study

The present work has been concerned with the specific legal circumstances which may expose the EU and its Member States to incurring responsibility for breaches of the principle of non-refoulement in Frontex's joint operations. First, this analysis studied the intricacies of the functioning of Frontex, its relationship with the EU, as well as the way the Agency works together with the Member States. Second, the analysis focused on the extent to which international responsibility for internationally wrongful acts can be ascribed to the EU and its Member States for violations committed in the context of Frontex's operations. Third, the

---

[7] Article 26a of the Frontex Regulation; Frontex, 'Frontex Fundamental Rights Strategy', Preamble, 31 May 2011.

analysis moved to the principle of non-refoulement and its territorial reach under international law and EU law. Here, the focus was the extent to which the principle accords with the actions of Frontex and the EU in the context of border control operations. Finally, scenarios were created which identified courses of action in Frontex's joint operations which may trigger the responsibility of the EU and its Member States.

Frontex not only provides technical and operational assistance to the border control activities conducted by the EU Member States. It also performs a leading role in joint operations. This is a consequence of a supranationalisation dynamic which concerns the EU institutions and the EU Member States in the EU common policy on border control (of which operational cooperation under Frontex is part). Nevertheless, concerning the matter of effective control, one of the requirements for determining the international responsibility of the EU, it is the Member State hosting the operation that has effective control of the operations and not the EU through Frontex (Chapter 3 and 4). This is because, according to the division of competence between the EU and its Member States in the EU common policy on external borders control, only the Member States have competence to exercise law-enforcement power when enforcing measures adopted pursuant to EU provisions on joint operations (Chapter 2). As an additional matter, the EU, through Frontex and its Member States, may incur derivative responsibility for aid and assistance to another Member State which commits an internationally wrongful act. In practical terms, let us take the example of a joint operation, hosted by Italy, in which other EU Member States, including Greece, take part. If a Greek border guard commits an internationally wrongful act, the Member State responsible for the violation will be Italy, since it is the Member State hosting the joint operation. Also, if Italy has received aid and assistance from the EU, through Frontex, in the coordination of the operation, the EU may also incur derivative responsibility. Equally, the derivative responsibility of Greece, home Member State, for aid or assistance, may be established in the case of the secondment of personnel from Greece to European Border Guard Teams receiving instructions from Italy, host Member State, if the international responsibility of Italy is established (Chapter 4).

Having clarified the matter of 'who does what' in the context of Frontex's joint operations, and having examined how the EU and its Member States may be held responsible for possible internationally wrongful acts, this book's analysis scrutinised the entity of potential violations (Chapter 5). The analytical task was then to establish whether the rule of law follows Frontex, *alias* the EU, and the Member States in their border control activities and prescribes to it the respect of the principle of non-refoulement when such activities are performed (Chapter 6). It was noted that Frontex's joint operations are carried out within the territories of the Member States, at their borders and outside their borders (i.e. on the high seas and, possibly in future, in the territories of third countries). Thus, breaches of the principle of non-refoulement during Frontex's joint operations may occur not only within the territories of the Member States but also beyond their borders. First, the analysis of international human rights law, refugee law and EU law showed that both the EU and its Member States are bound by the principle of non-refoulement under international law. It was also noted that within the EU legal order, protection against refoulement is clearly stated, and the standard of protection corresponds to that provided for under Article 3 ECHR. Moreover, the EU secondary legislation on joint operations through Frontex (the Schengen Borders Code, the Frontex Regulation, the Sea External Borders Regulation) requires Frontex and the Member States involved in joint operations to respect the principle of non-refoulement. Second, the study engaged with the case law of national and international decision-making bodies on this legal topic and showed that the principle of non-refoulement applies within the territory, at the borders and outside the borders whenever a State exercises effective control. Notably, the recent rulings of the European Court of Human Rights (ECtHR) in the *Al-Skeini* case, the *Hassan* case and the *Jaloud* case shed light on the extraterritorial reach of the ECHR and the exercise of effective control over individuals. The ECtHR's decision in the *Hirsi* case in 2012 has been important in establishing that the principle of non-refoulement applies on the high seas. The conclusion – that the principle of non-refoulement applies whenever the State exercises effective control – appears also to apply to the 1951 Refugee Convention if the methodological choice to use international human rights law as a supplementary means of interpretation of the Convention is endorsed. Under EU law, my analysis showed that the principle of non-refoulement enshrined in the EU Charter and the general principles of EU law applies within the territories of the Member States, and at their borders, when they conduct border control and border surveillance activities; it also applies when Frontex and the Member States implement legislation on joint operations outside the Member States' territories.

Focusing further on the Agency's action outside the EU's borders, the specificities of Frontex's mandate also led us to examine problematic aspects of Frontex's operations at sea (Chapter 7). First, the interconnection between respect of the principle of non-refoulement and the search and rescue at sea legal regime emerged clearly from the analysis of legal issues related to Frontex's surveillance operations. Here, disembarkation to a place of safety must not entail a violation of the principle of non-refoulement. Second, it was found that, despite pressure from public opinion and political circles, Frontex's joint operations cannot have an exclusive focus on search and rescue at sea. There are legal reasons which prevent such a move (i.e. the lack of a Frontex mandate; and, since Frontex is an EU agency, the lack of competence of the EU in this respect).

The book was then able to assess the emergent picture of the legal circumstances which may expose the EU and its Member States to incurring responsibility for breaches of the principle of non-refoulement in Frontex's joint operations: (i) the principle of non-refoulement is binding on the EU and its Member States when they carry out joint operations through Frontex, whether it is at the Turkish-Greek borders or during a surveillance operation on the high seas in the Mediterranean; (ii) legislation on joint operations through Frontex provides that Frontex and the Member States must act in accordance with the principle of non-refoulement. The Schengen Borders Code, the Frontex Regulation and the legislation regulating surveillance at the sea external borders, especially after the adoption of the Sea External Borders Regulation, are quite clear in this sense. Accordingly, it appears that the implementation of EU legislation by Frontex and the Member States does not lead to breaches of the principle. In other words, violations of the principle of non-refoulement, if registered in the context of Frontex's joint operations, generally would not derive from how the legislation concerning Frontex's joint operations is drafted. Mostly, violations of the principle would relate to how decisions are taken at the operational level. Significantly, in this respect, it is from the operational plans, which Frontex's Executive Director is involved in drawing up, that it may be possible to establish a derivative responsibility of the EU for breaches of the principle of non-refoulement in joint operations (Chapter 4).

At this juncture, the importance of having scenarios was reaffirmed. They highlight how violations at the operational level may occur and what courses of action performed in the context of Frontex's joint operations may trigger the responsibility of the EU and its Member States in this respect (Chapter 8). By way of example, the use of radar or thermos-visors at the EU's borders by Frontex may trigger with difficulty the responsibility of the EU and its Member States for violations of the principle of non-refoulement. Conversely, the derivative responsibility of the EU may be established when Frontex coordinates a joint sea operation involving both Member States and third countries if a migrant vessel is conducted to a third country, depending on the human rights records of the third country in question. This analysis points to where EU, Frontex and Member State action should be focused in order to prevent such violations in the context of joint operations. If the EU and its Member States want to honour their commitments to respect human rights and refugee rights when taking action to prevent and reduce irregular migration, then the focus should be on how Frontex's border control activities are planned so as not to breach the principle of non-refoulement.

Finally, the preceding chapters have examined some features of Frontex's activities which present problems and require action by the Agency if a proper balance between management of the EU external borders and respect of human rights and refugee rights is to be assured. Some specific reflections and recommendations pertaining to these unresolved issues are as follows.

The process described above, whereby Frontex has moved towards a more explicit fundamental rights orientation, has not been a smooth, uninterrupted process if one looks at the major problematic features of Frontex's activities identified in my study. Besides the matter of Frontex's working arrangements with third countries showing poor human rights records, the inadequacy of a self-monitoring mechanism within the Agency's structure regarding compliance with fundamental rights obligations constitutes a serious gap. On this point, as analysed in Chapter 3, the Agency has not yet adopted adequate procedural safeguards on the circumstances in which operations should be suspended or terminated because of the occurrence of fundamental rights violations in the context of joint operations. Establishing adequate procedural safeguards in compliance with the EU Charter, as recommended by the European Ombudsman in his own inquiry, would allow a concrete use of Article 3(1a) of the Frontex Regulation.[8] If such safeguards are lacking, this provision risks being disregarded (and not applied) given its unspecific wording in defining when joint operations should be suspended or terminated.

---

[8] Article 3(1a) of the Frontex Regulation states (first indent): 'The Agency may terminate, after informing the Member States concerned, joint operations and pilot projects if the conditions to conduct those joint operations or pilot projects are no longer fulfilled'.

Here, we might also venture a reflection on the transparency of Frontex's work and the accessibility of information about its operations. The Agency should increase the comprehensibility and visibility of what it does in the context of joint operations. It should be more open about how such operations are planned. Given the importance of the operational plan in determining whether the EU and/or its Member States may incur responsibility for internationally wrongful acts, such information should be made available to the public to the largest possible extent. Specifically, it is crucial to know which third countries are involved in the implementation of the operational plans, and it is essential to be informed about any specific acts of interception of persons in joint operations. As explained in Chapter 8, this information has not been disclosed by Frontex in response to my request for access to the operational plans of Joint Operation Hera 2011 and Joint Operation Hermes 2011. This practice has a profound (and negative) impact on the transparency of the work of the Agency. At the same time, it limits the success and scope of the project outlined above which aims to embed the EU and Frontex's actions in a fundamental rights–oriented process.

BIBLIOGRAPHY

Ahmed, Tawhida, and de Jesus Butler, Israel, 'The European Union and Human Rights: An International Law Perspective' (2006) 17 *European Journal of International Law* 771.

Allain, Jean, 'The Jus Cogens Nature of Non-refoulement' (2002) 13 *International Journal of Refugee Law* 533.

Alvarez, José, 'Misadventures in Subjecthood' (2010) *EJIL: Talk!.*

Azoulai, Loic (ed.), *The Question of Competence in the European Union* (Oxford University Press, 2014).

Baldaccini, Anneliese, 'Extraterritorial Border Controls in the EU: The Role of Frontex in Operations at Sea' in Ryan, Bernard, and Mitsilegas, Valsamis (eds.), *Extraterritorial Immigration Control – Legal Challenges* (Martinus Nijhoff Publishers, 2010).

Barnes, Richard, 'Refugee Law at Sea' (2004) 53 *The International and Comparative Law Quarterly* 47.

Barnes, Richard, 'The International Law of the Sea and Migration Control' in Ryan, Bernard, and Mitsilegas, Valsamis (eds.), *Extraterritorial Immigration Control – Legal Challenges* (Martinus Nijhoff Publishers, 2010).

Battjes, Hemme, *European Asylum Law and International Law* (Martinus Nijhoff Publishers, 2006).

Berman, Frank, 'Treaty Interpretation in a Judicial Context' (2004) 29 *Yale Journal of International Law* 315.

Bigo, Didier, 'The Transformation of European Border Controls' in Ryan, Bernard, and Mitsilegas, Valsamis (eds.), *Extraterritorial Immigration Control: Legal Challenges* (Martinus Nijhoff Publishers, 2010).

Börzel, Tanja A., 'Mind the Gap! European Integration between Level and Scope' (2005) 12 *Journal of European Public Policy* 217.

Boulesbaa, Ahcene, 'The Nature of the Obligations Incurred by States under Article 2 of the UN Convention against Torture' (1990) 12 *Human Rights Quarterly* 53.

Brownlie, Ian, *Principles of Public International Law* (Oxford University Press, 2012).

Brücker, Herber, and Others, 'Managing Migration in the European Welfare State', www.frdb.org.

Bruin, Rene, and Wouters, Kees, 'Terrorism and the Non-derogability of Non-refoulement' (2003) 15 *International Journal of Refugee Law* 5.

Bryan, Ian, and Langford, Peter, 'Impediments to the Expulsion of Non-nationals: Substance and Coherence in Procedural Protection under the European Convention on Human Rights' (2010) 79 *Nordic Journal of International Law* 457.

Burgers, J. Herman, and Danelius, Hans, *The United Nations Convention against Torture: A Handbook on the Convention against Torture and Other Cruel Inhuman or Degrading Treatment or Punishment* (Martinus Nijhoff Publishers, 1988).

Busuioc, Madalina, 'Accountability, Control and Independence: The Case of European Agencies' (2009) 15 *European Law Journal* 599.

Cannizzaro, Enzo, 'Beyond the Either/Or: Dual Attribution to the European Union and to the Member State for Breach of the ECHR' in Evans, Malcom, and Koutrakos, Panos (eds.), *The International Responsibility of the European Union: European and International Perspectives* (Hart Publishing, 2013).

Cannizzaro, Enzo, 'Postscript to Chapter 12' in Evans, Malcom, and Koutrakos, Panos (eds.), *The International Responsibility of the European Union: European and International Perspectives* (Hart Publishing, 2013).

Carrera, Sergio, 'The EU Border Management Strategy – Frontex and the Challenges of Irregular Migration in the Canary Islands', *CEPS Working Document* No. 261/March 2007.

Carrera, Sergio, and den Hertog, Leonhard, 'Whose Mare? Rule of Law Challenges in the Field of European Border Surveillance in the Mediterranean' *CEPS Paper in Liberty and Security in Europe* No. 79/January 2015.

Caron, David D., 'The ILC Articles on State Responsibility: The Paradoxical Relationship between Forma and Authority' (2002) 96 *The American Journal of International Law* 857.

Casolari, Federico, *L'Incorporazione del Diritto Internazionale nell'Ordinamento del Diritto dell'Unione Europea* (Giuffré, 2008).

Cassese, Antonio, *International Law* (Oxford University Press, 2005).

Chetail, Vincent, 'Le Droit des Refugiés à l'Epreuve de la Jurisprudence de la Cour Europèenne des Droit de l'Homme sur l'Interdiction de Renvoi des Etrangers Menacés de Torture et de Traitements Inhumains ou Dégradants' (2004) 1 *Revue Belge de Droit International* 155.

Chiti, Edoardo, 'An Important Part of the EU's Institutional Machinery: Features, Problems and Perspectives of European Agencies' (2009) 46 *Common Market Law Review* 1395.

Churchill, Robin R., and Lowe, Vaughan A., *The Law of the Sea* (Manchester University Press, 1999).

Coleman, Nils, 'Non-refoulement Revisited: Renewed Review of the Status of the Principle of Non-refoulement as Customary International Law' (2003) 5 *European Journal of Migration and Law* 23.

Coleman, Nils, *European Readmission Policy: Third Country Interests and Refugee Rights* (Martinus Nijhoff Publishers, 2009).

Costello, Cathryn, 'The Bosphorus Ruling of the European Court of Human Rights: Fundamental Rights and Blurred Boundaries in Europe' (2006) 6 *Human Rights Law Review* 88.

Costello, Cathryn, 'Courting Access to Asylum in Europe: Recent Supranational Jurisprudence Explored' (2012) 12 *Human Rights Law Review* 287.

Craig, Paul P., 'Competence and Member State Autonomy: Causality, Consequence and Legitimacy' in Micklitz, Hans W., and de Witte, Bruno (eds.), *The European Court of Justice and the Autonomy of the Member States* (Intersentia, 2012).

Craig, Paul P., 'EU Accession to the ECHR: Competence, Procedure and Substance' (2013) 6 *Fordham International Law Journal* 1114.

Cremona, Marise, 'The European Union as an International Actor: The Issues of Flexibility and Linkage' (1998) 3 *European Foreign Affairs Review* 67.

Cremona, Marise, 'External Relations of the EU and the Member States: Competence, Mixed Agreements, International Responsibility, and Effects of International Law' (2006) *EUI Working Papers Law* No. 2006/22.

Cremona, Marise, 'Defining Competence in EU External Relations: Lessons from the Treaty Reform Process' in Dashwood, Alan and Maresceau, Marc (eds.), *Law and Practice of EU External Relations: Salient Features of a Changing Landscape* (Cambridge University Press, 2008).

Dashwood, Alan, 'The Relationship between the Member States and the European Union/European Community' (2004) 41 *Common Market Law Review* 355.

Dashwood, Alan, Dougan, Michael, Rodger, Barry, Spaventa, Eleanor, and Wyatt, Derrick, *European Union Law* (Hart Publishing, 2011).

d'Aspremont, Jean, 'The Articles on the Responsibility of International Organizations: Magnifying the Fissures in the Law of International Responsibility' (2012) 9 *International Organizations Law Review* 15.

de Burca, Grainne, 'The European Court of Justice and the International Legal Order after Kadi' (2010) 51 *Harvard International Law Journal* 1.

Dehousse, Renaud, 'Misfits: EU Law and the Misfits of European Governance', *Jean Monnet Working Paper* No. 2/2002, 13.

de Schoutheete, Philippe, and Andoura, Sami, 'The Legal Personality of the European Union' (2007) *LX Studia Diplomatica*, EGMONT, Brussels.

Di Filippo, Marcello, 'Irregular Migration and Safeguard of Life at Sea. International Rules and Recent Developments in the Mediterranean Sea' in Del Vecchio, Angela (ed.), *International Law of the Sea: Current Trends and Controversial Issues* (Eleven International Publishing, 2014).

Douglas-Scott, Sionaidh, 'The European Union and Human Rights after the Treaty of Lisbon' (2011) 11 *Human Rights Law Review* 671.

den Heijer, Maarten, 'Whose Rights and Which Rights? The Continuing Story of Non-refoulement under the European Convention on Human Rights' (2008) 10 *European Journal of Migration and Law* 277.

den Heijer, Maarten, 'Europe beyond its Borders: Refugee and Human Rights Protection in Extraterritorial Migration Control' in Ryan, Bernard, and Mitsilegas, Valsamis (eds.), *Extraterritorial Immigration Control: Legal Challenges* (Martinus Nijhoff Publishers, 2010).

den Heijer, Maarten, *Europe and Extraterritorial Asylum* (Hart Publishing, 2012).

den Heijer, Maarten, 'Reflections on Refoulement and Collective Expulsion in the Hirsi Case' (2013) 25 *International Journal of Refugee Law* 265.

den Heijer, Maarten, 'Article 18' in Peers, Steve, Hervey, Tamara, and Others (eds.), *The EU Charter of Fundamental Rights: A Commentary* (Hart/Beck, 2014).

den Heijer, Maarten, and Lawson, Rick, 'Extraterritorial Human Rights and the Concept of 'Jurisdiction' " in Langford, Malcom, Wouter, Vandenhole, Scheinin, Marten, and Genugten, Willem (eds.), *Global Justice, State Duties: The Extraterritorial Scope of Economic, Social, and Cultural Rights in International Law* (Cambridge University Press, 2014).

Dennis, Michael J., 'Application of Human Rights Treaties Extraterritorially in Times of Armed Conflict and Military Occupation' (2005) 99 *The American Journal of International Law* 119.

de Wet, Erika, *The Chapter VII Powers of the United Nations Security Council* (Hart Publishing, 2004).

de Wet, Erika, 'The Prohibition of Torture as an International Norm of Jus Cogens and Its Implications for National and Customary Law' (2004) 15 *European Journal of International Law* 97.

de Witte, Bruno, 'Direct Effect, Primacy and the Nature of the Legal Order' in Craig, Paul P., and de Burca, Grainne (eds.), *The Evolution of EU Law* (Oxford University Press, 2011).

de Witte, Bruno, 'The EU and the International Legal Order: The Case of Human Rights' in Evans, Malcom, and Koutrakos, Panos (eds.), *Beyond the Established Legal Orders: Policy Interconnections between the EU and the Rest of the World* (Hart Publishing, 2011).

d'Aspremont, Jean, and Dopagne, Frederic, 'Kadi: The ECJ's Reminder of the Elementary Divide between Legal Orders' (2008) 5 *International Organizations Law Review* 371.

Direk, Omer F., 'Responsibility in Peace Support Operations: Revisiting the Proper Test for Attribution Conduct and the Meaning of the "Effective Control" Standard' (2014) 61 *Netherlands International Law Review* 1.

Dörr, Oliver, and Schmalenbach, Kirsten (eds.), *Vienna Convention on the Law of the Treaties: A Commentary* (Springer, 2012).

Duffy, Aoife, 'Expulsion to Face Torture? Non-refoulement in International Law' (2008) 20 *International Journal of Refugee Law* 373.

Eckes, Christina, 'Does the European Court of Human Rights Provide Protection from the European Community? – The Case of Bosphorus Airways' (2007) 13 *European Public Law* 47.

Eckes, Christina, 'EU Accession to the ECHR: Between Autonomy and Adaptation' (2013) 76 *The Modern Law Review* 254.

Fink, Melanie, 'Frontex Working Arrangements: Legitimacy and Human Rights Concerns Regarding "Technical Relationships" ' (2012) 75 *Merkourios – Utrectht Journal of International and European Law* 20.

Fischer-Lescano, Andreas, Löhr, Tillmann, and Tohidipur, Timo, 'Border Controls at Sea: Requirements under International Human Rights and Refugee Law' (2009) 21 *International Journal of Refugee Law* 256.

Foster, Michelle, *International Refugee Law and Socio-Economic Rights: Refuge from Deprivation* (Cambridge University Press, 2007).

Gaja, Giorgio, 'Accession to the ECHR' in Biondi, Andrea, Eeckhout, Piet, and Ripley, Stefanie (eds.), *EU Law after Lisbon* (Oxford University Press, 2012).

Gallagher, Anne T., 'Human Rights and the New UN Protocols on Trafficking and Migrant Smuggling: A Preliminary Analysis' (2001) 23 *Human Rights Quarterly* 975.

Gammeltoft-Hansen, Thomas, and Gammeltoft-Hansen, Hans, 'The Right to Seek – Revisited. On the UN Human Rights Declaration Article 14 and Access to Asylum Procedures in the EU' (2008) 10 *European Journal of Migration and Law* 439.

Gammeltoft-Hansen, Thomas, *Access to Asylum: International Refugee Law and the Globalisation of Migration Control* (Cambridge University Press, 2011).

Gardiner, Richard K., *Treaty Interpretation* (Oxford University Press, 2008).

Giannelli, Alessandra, 'Customary International Law in the European Union' in Cannizzaro, Enzo, Palchetti, Paolo, and Wessel, Ramses A. (eds.), *International Law as Law of the European Union* (Brill Nijhoff, 2011).

Giuffré, Mariagiulia, 'Watered-down Rights on the High Seas: Hirsi Jamaa and Others v Italy' (2012) 61 *International and Comparative Law Quarterly* 728.

Giuffré, Mariagiulia, 'State Responsibility Beyond Borders: What Legal Basis for Italy's Push-backs to Libya?' (2012) 24 *International Journal of Refugee Law* 692.

Gil-Bazo, María-Teresa, 'Refugee Status, Subsidiary Protection, and the Right to be Granted Asylum under Refugee Law' (2006) *New Issues in Refugee Research*, Research Paper No. 136, Refugee Studies Centre Oxford.

Gil-Bazo, María-Teresa, 'The Charter of Fundamental Rights of the European Union and the Right to Asylum in the Union's Law' (2008) 27 *Refugee Survey Quarterly* 33.

Gondek, Michal, 'Extraterritorial Application of the European Convention on Human Rights: Territorial Focus in the Age of Globalization?' (2005) 52 *Netherlands International Law Review* 349.

Goodwil-Gill, Guy S., and McAdam, Jane, *The Refugee in International Law* (Oxford University Press, 2007).

Goodwin-Gill, Guy S., 'The Right to Seek Asylum: Interception at Sea and the Principle of Non-refoulement' (2011) 23 *International Journal of Refugee Law* 443.

Graefrath, Bernhard, 'Complicity in the Law of International Responsibility' (1996) 29 *Revue Belge de Droit International* 371.

Grahl-Madsen, Atle, *The Status of Refugees in International Law*, vol. 2 (A.W. Sijthoff – Leiden, 1972).

Gronnegaard Christensen, Joergen, 'Administrative Capacity, Structural Choice and the Creation of EU Agencies' (2010) 17 *Journal of European Public Policy* 176.

Guild, Elspeth, 'Moving the Borders of Europe', Inaugural Lecture at the University of Nijmegen, 30 May 2001.

Guild, Elspeth, 'Article 19' in Peers, Steve, Hervey, Tamara, Kenner, Jeff, and Ward, Angela (eds.), *The EU Charter of Fundamental Rights: A Commentary* (Hart/Beck, 2014).

Hailbronner, Kay, 'Non-refoulement and "Humanitarian" Refugees: Customary International Law or Wishful Legal Thinking?' (1986) 26 *Virginia Journal of International Law* 857.

Hailbronner, Kay, 'Introduction into the EU Immigration and Asylum Law' in Hailbronner, Kay (ed.), *EU Immigration and Asylum Law: Commentary on EU Regulations and Directives* (C.H. Beck Hart Nomos, 2010).

Haraszti, Gabor, *Some Fundamental Problems of the Law of Treaties* (Akademiai Kiado Budapest, 1973).

Harpaz, Guy, 'The European Court of Justice and Its Relations with the European Court of Human Rights: The Quest for Enhanced Reliance, Coherence and Legitimacy' (2009) 46 *Common Market Law Review* 105.

Harvey, Colin, 'The Right to Seek Asylum in the European Union' (2004) 1 *European Human Rights Law Review* 17.

Hathaway, James C., *The Rights of Refugees under International Law* (Cambridge University Press, 2005).

Hathaway, James C., and Foster, Michelle, *The Law of Refugee Status* (Cambridge University Press, 2014).

Hobbing, Peter, 'Integrated Border Management at the EU Level' in Carrera, Sergio, and Balzacq, Thierry (eds.), *Security versus Freedom? A Challenge for Europe's Future* (Ashgate Publishing, 2006).

Hoffmeister, Frank, 'Litigating against the European Union and Its Member States: Who Responds under the ILC's Draft Articles on International Responsibility of International Organizations?' (2010) 21 *European Journal of International Law* 723.

Holberg, Ross K., 'Italy's Policy of Pushing Back African Migrants on the High Seas Rejected by the European Court of Human Rights in the Case of Hirsi Jamaa & Others v. Italy' (2012) 26 *Georgetown Immigration Law Journal* 467.

Holdgaard, Rass, *External Relations Law of the European Community* (Wolters Kluwer, 2007).

Howley, Jacob D., 'Unlocking the Fortress: Protocol No. 11 and the Birth of Collective Expulsion Jurisprudence in the Council of Europe System' (2006) 21 *Georgetown Immigration Law Journal* 117.

Jacob, Francis J., 'Direct Effect and Interpretation of International Agreements in the Recent Case Law of the European Court of Justice' in Dashwood, A., and Maresceau, M. (eds.), *Law and Practice of EU External Relations: Salient Features of a Changing Landscape* (Cambridge University Press, 2008).

Janik, Cornelia, and Kleinlein, Thomas, 'When Soering Went to Iraq: Problems of Jurisdiction, Extraterritorial Effect and Norm Conflicts in the Light of the European Court of Human Rights' Al-Saadoon Case' (2009) 1 *Goettingen Journal of International Law* 459.

Janmyr, Maja, *Protecting Civilians in Refugee Camps: Issues of Responsibility and Lessons from Uganda* (DPhil thesis, University of Bergen, 2012).

Jessup, Philip C., *The Law of Territorial Waters and Maritime Jurisdiction* (G.A. Jennings Co., 1927).

Joseph, Sarah, and Castan, Melissa, *The International Covenant on Civil and Political Rights: Cases, Materials, and Commentary* (Oxford University Press, 2013).

Jorrit, Helene, 'Construction of a European Institutional Model for Managing Operational Cooperation at the EU's External Borders: Is the Frontex Agency a Decisive Step Forward?', *CEPS Challenge Paper* No. 6, *CEPS Challenge*, Brussels, 2007.

Kälin, Walter, Caroni, Martina, and Heim, Lukas, 'Article 33, para 1' in Zimmermann, Andreas (ed.), *The 1951 Convention Relating to the Status of Refugees and Its 1967 Protocol: A Commentary* (Oxford University Press, 2011).

Klug, Anja, and Howe, Tim, 'The Concept of State Jurisdiction and the Applicability of the Non-refoulement Principle to Extraterritorial Interception Measures' in Ryan, Bernard, and Mitsilegas, Valsamis (eds.), *Extraterritorial Immigration Control: Legal Challenges* (Martinus Nijhoff Publishers, 2010).

Klug, Anja, 'Strengthening the Protection of Migrants and Refugees in Distress at Sea through International Cooperation and Burden-sharing' (2014) 26 *International Journal of Refugee Law* 48.

Kokott, Juliane, and Sobotta, Christoph, 'The Kadi Case – Constitutional Core Values and International law – Finding the Balance?' (2012) 23 *European Journal of International Law* 1016.

Kopacz, Zdzislaw, Morgas, Waclaw, and Urbanski, Jozef, 'The Maritime Safety System: Its Main Components and Elements' (2001) 54 *The Journal of Navigation* 199.

Kostakopoulou, Dora, 'An Open and Secure Europe? Fixity and Fissures in the Area of Freedom Security and Justice after Lisbon and Stockholm' (2010) 19 *European Security* 151.

Kritzman-Amir, Tally, and Spijkerboer, Thomas, 'On the Morality and Legality of Borders: Border Policies and Asylum Seekers' (2013) 26 *Harvard Human Rights Journal* 1.

Kuijper, Pieter J., 'Customary International Law, Decisions of International Organisations and Other Techniques for Ensuring Respect for International Legal Rules in European Community Law' in Wouters, Jan (ed.), *International Law in the EU and its Member States* (T.M.C. Asser Press, 2008).

Kuijper, Jan Pieter, and Paasivirta, Esa, 'EU International Responsibility and its Attribution: From the Inside Looking Out' in Evans, Malcom, and Koutrakos, Panos (eds.), *The International Responsibility of the European Union: European and International Perspectives* (Hart Publishing, 2013).

Lambert, Helene, 'Protection Against Refoulement from Europe: Human Rights Law Comes to the Rescue' (1999) 48 *International Comparative Law Quarterly* 519.

Lambert, Helene, 'The European Convention on Human Rights and the Protection of Refugees: Limits and Opportunities' (2005) 24 *Refugee Survey Quarterly* 39.

Lambert, Helene, Messineo, Francesco, and Tiedemann, Paul, 'Comparative Perspectives of Constitutional Asylum in France, Italy and Germany: Resquiescat in Pace?' (2008) 27 *Refugee Survey Quarterly* 16.

Larsen, Kjetil Mujezinovic, 'Attribution of Conduct in Peace Operations: The "Ultimate Authority and Control" Test' (2008) 19 *European Journal of International Law* 50.

Lauterpacht, Elihu, and Bethlehem, Daniel, 'The Scope and the Content of the Principle of Non-refoulement: Opinion' in Feller, Erika, Türk, Volker, and Nicholson, Frances (eds.), *Refugee Protection in International Law: UNHCR's Global Consultation on International Protection* (Cambridge University Press, 2003).

Lawson, Rick, 'Life After Bankovic: On the Extraterritorial Application of the European Convention on Human Rights' in Coomans, Fons, and Kamminga, Menno, T. (eds.), *Extraterritorial Application of Human Rights Treaties* (Intersentia, 2004).

Legomsky, Stephen H., 'The US and the Caribbean Interdiction Program' (2006) 18 *International Journal of Refugee Law* 677.

Lenaerts, Koen, 'Exploring the Limits of the EU Charter of Fundamental Rights' (2012) 8 *European Constitutional Law Review* 375.

Linderfalk, Ulf, *On the Interpretation of Treaties: The Modern International Law as Expressed in the 1969 Vienna Convention on the Law of Treaties* (Springer, 2007).

Lock, Tobias, 'Beyond Bosphorus: The European Court of Human Rights' Case Law on the Responsibility of Member States of International Organisations under the European Convention on Human Rights' (2010) 10 *Human Rights Law Review* 529.

Lock, Tobias, 'End of an Epic? The Draft Agreement on the EU's Accession to the ECHR' (2012) 31 *Yearbook of European Law* 162.

Mallory, Conall, 'European Court of Human Rights Al-Skeini and Others v. United Kingdom (Application No. 55721/07) Judgment of 7 July 2011' (2012) 61 *International and Comparative Law Quarterly* 301.

Mantouvalou, Virginia, 'Extending Judicial Control in International Law: Human Rights Treaties and Extraterritoriality' (2005) 9 *International Journal of Human Rights* 147.

Martínez, Hinojosa, and Luis, M., 'Bad Law for Good Reasons: The Contradictions of the Kadi Judgment' (2008) 5 *International Organizations Law Review* 339.

McGoldrik, Dominic, 'Extraterritorial Application of the International Covenant on Civil and Political Rights' in Coomans, Fons, and Kamminga, Menno, T. (eds.), *Extraterritorial Application of Human Rights Treaties* (Intersentia, 2004).

Meron, Theodor, 'Extraterritoriality of Human Rights Treaties' (1995) 89 *The American Journal of International Law* 78.

Messineo, Francesco, 'The House of Lords in Al-Jedda and Public International Law: Attribution of Conduct to Un-authorized Forces and the Power of the Security Council to Displace Human Rights' (2009) 56 *Netherlands International Law Review* 35.

Messineo, Francesco, 'Multiple Attribution of Conduct', *SHARES Research Paper* No. 2012-11.

Messineo, Francesco, 'Non-refoulement Obligations in Public International Law: Towards a New Protection Status?' in Juss, Satvinder (ed.), *The Ashgate Companion to Migration Law, Theory and Policy* (Ashgate, 2013).

Milanovic, Marko, 'From Compromise to Principle: Clarifying the Concept of State Jurisdiction in Human Rights Treaties' (2008) 8 *Human Rights Law Review* 411.

Milanovic, Marko, and Papic, Tatjana, 'As Bad as it gets: The European Court of Human Rights' Behrami and Saramati Decision and General International Law' (2009) 58 *International and Comparative Law Quarterly* 267.

Milanovic, Marko, *Extraterritorial Application of Human Rights Treaties* (Oxford University Press, 2011).

Milanovic, Marko, 'Al-Skeini and Al-Jedda in Strasbourg' (2012) 23 *European Journal of International Law* 121.

Miller, Sarah, 'Revisiting Extraterritorial Jurisdiction: A Territorial Justification for Extraterritorial Jurisdiction under the European Convention' (2009) 20 *European Journal of International Law* 1223.

Mole, Nuala, and Meredith, Catherine, *Asylum and the European Convention on Human Rights* (Council of Europe Publishing, 2010).

Monzini, Paola, 'Sea-border Crossings: The Organisation of Irregular Migration to Italy' (2007) 12 *Mediterranean Politics* 163.

Moravcsik, Andrew, 'Preferences and Power in the European Community: A Liberal Intergovernmentalist Approach' (1993) 31 *Journal of Common Market Studies* 473.

Moreno-Lax, Violeta, 'The EU Regime on Interdiction, Search and Rescue, and Disembarkation: The Frontex Guidelines for Intervention at Sea' (2010) 25 *The International Journal of Marine and Coastal Law* 621.

Moreno-Lax, Violeta, '(Extraterritorial) Entry Controls and (Extraterritorial) Non-refoulement in EU Law' in Foblets, Marie-Claire, and De Bruycker, Philippe (eds.), *The External Dimension(s) of EU Asylum and Immigration Policy* (Bruylant, 2011).

Moreno-Lax, Violeta, 'Seeking Asylum in the Mediterranean: Against a Fragmentary Reading of EU Member States' Obligations Accruing at Sea' (2011) 23 *International Journal of Refugee Law* 174.

Moreno-Lax, Violeta, 'Frontex as a Global Actor: External Relations with Third Countries and International Organizations' in Dony, Marianne (ed.), *The External Dimension of the Area of Freedom, Security and Justice* (Universite Libre de Bruxelles Press, 2012).

Moreno-Lax, Violeta, 'Hirsi Jamaa and Others v Italy or the Strasbourg Court versus Extraterritorial Migration Control?' (2012) 12 *Human Rights Law Review* 574.

Moreno-Lax, Violeta, and Costello, Cathryn, 'The Extraterritorial Application of the EU Charter of Fundamental Rights: From Territoriality to Facticity, the Effectiveness Model' in Peers, Steve, Hervey, Tamara, Kenner, Jeff, and Ward, Angela (eds.), *The EU Charter of Fundamental Rights: A Commentary* (Hart/Beck, 2014).

Nahapetian, Kate, 'Confronting State Complicity in International Law' (2002) 7 *UCLA Journal of International Law and Foreign Affairs* 99.

Nathwani, Niraj, *Rethinking Refugee Law* (Martinus Nijhoff Publishers, 2003).

Nedeski, Natasa, and Nollkaemper, André, 'Responsibility of International Organizations in Connection with Acts of States' (2012) 9 *International Organizations Law Review* 33.

Noll, Gregor, *Negotiating Asylum: The EU Acquis, Extraterritorial Protection and the Common Market of Deflection* (Martinus Nijhoff Publishers, 2000).

Noll, Gregor, 'Seeking Asylum at Embassies: A Right to Entry under International Law?' (2005) 17 *International Journal of Refugee Law* 542.

Nollkaemper, André, and Jacobs, Dov, 'Shared Responsibility in International Law: A Conceptual Framework', *SHARES Research Paper* 03 (2011).

Nolte, Georg and Aust, Helmut Philipp, 'Equivocal Helpers – Complicit States, Mixed Messages and International Law' (2009) 58 *International and Comparative Law Quarterly* 1.

Nowak, Manfred, *U.N. Covenant on Civil and Political Rights, CCPR Commentary* (N.P. Engel, 2005).

Nowak, Manfred, and McArthur, Elizabeth, *The United Nations Convention Against Torture* (Oxford University Press, 2008).

Noyes, John E., 'Ships in Distress' in Wolfrum, Rüdiger (ed.), *Max Planck Encyclopedia of Public International Law* (Oxford University Press, 2007).

Obokata, Tomoya, 'The Legal Framework Concerning the Smuggling of Migrants at Sea under the UN Protocol an the Smuggling of Migrants by Land, Sea and Air' in Ryan, Bernard, and Mitsilegas, Valsamis (eds.), *Extraterritorial Immigration Control – Legal Challenges* (Martinus Nijhoff Publishers, 2010).

Orakhelashvili, Alexander, 'Restrictive Interpretation of Human Rights Treaties in the Recent Jurisprudence of the European Court of Human Rights' (2003) 14 *European Journal of International Law* 529.

Orakhelashvili, Alexander, *Peremptory Norms in International Law* (Oxford University Press, 2006).

Orakhelashvili, Alexander, 'R(on the Application of Al-Jedda) (FC) v. Secretary of State for Defence [2007] UKHL 58' (note) (2008) 102 *The American Journal of International Law* 337.

Pallis, Mark, 'Obligations of States Towards Asylum Seekers at Sea: Interactions and Conflicts Between Legal Regimes' (2002) 14 *International Journal of Refugee Law* 329.

Papastavridis, Efthimios, ' "Fortress Europe" and Frontex: Within or Without International Law?' (2010) 79 *Nordic Journal of International Law* 75.

Papastavridis, Efthimios, 'European Court of Human Rights Medvedyev Et Al V France (Grand Chamber, Application No. 3394/03) Judgment of 29 March 2010' (2010) 59 *International and Comparative Law Quarterly* 867.

Papastavridis, Efthimios, *The Interception of Vessels on the High Seas: Contemporary Challenges to the Legal Order of the Oceans* (Hart Publishing, 2013).

Papastavridis, Efthymios, 'The EU and the Obligation of Non-refoulement at Sea' in F. Ippolito and Seline Trevisanut (eds.), *Migration in the Mediterranean: Mechanisms of International Cooperation*, (Cambridge University Press, 2016).

Parry, Clive, *The Sources and Evidences of International Law* (Manchester University Press, 1965).

Pastore, Ferruccio, Monzini, Paola, and Sciortino, Giuseppe, 'Schengen's Soft Underbelly? Irregular Migration and Human Smuggling Across Land and Sea Borders to Italy' (2006) 44 *International Migration* 95.

Peers, Steve, 'Taking Rights Away? Limitations and Derogations' in Steve, Peers, and Angela, Ward (eds.), *The European Union Charter of Fundamental Rights* (Hart Publishing, 2004).

Peers, Steve, 'Human Rights, Asylum and European Community Law' (2005) 24 *Refugee Survey Quarterly* 24.

Peers, Steve, 'Bosphorus – European Court of Human Rights – Limited Responsibility of European Union Member State for Actions within the Scope of Community law. Judgment of 30 June 2005, Bosphorus Airways v. Ireland, Application No. 45036/98' (2006) 2 *European Constitutional Law Review* 443.

Peers, Steve, *EU Justice and Home Affairs Law* (Oxford University Press, 2011).

Peers, Steve, 'Immigration, Asylum and the European Union Charter of Fundamental Rights' in Guild, Elspeth, and Minderhoud, Paul E. (eds.), *The First Decade of EU Migration and Asylum Law* (Martinus Nijhoff Publishers, 2012).

Peers, Steve, 'New Rules on Maritime Surveillance: Will They Stop the Deaths and Push-backs in the Mediterranean?' – Statewatch Analysis, February 2014.

Pollak, Johannes, and Slominski, Peter, 'Experimentalist but Not Accountable Governance? The Role of Frontex in Managing the EU's External Borders' (2009) 32 *West European Politics* 904.

Reinisch, August, 'Aid or Assistance and Direction and Control between States and International Organizations in the Commission of Internationally Wrongful Acts' (2010) 7 *International Organization Law Review* 63.

Rijpma, Jorrit and Cremona, Marise, 'The Extra-Territorialisation of EU Migration Policies and the Rule of Law' (2007) *EUI Working Papers Law* 2007/01.

Rijpma, Jorrit, 'Building Borders: The Regulatory Framework for the Management of the External Borders of the European Union' (DPhil thesis, European University Institute, 2009).

Rijpma, Jorrit, 'Frontex: Successful Blame Shifting of the Member States?' (2010) 69 *Real Instituto Elcano (ARI)*, www.realinstitutoelcano.org.

Rijpma, Jorrit, 'Hybrid Agencification in the Area of Freedom, Security and Justice and Its Inherent Tensions: The Case of Frontex' in Busuioc, Madalina, Groenleer, Martijn, and Trondal, Jarle (eds.), *The Agency Phenomenon in the European Union – Emergence, Institutionalization and Everyday Decision-making* (Manchester University Press, 2012).

Rijpma, Jorrit, 'The Patrolling of the European Union's External Maritime Border: Preventing the Rule of Law from Getting Lost at Sea' in Del Vecchio, Angela (ed.), *International Law of the Sea: Current Trends and Controversial Issues* (Eleven International Publishing, 2014).

Robinson, Nehemiah, *Convention Relating to the Status of Refugees: Its History, Contents and Interpretation* (Institute of Jewish Affairs 1953, reprinted by UNHCR 1997).

Rosas, Allan, 'Fundamental Rights in the Luxembourg and Strasbourg Courts' in Baudenbacher, Carl, Tresselt, Per, and Orlygsson, Thorgeir (eds.), *The EFTA Court: Ten Years On* (Hart Publishing, 2005).

Rosas, Allan, 'International Human Rights Instruments in the Case Law of the Court of Justice' in *Law in the Changing Europe: Liber Amicorum Pranas Kuris* (Mykolo Romerio Universiteto, 2008).

Rosas, Allan, 'The Charter and Universal Human Rights Instruments' in Peers, Steve, Hervey, Tamara, Kenner, Jeff, and Ward, Angela (eds.), *The EU Charter of Fundamental Rights: A Commentary* (Hart/Beck, 2014).

Sandholtz, Wayne, 'European Integration and Supranational Governance' (1997) 4 *Journal of European Public Policy* 297.

Sari, Aurel, and Wessel, Ramses A., 'International Responsibility for EU Military Operations: Finding the EU's Place in the Global Accountability Regime' in van Vooren, Bart, Blockmans, Steven, and Wouters, Jan (eds.), *The EU's Role in Global Governance: The Legal Dimension* (Oxford University Press, 2012).

Sarooshi, Danesh, *The United Nations and the Development of Collective Security* (Oxford University Press, 2000).

Scheinin, Martin, 'Extraterritorial Effect of the International Covenant on Civil and Political Rights' in Coomans, Fons, and Kamminga, Menno, T. (eds.), *Extraterritorial Application of Human Rights Treaties* (Intersentia, 2004).

Scheinin, Martin, 'Is the ECJ Ruling in Kadi Incompatible with International Law?' (2008) 28 *Yearbook of European Law* 637.

Shapiro, Martin, 'Independent Agencies' in Craig, Paul P., and de Burca, Grainne (eds.), *The Evolution of EU Law* (Oxford University Press, 2011).

Shaw, Malcom N., *International Law* (Cambridge University Press, 2008).

Shearer, Ivan A., *Starke's International Law* (Butterworths, 1994).

Spijkerboer, Thomas, 'The Human Costs of Border Control' (2007) 9 *European Journal of Migration and Law* 127.

Tanaka, Yoshifumi, *The International Law of the Sea* (Cambridge University Press, 2012).

Tomuschat, Christian, 'The International Responsibility of the European Union' in Cannizzaro, E. (ed.), *The European Union as an Actor in International Relations* (Kluwer Law International, 2002).

Tomuschat, Christian, 'The Kadi Case: What Relationship is There between the Universal Legal Order under the Auspices of the United Nations and the EU Legal Order?' (2009) 28 *Yearbook of European Law* 654.

Tomuschat, Christian, 'Attribution of International Responsibility: Direction and Control' in Evans, Malcom, and Koutrakos, Panos (eds.), *The International Responsibility of the European Union: European and International Perspectives* (Hart Publishing, 2013).

Trevisanut, Seline, 'Search and Rescue Operations in the Mediterranean: Factor of Cooperation or Conflict?' (2010) 25 *The International Journal of Marine and Coastal Law* 523.

Trevisanut, Seline, 'The Principle of Non-refoulement and the Deterritorialisation of Border Control at Sea' (2014) 27 *Leiden Journal of International Law* 661.

UNHCR, 'The Haitian Interdiction Case 1993 Brief Amicus Curiae' (1994) 6 *International Journal of Refugee Law* 85.

van den Herik, Larissa, and Schrijver, Nicolaas J., 'Eroding the Primacy of the UN System of Collective Security: The Judgment of the European Court of Justice in the Cases of Kadi and Al Barakaat' (2008) 5 *International Organizations Law Review* 329.

von Bogdandy, Armin, and Bast, Jürgen, 'The Federal Order of Competences' in Armin von, Bogdandy, and Jürgen, Bast (eds.), *Principles of European Constitutional Law* (Hart CH Beck Nomos, 2011).

von Bogdandy, Armin and Steinbrück Platise, Mateja, 'ARIO and Human Rights Protection: Leaving the Individual in the Cold' (2012) 9 *International Organizations Law Review* 67.

Vos, Ellen, 'Reforming the European Commission: What Role to Play for EU Agencies?' (2000) 37 *Common Market Law Review* 1113.

Weiler, Joseph H.H., 'Eurocracy and Distrust: Some Questions Concerning the Role of the European Court of Justice in the Protection of Fundamental Human Rights within the Legal Order of the European Communities' (1986) 61 *Washington Law Review* 1103.

Weis, Paul, *The Refugee Convention, 1951: The Travaux Préparatoires Analyzed with a Commentary by Dr Paul Weis* (Cambridge University Press, published posthumously 1995).

White, Nigel D., and MacLeod, Sorcha, 'EU Operations and Private Military Contractors: Issues of Corporate and Institutional Responsibility' (2008) 19 *European Journal of International Law* 965.

Wonka, Arndt, and Rittberger, Bertold, 'Credibility, Complexity and Uncertainty: Explaining the Institutional Independence of 29 EU Agencies' (2010) 33 *West European Politics* 730.

Wouters, Kees, *International Legal Standards for the Protection from Refoulement* (Intersentia, 2009).

Wouters, Jan, and Van Eeckhoutte, Dries, 'Giving Effect to Customary International Law Through European Community Law' in Prinssen, Jolande M., and Schrauwen, Annette (eds.), *Direct Effect* (Europa Law Publishing, 2004).

Zgonec-Rozej, Misa, 'Al-Skeini v. United Kingdom' (2012) 106 *American Journal of International Law* 131.

INDEX

Lightning Source UK Ltd.
Milton Keynes UK
UKHW022348151021
392306UK00019B/414